gilli danda to golf

a memoir

ram varma

RUPA

Published by
Rupa Publications India Pvt. Ltd 2021
7/16, Ansari Road, Daryaganj
New Delhi 110002

Sales centres:
Allahabad Bengaluru Chennai
Hyderabad Jaipur Kathmandu
Kolkata Mumbai

ISBN: 978-93-90356-95-9

First impression 2021

10 9 8 7 6 5 4 3 2 1

Printed at Thomson Press India Ltd, Faridabad

I celebrate myself, and sing myself!

—Walt Whitman

CONTENTS

1

MOTHER

I was born in fulfillment of a prophecy. My mother, Pyari, 'the beloved', or more formally, Ram Pyari, 'darling of Lord Rama', was blessed by the priest of a rock shrine, high on a rugged hill near her birthplace Samod, that her anguished prayers before the goddess Mahamai, the Great Mother, would be answered, and she would beget two sons.

•◆

My mother's life had been traumatic after marriage. Born in a family of Khandwals, stoneworkers and statue carvers in Samod, near Jaipur, she was married at the tender age of 15 to the 18-year-old Ram Chandra, into a family of stone masons and bricklayers, in Sri Madhopur, a town on the periphery of Shekhawati, about 50 miles from Samod. Sri Madhopur was a new town, founded during Maharaja Madho Singh's time and named after him, and built on Jaipur's geometric grid pattern.

Unfortunately, Ram Pyari's husband died of pneumonia after about three years of marriage, just when they were beginning to know each other, after her muklava[1]. Ram Pyari was widowed at the threshold of her youth.

[1]In Rajasthan, girls used to be married off when they were very young, and after a ceremonial visit to the sasural (marital home), they returned to their parents' house. Marriages were consummated one or two years later, after the muklava ceremony.

Neither did Ram Chandra have a younger brother with whom she could be remarried according to the custom of the community, nor was there an unmarried boy in the requisite age group in the small Loharwadia clan of her deceased husband. The clan elders therefore brought an 18-year-old boy of the Loharwadia gotra from a dhani[2] near the neighbouring town, Ringus. The boy, Bhura Mal, was renamed Ram Chandra and after a brief nuptial ceremony was installed in Ram Pyari's house as her new husband. Ram Pyari erased the memory of her previous short-lived marriage and started life all over again. Destiny had brought these two luckless souls together.

Bhura Mal too had his own share of misfortune. His father had died a few years ago in a tragic accident while drawing water from a kuccha dug-well without any masonry structure in a dry riverbed, where he had been employed by a neighbour to irrigate the fields.

Water used to be drawn from these dug-wells with the help of a yoked pair of oxen. A huge cowhide receptacle, called charsa, was tied to a thick rope and lowered into the well, over a wooden wheel fixed on a pulley. The rope was pulled up by the yoked oxen driven by another man. As the charsa rose up the well, the man standing under the pulley caught it and placed it on a stone slab. Water was drained when the rope was released by the man driving the oxen.

This was a primitive system of drawing water that had worked for generations. The man standing in the trough to receive the water-filled charsa was the pivotal figure. He would sing an impromptu ditty in his high-pitched voice to give a signal to his teammate driving the oxen to release the rope after he had got hold of the charsa: *'Ab khol de re keeli, mera bhayala!'* (Now release the rope, my friend!) His song would reverberate in the silence of the dawn.

---

[2]A small habitation

It was crucial that the rope was released *after* the charsa had been caught and placed squarely on the stone slab.

Bhura's father had been standing under the wooden pulley to catch the charsa and drain the water. Accidentally, the rope was released before he had caught the water-filled charsa, *when the charsa was still dangling free*. In a flash, the rope whipped back like a giant coiled serpent, taking the pulley, wheel and his father into the well.

Everyone in the guwadi[3] addressed Ram Chandra aka Bhura Mal as 'Chandra Kaka[4]' because he was their uncle by relation, though younger in age. He had grown up doing odd chores as a farm helper and was not trained to be a bricklayer. He began to learn masonry in his new home, with the tools of his predecessor.

The small town of Sri Madhopur did not have enough work opportunities for the sizeable chejara[5] community and most young men had to go to distant cities like Bombay, Indore, Raigarh or Barwani, where new cotton mills and factories were coming up. The men said they went to pardes[6], because these faraway metropoles were as alien as foreign shores.

The mill owners allowed the men to live at the worksites in makeshift tenements, and in the evening they cooked their own spartan meal of daal-roti. They went to work in the morning after eating the leftovers for breakfast.

While the daily wage for a mason in Sri Madhopur was ₹1, they earned ₹2 a day in pardes. On an average, they were employed for 20 to 25 days in a month. Every two months, Ram Chandra would send a money order of ₹70-80 to his wife, spending less than ₹10 a month on himself. He spent about eight months of a

---

[3]A group of houses enclosed by a common wall with a single entrance

[4]'Kaka' means 'uncle' in Rajasthan, though it means 'son' in Punjabi

[5]Mason

[6]Foreign land

year in pardes: when the rainy season interrupted work, he would catch a train home.

◆

Pyari conceived after a few months of her remarriage, but she miscarried. After a year, she conceived again, but delivered a deformed male child, who died soon after birth. Drained and distraught, she went to live for a while with her widowed mother, Heeran, in Samod.

On an auspicious day, Heeran took her to the Mahamai shrine, carrying on her head a basketful of pooye, poories, pakori and kheer, which she had cooked during the night, as offerings to propitiate the goddess.

This was a shrine where young mothers brought their children for their first tonsuring. Heeran was singing hymns in praise of the goddess as they went up the hilly track. Before her marriage, Pyari used to bring the family cows and goats to graze on that wooded hillside. She was delighted to revisit her childhood haunts. Her heart ached as memories of her happy childhood came flooding back.

Devotees were flocking to the shrine from all directions. Heeran presented her offerings to the priest, who was from Samod and knew them well. Pyari rang the temple bell and prostrated herself on the floor before the Devi, mumbling her prayers. Tears welled up in her eyes; she was writhing helplessly and cried out aloud: 'What is my sin, O Great Mother? Why are you punishing me so severely?'

Heeran lifted her sobbing daughter, took her in her arms and they stood before the Devi with folded hands. The priest drew the shrine's silk curtain and took the offerings inside the shrine. He came out, parting the curtain, a few minutes later and returned the sanctified prasad to Heeran. He blessed Pyari then, placing his hand on her head in benediction: 'Don't you grieve for your lost children, Pyari. Mahamai will bless you with two sons.'

She returned to her husband rejuvenated in body and spirit. After a year, she gave birth to a healthy baby girl: they named her Chhoti, the little one.

When Chhoti was four years old, playing by herself, Ram Pyari noticed that she seemed to be talking to somebody although there was no one near her. As Chhoti reprimanded an unruly child, Pyari enquired who she was talking to. 'This little one, can't you see?' Chhoti replied. 'He's so naughty; runs around all the time, doesn't let me have a moment's rest.' Pyari's eyes grew misty; she remembered the priest's prophecy.

That evening, Ram Chandra came home with two other fellow migrants from Indore, bringing a colourful frock for Chhoti and a length of chintz for his wife's lehenga[7].

Some time after Ram Chandra left for Barwani, Pyari missed her menses and in a couple of months, the town's midwife confirmed her pregnancy. About three months later, Pyari got a school-going boy from the guwadi to write a postcard to her husband: '*Nayi aas lagi hai!* (There is new hope!) Your presence is required at home urgently.' She dropped it in the red letterbox of the post office. Ram Chandra came home within a month of receiving the postcard. He was delighted to see his blossoming wife.

One day in the month of Ashvin, when it was raining intermittently, Pyari asked her husband to go to the midwife's house and bring her along. Ram Chandra hastened to her house, that was about a mile and a half away. She knew about the impending event and came with him at once.

Late in the evening, Ram Pyari delivered the baby. Two other ladies from the guwadi were also in attendance. Holding the newborn baby in her hands, the midwife exclaimed with joy: 'It's

---

[7]A long traditional skirt

a boy!' One of the ladies picked up a nickel thali[8] and sounded it like a gong to announce the arrival of a male child to the world.

The boy was named Bhagirath, after the mythical king of the Ikshvaku dynasty and a celebrated ancestor of Lord Rama, whose prayers had brought the sacred Ganga to earth.

Ram Pyari was happy, but only a part of the prophecy had been fulfilled. Sure enough, after two years she conceived again, and in the rainy month of Shravan she gave birth to another boy. He was named Ram Sahai, Lord Rama's helper. Ram Chandra fancied this name: Ram Sahai Thekedar was one of the wealthiest stone merchants belonging to our community in the town, wishing for his child a similar prosperous future.

•◆

When I was about six years old, Mother took my brother and me to the shrine of Mahamai to perform our ritual tonsure, jadoola. By that time, her mother had left for Jaipur to live with my Mamaji. We boarded the Jaipur-bound train and alighted at the Chomu station. From there we walked for a few miles along the road to Samod. I remember running after my brother under the shade of the mango trees that lined the road, picking up half-ripe mangoes pecked by birds and taking a tongue-tingling sweet-sour bite. I was thrilled to discover mango trees; our town had only neem and peepal trees. Mother carried a basket on her head, full of halwa, poori and gulgula, to offer to the goddess.

A few miles before Samod we turned left and went up to the shrine. A barber shaved our heads and Mother picked up the shorn hair and dropped it into a drum. The priest recognized my mother and blessed us, putting his hands on our bald pates. She had fulfilled an old vow.

---

[8]A large round plate for food

When we returned home, one of the women in the guwadi, Gulab bhabhi[9] asked me where we had gone. I told her about the Mahamai shrine and suggested that she should also visit it. Although married for almost six years, she was yet to have a child, and her face clouded over. 'Whose jadoola would I offer to the goddess, Ram Sahaiji?' she asked me. 'Why? You take Laxman bhaiyya[10] with you and offer his jadoola,' I answered, undeterred. Her husband Laxman Ram had returned a few days back, from Indore, where he also worked. Coincidentally, she conceived soon after and always believed that my words had been prophetic.

---

[9]Older brother's wife, often used as a term of address for young married women
[10]Older brother, often used as a term of address for young men

2

FATHER

Ram Chandra had come home on his annual furlough, bringing some clothes for his wife and their two children, besides a princely sum of ₹100 in his pocket. Chhoti had been married a few years back and had gone to live in her sasural at Khetri.

Pyari told her husband they should buy a cow: the boys needed to drink milk. Ram Chandra went to meet the town cowherd, Sonu Ram Padhya (rustic form of 'Upadhaya'), who took the town's cows to graze during the day in the scrubland around a natural pond called Bhojalai, over a mile from the town. Sonu Ram told him about a cow, Neeli, in her second calving, that belonged to Pundit Ram Prasad, who had asked him to look for a buyer. Ram Chandra proceeded to the Pundit's house in the west of the town and saw the bluish grey cow and her newborn male calf. It was love at first sight. The pundit demanded ₹60; Ram Chandra offered ₹50. The deal was struck at ₹55 and he brought Neeli home, with her calf trotting behind her. A thrilled Ram Pyari tended to the cow like a daughter and Neeli yielded about a seer[11] of milk that evening. The yield doubled within a month, as Pyari nourished the cow with boiled and crushed cotton seeds, mixed with soaked sesame oilcakes.

As a natural corollary to owning a cow, Ram Pyari wanted to

[11]Unit of old system of weight, slightly less than a kilogram or litre

have some farmland to grow fodder. She leased a small piece of unirrigated arable land for ₹60 per crop season. Situated about two miles north-east of the town, in the territory of the Thakur of Mau, it measured 'four ploughs' in local terminology, which meant four ploughs were needed to work it. She hired some Jat cultivators to plough and seed it after the first good rainfall in early July. Every morning, Pyari went to her khet[12] to work and returned carrying a load of green fodder on her head for the cow.

Ram Chandra came home before the festival of Dasehra in September, in time for harvesting. He liked farming infinitely more than the drudgery of bricklaying. When the ears of the bajra crop were ripening, he made himself a machan[13] on a khejri tree in the middle of the field. After eating his frugal evening meal, he stretched himself out on the machan and surveyed his little kingdom, happiness welling in his heart. He slept under the starry sky, keeping a night vigil.

The doughty husband-wife team first harvested the crop of moong, moth and guar with sickles and scythes, moving in tandem, and left the stacks to dry. The main bajra crop ripened meanwhile. Its hardy stalks demanded all their strength to harvest and took a week or two. They prepared a mud-plastered threshing floor and beat the dry cobs with clubs, winnowed on a windy day and separated the grains from the chaff, which was as precious as the grains and served as nutritious dry fodder for the cow. They carried the grains and chaff home, on their heads, including the loads of long, dry stalks of bajra, called karbi.

Ram Chandra also harvested the thorny ber bushes that grew wild on the field's periphery, which provided protein-rich nutrition to the cow. He even carried thorny bundles of dry bush home,

---

[12]From the Sanskrit *kshetra*, meaning 'field'.

[13]A platform erected on a tree, used originally for hunting large animals and now for watching animals in wildlife reserves.

holding them high on his pitchfork, to make a hedge around the cowshed. In the end, he harvested the sarkanda[14] stalks that grew wild around the field, for thatch-making. We had two houses. The one in the front courtyard had a corrugated tin roof and the one at the back quadrangle had a thatched roof that required to be replaced every few years, for which the sarkanda stalks were used. He sold them if there was surplus, or wound them into a rough rope. By the end of the lease, they had extracted every useful bit from the piece of the land.

Mother leased this piece of land every year for four months. Although this field was far from home, it had fertile loamy soil. However, it was situated near a rivulet that swelled during the rains. Once, the rain-fed torrent washed away about a third of the field a few weeks before harvest. She came home dejected, and told us about the devastation. But, seeing my melancholy face, she narrated a tale about a camel farmer from the deserts of Jaisalmer. He was a grand old man with a large herd of a hundred male camels, a hundred female camels and a large family as well. Rainfall was scarce in the desert, but one dark night when they were asleep, a cloudburst and flood washed away the old man's herd of camels and his whole family. He was the sole survivor. When people came to commisserate with him and blamed the rains that had caused the devastation, the old man murmured: *'Sau karva, sau karvani, poot sapooti dhaya; Meha to barsya hi bhala, honi ho so hoye.'* (A hundred male camels and a hundred female camels, my sons and their mother have all been washed away, yet the rains are good for mankind, whatever happens!)

With a feeble smile on her gentle face, my mother reminded us that the loss we had suffered was inconsequential as the bountiful rain was beneficial to all.

[14] Reed

3

SRI MADHOPUR

The town I was born in, Sri Madhopur, is named after Maharaja Madho Singh I of Jaipur. A tale hangs behind its foundataion.

The beautiful city of Jaipur was founded in 1727 by Maharaja Sawai Jai Singh II, father of Madho Singh I, in the vicinity of the ancestral fort-palace of Amber. Jaipur perpetuates its founder's name and fame. It is deservedly famous for the architectural beauty of its palaces and even more for being planned in a geometric grid pattern: wide market streets were laid out from the imposing gates of the city wall, intersecting at right angles. At their intersections, spacious market squares called chowpars were created. The streets into the residential areas emanated from the market streets, and also intersected each other at right angles. In 1876, shop façades were painted bright pink to welcome visiting royalty, which gave it the sobriquet 'Pink City'. Jaipur was the first city of its kind in India.

In 1750, the Mughal empire had already waned when Ishwari Singh, the son of Sawai Jai Singh II and the princess of Jodhpur, was sitting on the throne of Jaipur. When Khande Rao Holker arrived at the gates of Jaipur with the Maratha army, Ishwari Singh chose honourable death over defeat and capture. With his demise, Madho Singh I, the son of Sawai Jai Singh II and the princess of

Udaipur Chandra Kunwar, was crowned King of Jaipur, in fateful fulfillment of a condition made long ago.

•◆

While the royal house of Jaipur had been embroiled in internal conflicts, the chiefs of the Shaikhawati region, under the leadership of the chief of Khandela, had stopped paying their annual tribute, in an attempt to assert their independence. Maharaja Madho Singh refused to tolerate this disobedience. In 1761, he sent his astute diwan[15] Khushali Ram Bohra with a contingent of Maratha soldiers to sort out the Shaikhawati chiefs and restore the state's suzerainty. His forces camped at the place where Sri Madhopur exists now. Legend has it that Khushali Ram Bohra planted a khejri sapling at a diminutive wayside Hanuman temple. A brief skirmish at a nearby village, Haanspur, resulted in a few deaths and brought the rebellious chiefs to heel. They reached Jaipur and made obeisance to the king, sought his pardon and promised to pay the outstanding tribute.

However, the Shaikhawati chiefs defaulted in the following years and Khushali Ram arrived with a contingent again in 1763. While camping there this time, he constructed a small Garh[16], indicating that an army unit would be permanently stationed there. He was happy to see that the khejri sapling had grown into a luxuriant young tree. Taking it to be a good omen, he decided to found a new town at the site. This time, the chiefs immediately presented themselves before him, explaining that acute drought had resulted in crop failure, and assured him of their unflinching loyalty.

Today, over two and a half centuries later, the khejri tree stands majestically at the foot of the ancient statue of Hanuman, at the

---

[15]Chief minister and army commander

[16]Fortress

main chowpar of the new town that was built subsequently.

◆

Sri Madhopur is situated about 15 miles north of the old town of Khandela. Unlike Khandela, which is perched on a hillock, Sri Madhopur stretches itself on level ground. The small Garh constructed by Khushali Ram Bohra appears to be its focal point.

Sri Madhopur was not a walled town, but grand entrance gates were constructed in stone and lime mortar. A broad market street was planned from the Garh towards Hanuman Garhi and beyond, in the direction of Khandela. This north-south axis came to be called the Khandela Bazaar. Another market street, called the Sikar Bazaar, was planned along the east-west axis in the direction of Sikar. Hanuman Garhi stood at the intersection, and a spacious chowpar was created there. A beautiful temple dedicated to Shiva was constructed next to Hanuman Garhi. The extension of Sikar Bazaar to the east, beyond the chowpar, was named Surani Bazaar, after a town in the east.

A Muslim mohalla came up at the end of Surani Bazaar. The workshops of hard-working lohars[17] fabricated masonry tools, iron containers for mortar and agricultural implements for the large farming community. A stately mosque with towering minarets came up in the east.

In time, the municipal office, the tehsildar's court, the police station, a dispensary and a middle school (which later became a high school) came up on a broad road from the Garh, at right angles to the Khandela Bazaar. The railway station was built later, during British times, and the Patwari Dharamshala was built next to it by a wealthy trader. The Dharamshala was also the venue of plays and dance performances by the school boys.

---

[17]Ironsmiths

Residential blocks were carved out in-between the major arteries and main bazaars, adhering to the grid pattern. Most of the houses were one-storeyed, made of brick or stone, plastered with lime-mortar and arranged around a sand-filled unpaved courtyard. There were many havelis, and the bigger ones were double-storeyed, with two or three courtyards.

Sri Madhopur was a khalsa town, directly administered by the state, and was made the estate of one of the queens.[18] The Garh, which was never used to quarter army units and had remained unoccupied, was later converted into a primary school. My father took me to this school in July 1945, to launch me on my academic career.

•◆

Till 1956, when I graduated from the high school, all the streets were kuccha, filled with fine-grained sand, except the one leading to the railway station, which was pucca. Let alone a motor vehicle, no one owned even a lowly bicycle, for a simple reason: you just couldn't ride it in the sand-filled streets! There were no tongas or rickshaws: everyone walked to their places of work, gentry or commoner–the Tehsildar (highest civil official of the town), the doctor, the headmaster and teachers and the rich Seths.

The town had no electricity till then and went to sleep early. Tiny ink-pot-sized kerosene lamps (called chimney) were used in houses and hurricane lanterns were used in big shops. Dazzling petromax lamps, available on hire, were carried in wedding processions or used by itinerant theatre groups while staging Ramlila performances a fortnight before Dasehra.

There was no piped water supply in town: women, irrespective

---

[18]James Tod, *Annals and Antiquities of Rajasthan*, Motilal Banarasidass, Delhi, 1971, vol. III, p. 1412.

of social or economic status, fetched water from sweetwater wells outside town. They carried the water in brass or earthen pitchers, balancing them on their heads.

My cousin Govind Sahai was probably the first graduate from the town. He was married to the daughter of the manager of the salt mines of Sambhar, a town which had tarred streets and piped water supply. His bride, Sushila, had studied till middle school and had never carried water on her head. She was bewildered when her jethani[19] asked her to accompany her to the well, carrying a pitcher on her head. She bore her lot bravely for a month or so. Luckily, Govind Sahai got a job in Jaipur, which saved her from this mortifying daily ordeal.

With no piped water supply, household latrines were non-existent. At dawn, holding lotas in their hands and tucking their dhotis around their waists, people would walk to the open fields outside town to relieve their bowels. While bathing with water drawn from wells, they called upon the sacred rivers of India—Ganga, Yamuna, Saraswati, Gomati, Godawari and Narmada—exhorting them to come and purify them.

◆

In our mohalla[20] of raj-mistris, who built beautiful havelis for the Seths and the imposing temples of the town, there were many havelis too, some very large and imposing. But it was a poor community and there was a preponderance of houses with tin or thatched roofs. Our guwadi, which lodged about 10 families, was spread out across four chowks, with only one single-storeyed old haveli.

The women swept and dusted the houses in the morning, and once a year, before Diwali, they hand-plastered the walls with a

---

[19]Wife of the husband's elder brother

[20]Sector or ward

mixture of mud and cowdung. The chowks and common areas were swept clean by a sweeper woman, who came every morning, carrying a big broom in her hand and a basket on her head to carry the sweepings. No one seemed to know her real name. Everyone called her 'Mooliya ki bahu'; probably her husband's name was Mool Chand. After sweeping the dusty chowks of the guwadi with her big broom and collecting the garbage in her basket, she would stand in front of the door of every house and spread out her soiled odhani[21]. Each housewife dropped into it a thick roti of barley or bajra, left over from the previous evening. She was humility incarnate; her face was a picture of serenity—an image of 'karuna'.

An early memory about her clings to my mind. I was a child of about five years then. As she was waiting for my mother to give her the roti, on a sudden impulse I rushed to her and enclosed her in my little arms in an expression of affection. I liked her—her gentle face, soft speech and subdued demeanour. She was aghast and my mother was horrified. 'No, Ram Sahaiji,' she chided me in her sweet voice and quickly disengaged herself. 'We are bhangis[22], achhoot! You should never touch me!'

My mother took some water in her palm, dipped her little gold pendant in it and sprinkled it on me to wash away the pollution and administered a stern warning never to do it again.

◆

Not very far from our humble guwadi, the rich men of our community had built their magnificent havelis. Suwalal Khowal and his brothers owned stone godowns and workshops; Ram Sahai Thekedar was the biggest stone merchant in town and employed about two dozen young artisans from our community in his stone-

---

[21]Long scarf used to cover the face and head

[22]Sweepers

carving workshop, where they hammered, chiselled and carved, enveloped in a cloud of stone dust, looking ghastly; Mahadevji Thekedar's haveli was a painted mansion, decorated with frescos depicting scenes from the Ramayana and Lord Krishna's Raas Lila[23]. His son, Inder Sahai, had made big money in road-building contracts in Udaipur and had settled there. He had built a Shiva temple near our community's shamshan ghat[24], and a sweetwater well for ritual ablutions after cremation. It had become a popular haunt of itinerant sadhus. A renowned sage called Tiddinath Baba (King of the Locusts) had come to lodge at the temple: he kept his body bare in sun, rain or shivering cold, save for a skimpy langot (genital cover). He had penetrating eyes and his braided jata came down to his knees.

Mahadevji had also built a gau-shala[25] about a mile away from the town, on the Khandela road, with a dedicated farmland for growing fodder for the cows. A deep tube well had been bored and pumpsets installed for drawing water.

[23]Dancing with maidens in the moonlight in the forest

[24]Cremation ground

[25]Cow shelter

4

CHILDHOOD

About a month before my sixth birthday, I was admitted to school. I distinctly remember donning a new white shirt and khaki shorts on that hot and sultry day in early July. My father and I first went to the Murli Manoharji temple to make obeisance to the family deity and receive a few drops of holy charan-amrit[26] for an auspicious start. Durga Prasad, a boy from our guwadi, who was a few months older than me, had also come along with us, as his father was away working in the stone mines.

The dour and rugged ramparts of the Garh School, beyond a vast open ground, were built on a high plinth. Blackened with age, the walls were topped with turrets at the corners. The entrance at the base of the towering wall looked like a tiny hole. Inside the Garh, there was a spacious sand-filled quadrangle, lined with single-storeyed tin-roofed classrooms along the left and right, and a double-storeyed block in front.

Father walked us to a teacher popularly known as Munshiji. He had radiant fair skin, and sat on a chair under a neem tree, looking majestic in his yellow safa[27]. He had been crippled by polio and his shrivelled legs were tucked up on the chair. He belonged to our community and knew my father well. About 20 boys were

---

[26]Lit. Charan (foot)-Amrit (nectar), 'Nectar from the feet of the Lord', sanctified water that was used to wash the deity's feet in the morning

[27]Headgear

squatting in front of him on the sand. As my father saluted him with folded hands, saying, 'Jai Ramji ki, Munshiji,' he responded warmly and said, 'Jai Ramji ki, Patelji!' (as my father was commonly addressed).

Munshiji enrolled both of us in pre-primary class 'A'. Though I was less than six years old at that time, Munshiji recorded my age as seven years, without asking my father. The day of admission conveniently became my official date of birth. Ditto for Durga Prasad.

After six months, at the end of winter break, we were promoted to class 'B' and after the summer holidays, when the school reopened in July, we were promoted to class 1. No room had been assigned for the preparatory classes A and B: we sat in the shade of the neem tree.

Our teachers carried a danda[28] in their hand, about two feet in length and an inch in diameter. It was issued by the school as a sort of essential equipment, and was used liberally to punish erring boys; the number of blows depended on the nature and severity of the misdemeanour. This was an accepted practice at that time and no one took offence, but some teachers were known to take special relish in performing this corrective task.

Munshiji taught us to write the alphabet and numerals on a slate. As homework, called 'sulekh' (beautiful writing), we had to write them in bold letters on a 2 × 1 foot wooden board called 'takhti'. We wrote in black ink with a 'kalam' (pen) made of reed and took it to school. My brother taught me to wash the takhti, give it a coating of yellowish multani mitti and write carefully, after drying it. This daily ritual made my handwriting artistic, almost calligraphic, which became my most valuable asset in getting top marks.

---

[28]From the Sanskrit word 'dand', meaning punishment; wooden staff

An incident from when I was in class B is clearly etched in my memory. Our class teacher was Badri Narainji, a tall man with the body of a wrestler. We were terrified of him; he never overlooked any lapse and never spared the rod. However, he liked me and had made me the monitor of the class. He also made me fetch a large brass tumbler full of buttermilk from his house after the second period. His house was about a kilometre away, beyond Surani Bazaar. After downing the drink, he would give us some sums to do and then doze off.

Shiv Dayal, who we called Shyol, was a year older than me and lived in our guwadi. He had failed in class B and become my classmate. One day, a sleeping Badri Narainji woke up with a start and saw Shyol throwing a paper airplane at another boy. Enraged, he picked up the lanky Shyol with his right hand and threw him in the air like a ball, as we watched in horror. Shyol crashed to the ground with a thud. Mercifully, he was unharmed. He got up and ran off as fast as his legs could carry him, leaving his things behind. He never went back to school, and a nascent spark of scholarship was rudely snuffed out.

My brother Bhagirath, who was in class 2 when I started school, had joined the middle school which ran classes from 3 to 7. Class 3 was considered an important stage in one's academic career, as one started studying English.

Learning the English language bestowed a special status on a person. In those days, telegrams could be written only in English and were mostly used to convey the dire news of relatives passing away in far-off towns. People who received telegrams were compelled to go looking for someone who could decipher the message for them, like Babu Gopichand Rajoria, who was the only 'middle pass' man in the whole town!

I wanted to grow up quickly, start middle school and begin learning English—join the charmed circle of English-knowing people. But little did I know that I would have to wait three extra years.

◆

In class 1, we moved to a proper room on the ground floor. We sat on jute mats on the floor, the teacher sat on a grey cushion. He had a small wooden desk and his trusted danda.

I had scored the highest marks in class and was made the class monitor, which gave me the privilege of occupying the first place to the right of the teacher. In the morning, I went to collect a couple of sticks of chalk from the Headmaster's room, in a turret. He sat at his desk, dwarfed by a life-sized portrait of the handsome Maharaja Man Singh II, the ruler of Jaipur, hanging on the wall behind his chair.

My other duties included cleaning the blackboard, leading the boys in reciting numerical tables and minding the class when the teacher was away or snoozing.

Our curriculum included learning the art of spinning—not on a regular spinning wheel like Mahatma Gandhi, but on a tiny taqli, which was a simple handheld tool. Holding a roll of pressed cotton in the left hand, one had to spin the taqli with the right hand to make thread. The last period was for learning craft and Jagdishji Nan-ka-Joshi was our craft teacher. All he did by way of teaching was to ask us to take out our taqlis and start spinning. He would doze off then, waking up only when the school gong struck for chhutti[29] and the boys sprang to their feet and bolted for freedom.

A boy named Mukti Lal Thoiwala always used to play pranks on others but was much too smart to be caught. One day, he

[29]Lit. release; end of school time

was sitting with Kalu Ram who was dull in the head. Kalu Ram was concentrating hard on the task of yarn-making but Mukti Lal would flick a finger and break his thread again and again, which angered Kalu Ram and he hit him. Jagdishji's nap was disturbed by the sound. He saw Kalu Ram's raised hand. His eyes flashed in anger and he shouted at him: '*Idhar aaja, meri shikaar!*' (Come here, my prey)—those were his very words. Bending the fingers of his right hand into a claw, he stretched it towards him and a frightened Kalu Ram walked towards him, as if spellbound. Jagdishji gave a resounding slap on his face, and then with the danda in his hand, he gave him a sound thrashing. Jagdishji then glowered at me, as if it was my fault. Mercifully at that same instant the gong struck—Chhutti!

◆

I have happy memories of class 2. Just a month after the school opened in July 1947, independence was dawning on the country. There was euphoria in the air, although there was to be no apparent change in our lives, as the Maharaja of Jaipur would continue to be our ruler.

Our Headmaster Tara Chand Sharma decided that the boys of class 2, the highest class of the school, should take out prabhat pheris[30] in town, during the week before Independence Day. As the monitor of the class, I led the motley group of schoolboys and our drill master trailed behind. We marched through the sleepy lanes of the town, shouting 'Mahatma Gandhi ki Jai', 'Bharat Mata ki Jai', while singing the standard prabhat pheri song, 'Uth jaag musafir bhor bhai, ab rain kahan jo sowat hai'[31] and bhajans[32] popularized

[30]Early morning rallies

[31]Awake and arise, O traveller, the dawn is breaking; shed your slumber, for the night is past

[32]Religious songs

by Gandhiji, like 'Raghupati Raghav Raja Ram'.

I tremendously enjoyed leading these rallies; my enthusiasm endeared me to the Headmaster, who joined us sometimes. On 15 August, we were required to wear caps dyed in kesaria[33] colour. Everyone got their caps dyed by the local rangrez[34] by paying him an anna[35] but my thrifty mother dyed my cap, herself, with turmeric powder, singling me out and plunging me into eternal shame. Notwithstanding my not-so-bright pale-yellow cap, when the Headmaster unfurled the tricolour on the ramparts of the old Garh, I was the lead singer on the dais, leading the rapturous school assembly in singing 'Jhanda uncha rahe hamara' (Let our flag fly high)!

◆

The task of leading the morning school prayer was assigned to me when the previous leader went to middle school. Our school prayer used to be a religious song: 'Hey Prabho, ananda-data, gyan humko deejiye!' (O Lord, giver of bliss, give us knowledge!) One day, the Headmaster handed me a long poem printed on cardboard: it was the new school prayer, Rabindranath Tagore's long poem 'Jana gana mana adhinayak jai he, Bharat bhagya vidhata', which had been adopted as the country's national anthem. I had never read the poem before, nor learnt the tune, so I sang haltingly. Unlike me, the boys didn't have the text before them, and the result was a discordant medley of sounds. Most of the words were beyond our comprehension and it was inordinately long to recite.

However, after some days, a message was received that only the first stanza was to be recited in daily prayer. That was a huge relief and we soon became quite adept at singing it. Instead of the

---

[33]Saffron

[34]Dyer

[35]4 paisa coin, equivalent to one-sixteenth of a rupee

religious content of the former morning prayer, our new school prayer had a vibrant nationalistic fervour.

◆

After the winter break, in January we learnt that the Inspector of Schools of Sikar district would arrive soon for inspection. The headmaster decided to put up an exhibition of paintings and handicrafts made by students, and stage a one-act play for the visitor.

The drawing master, Madan Lal Sharma, told me to paint portraits of Mahatma Gandhi and Jawaharlal Nehru, and to draw Bharat Mata holding the tricolour in her hand against the backdrop of the map of India. He guided me at every step. Indeed, he sketched the portraits himself in pencil, in amazing likeness of the two leaders, and 'helped' me colour them. Though the honour was bestowed upon me, they were his creations in all but name.

The Hindi teacher, Mangi Lal Sharma, was in charge of the one-act play. He chose a short play, *Daan Veer Karna,* narrating an episode from the Mahabharat where the crafty Krishna cajoles chivalrous (and charitable-to-a-fault) Karna to promise that he would not harm Arjun. My classmates Nagarmal Tewari and Tara Chand Gopalka were chosen for the roles of Krishna and Karna respectively and I played the role of Arjun. He made us rehearse the play several times. I distinctly remember the three of us draped in colourful silk costumes, wearing glittering diadems on our heads, our faces painted with heavy make-up. Shri Krishna held a flute in his hand while the two warriors carried bamboo-stick bows. We confidently acted our parts, reciting our dialogues in high-pitched theatrical voices. A stage was erected in the open ground outside the Garh, against the backdrop of the eastern wall. The students squatted on durries and the chief guest and teachers occupied chairs.

At the prize distribution ceremony, I received prizes for chart-making, singing, acting and being the highest scorer in my class.

As the Inspector handed out books, pens and pencils to me, I strutted about like a peacock. There was no tradition of naming the best student, but by showering most of the prizes on me, the Headmaster had made it amply clear.

◆

I had hoped to enter middle school in July, but that was not to be. It was decided that both the schools would be upgraded: the middle school into a high school and the Garh school into an upper primary school. So we stayed put in the Garh school till class 5.

I was sorely disappointed. Even the introduction of English from class 3 was deferred; it was to commence from class 6. But there was a bright side to it: our class continued to be the senior class of the school for the next three years! Tara Chand Sharma continued to be our Headmaster and I retained my favourite status, monitor of the senior class and de facto head boy of the school!

◆

Our school had no facilities for games and sports. The boys in our mohalla mostly played kabaddi, in the sand-filled lane in the evening.

Sometimes we played a fascinating game called gillidanda. While kabaddi is a sport of strength, gillidanda is a game of skill, like cricket: indeed, there is some resemblance between this game and cricket. The ball was replaced by a wooden gilli with perpendicular edges, and instead of a bat there was a danda. However, the gilli was not thrown to the man holding the danda, but placed on the ground and hit on the edge with the danda, in order to make it bounce and spin in the air. In that split second when the gilli is airborne, the man with the danda has to hit it hard and send it flying, over and above the reach of all other players who stand around him like fielders in cricket. The player is out if somebody catches the gilli in midair. The one who retrieves the gilli has to throw it back so as to hit the danda, which the player has placed on the ground meanwhile. If the gilli hits the danda, the player is out. Otherwise, he picks up the danda again and continues playing till he is out. The man who either takes a catch or hits the danda with the gilli then gets a turn to play. There are no teams in this game; it's one versus all. We used to play this game on holidays, outside the town, so as to avoid hitting passers-by in the lane.

Once, a boy got a big ball of rags made and we found some sticks which were curved at the end, and played a rustic version of hockey till the rag-ball was in tatters.

After coming home from school, I regularly played a game with cowries. This game could be played between two people, as well as among three or four. The game of cowries required precision. The cowries had to be thrown from a certain distance into a little hole made in hard ground, about two inches in diameter and of the same depth. Every player had to contribute a couple of cowries for each round of the game.

To determine who would have the first throw of the game, every player was required to throw his master cowry into the hole. The master cowry was special: bigger, heavier and filled with hot liquid nickel. The one who 'holed' the master cowry first, got the first throw. He collected cowries from each player and threw them into the hole, and won the ones which he 'holed'. He could win the ones lying outside by hitting a particular cowry indicated by his opponents, with his master cowry, but that was a rare feat. On the other hand, if he missed that particular cowry and hit another, he lost even the ones he had 'holed'. Generally, he missed the designated cowry, and the next boy threw the remaining cowries. The game continued till the last cowry was holed or hit, when the next round began.

Chauth Mal, about two years senior to me in age, had an uncanny knack and hit the jackpot often. He was named after the day he had been born on, the auspicious day of Karva Chauth, the fourth day of the bright half of the month of Kartik, when women observe a day-long fast to pray for the long lives of their husbands, and eat only after seeing the moon rise.

Very often, a boy exhausted his stock of cowries and had to buy cowries from Chauth Mal, at the rate of a paisa a dozen. At the end of the game, Chauth Mal was richer by a few annas, which wasn't a mean sum in those days. One anna could buy you a plateful of crisp pakoras from the famous Lala Halwai or a leaf-full of home-made ice-cream from Ramu Barfwalla.

I loved flying paper kites. Unlike cowries, it was an expensive pursuit; charkhis[36] of kite thread and big multi-coloured kites were beyond my means. I could only buy small kites worth a paisa or two, so I contented myself with the kites that came my way: the ones that were cut loose by other kites, and which I then chased down. Mercifully, kite-flying had a specific season: it began in late December, during the winter holidays for Christmas, and culminated with the festival of Makar Sakranti.

We did not have a terrace of our own from where I could fly a kite, so I had to go to someone's haveli. These restrictions never dampened my zeal: many a time I would fly my small kites standing precariously on the sloping tin roof of our house! I had to fly my kites low because of my measly stock of thread and also out of fear of getting entangled in a 'fight' with other kites and losing my kite.

Men, too, indulged in the game. One man, Goverdhan, was a passionate kite-flyer. He had big ornate kites and reels of thread coated with glass powder, which sliced the thread of other kites easily. He delighted in long-range kite fights and triumphantly shouted *'Woh kata!'* when he 'cut' other kites. On the other hand, if

---

[36]Spool or reel

his kite was 'cut', he became hell-bent on revenge and would send up another in the sky. Sometimes, he would allow me to fly his kite when there was no competition around, and rarely permitted me to engage in a fight with his kite.

•◆

There were no restaurants or eateries in the town; eating out was an unknown concept, even among the well-to-do. Halwai shops sold traditional sweets like barfi, kalakand or peda made from milk and laddoo or jalebi made from gram flour. The hot pakoras of the jocular Lala Halwai tempted me every evening, and I used to steal a chavanni[37] from my mother's meagre coffer once in a while to buy them. There was always a queue of men waiting for their turn for the pakoras, especially in winter.

Ramu Barfwala's creamy slices of ice were another mouth-watering temptation. He lived in a nearby settlement and came, with his wares in a wooden box, during the sizzling summer months. He would even give me goodies on credit, which soon became a problem; it wasn't possible to steal that often.

•◆

Independence had brought Partition in its wake, which turned the world topsy-turvy and the whole Muslim mohalla was thrown into turmoil. The Maharaja of Jaipur had assured the Muslim population that they could continue to stay in India if they wished to, so there was minimal migration from the Muslim mohallas of Jaipur.

Our mohalla was separated from the Muslim one, by one lane. Miru and Aladin Teli were our immediate neighbours. Often, I went to their large havelis to buy sesame or mustard oil. An

---

[37]Four-anna coin

ox, with blinkered eyes, went around the ghani[38] in the haveli's chowk, turning the enormous wooden pestle to crush the sesame or mustard seeds. Years of spilled oil had made the floor jet-black and sticky. Miru and Aladin Teli told my parents that they were all going to Pakistan. They offered an oil-soaked manjoosh[39], about 3 feet high, as a gift, and in thanks, my mother gave them a few rupees.

In the next few days, the Muslim mohalla became deserted. The sundry Muslim families elsewhere in the town also started leaving. A rumour started circulating that a rangrez from the main bazaar had been murdered, and panic stalked the town thereafter. Curfew was clamped on the town and the army began patrolling the streets.

My fevered imagination created gory visions of severed heads and limbs, slain by unknown assassins. Nightmares haunted me and I dared not go out.

◆

After a month of the Muslims' departure from the town, on a Sunday afternoon, curiosity drove me and my brother to enter the deserted mosque. We would have never dreamt of stepping inside when the Muslims were there, nor would they have allowed it: such an act was unthinkable then.

I had a certain dread of Muslims; with their piercing looks and long pointed beards, they had a fierce aspect. No Muslim boy studied in our school although a sizable Muslim population lived in the town. And although we lived in houses separated by just a lane, no Muslim boy ever came to play with us. We had some professional contact with them, buying cooking oil or an iron chain for the cow.

---

[38]Wooden oil press

[39]A wooden box

My brother and I tiptoed into the bare prayer hall of the mosque, paved with gleaming white ceramic tiles. It was bereft of all ornament; there was no painting or icon, so unlike our temples! I saw some glazed tiles lying in a corner and, on an impulse, picked them up. I thought of fixing them in the alcove where I kept my school books. Then, we began exploring the house beside the mosque. I found a tiny wooden sewing box, its top studded with little mirrors. I couldn't resist the temptation of picking it up as well. My brother saw a wooden pestle with iron bands fixed on its ends, lying in the corner of a room. The one we had in our house was heavy and unwieldy, this one was much lighter. 'Let's take this. Mother would be so pleased,' he said as he picked it up.

As we came out, Ruggha Meena, who lived further down the same lane, saw us carrying away those things. He was a police informer and took us to the police station near the Garh school. We were mortified; suddenly, from bright schoolboys we had turned into petty thieves.

Father came running to the thana with some men from the community but the thanedar refused to let us off. Only after the intervention of the Tehsildar, were we released on bail. The matter went up to the Munsiff Magistrate's court at Neem Ka Thana, two stations away by train. We appeared before him a few times over the next few months before he finally pardoned us on promise of good behaviour.

I was struck by the fragility of the frontiers of respectability, and realized how imperceptibly one could slip into the world of crime!

5

GROWING UP

We grew up solely in our mother's care, as our father was generally away in Indore, Raigarh or Barwani for most part of the year, on work.

My mother was a veritable powerhouse of energy and kept a punishing daily schedule of work for herself—with not a moment's rest during her waking hours. She had no time for molly-coddling us. Indeed, she was a stern parent, and if she harboured tender feelings for us, she kept them to herself, rarely exhibiting them.

Mother rose very early, when the stars still dazzled brightly in the firmament, and judged the time by the position of the stars in the sky. Indeed, the star-studded sky served as a kind of celestial clock to her. She recognized the three bright stars, which our ancient sages called Mrig-Shirsh (Head of the Deer) and had named the month of Margshirsha after them. It followed the month of Kartik. In the Western zodiac signs, it's called the Hunter's Belt. My mother called it by its Hindi name, 'Hirni' (a female deer). By looking at the position of the Hirni, in the eastern firmament, she could have a fair sense of time.

She began her day by grinding flour on her manually operated chakki[40], which consisted of two heavy circular stones about two feet in diameter. The lower stone was fixed, while the upper one was rotated by a handle to grind grains. Mother would squat on

[40]Grinding mill

the floor, her legs gripping the chakki, her right hand holding the wooden handle to turn the upper wheel clockwise, while her left hand dropped grains into the hole near the central shaft—her body moving in sync, her odhani slipping away from her head, her pigtail dancing. She did this in the dim light of a tiny kerosene lamp, while my brother and I slept on a cot nearby. I could dimly make out the vigorous rocking movements of her lean frame, although the chakki's sound acted like lullaby and sent us into deep sleep. In an hour or so, sweating all over, she was able to grind about two seers of barley flour, which was enough for the three of us.

There were days when she didn't have to grind the flour and it was too early to milk the cow. She would remain reclining in her bed adjacent to ours and sing bhajans in her sonorous voice.

> *Kali dah par khelan aayo ri, Jasoda tero Kanhaiyo.*
> O Yashoda, your Kanhaiya has come to sport and amuse himself on Kali Lake.

There was a flour-grinding mill in the town. The charges were minimal, a rupee for a maund[41], but my mother disapproved of the idea. She believed that the flourmill's fast, mechanical grinding process greatly diminished the vitality of the grain. Besides, she did not want her well-cleaned grains to mix with the weevil-infested stuff brought by others. In any case, she said, she couldn't abandon the good old chakki of her mother-in-law!

Flour grinding done, she retreated to the thatched house in the backyard, where the cow was tethered, just as the rosy tints of early dawn appeared on the eastern sky. She took the cow out, collected the dung in a basket and cleaned the stall. After milking the cow, she fed her cotton-seed cakes and crushed grains, and filled her trough with nutritious fodder. Thereafter, she mixed the

---

[41]A maund had 40 'seers'

cowdung with the remnants of fodder and made dung cakes called thapri, spreading them on the boundary wall to dry. The thapris made excellent fuel for her chulha[42].

She managed to accomplish all this about an hour before sunrise.

•◆

After tending to the cow she went to the kitchen, which was also in the backyard. She swept the kitchen floor and rekindled the fire in the chulha from the embers. The matchbox had arrived, but she was loathe to abandon the hallowed tradition of maintaining the fire. She preserved the embers carefully in the chulha, never allowing them to be extinguished, in deference to one of her mother-in-law's earliest diktats. At that time, safety matches had been unknown; if the home fire was extinguished, one had to go to a neighbour for live embers.

Barley was our staple diet. It was the cheapest foodgrain: five ser[43] of barley cost a rupee, the price of two ser of wheat. Mother used to keep some wheat flour in home-made papier-mâché containers called dhoomla. She had made these containers herself by spreading finely crushed paper pulp on inverted earthen pitchers. Wheat flour was kept in reserve for preparing sweetened fluffy gulgule or poories during festivals, or to make thin chapattis, called phulkas, for special guests like my sister's husband when he came visiting. Eating wheat was a status symbol and only the rich could afford it. In winter, we ate home-grown bajra. Mother made bajra rotis for lunch and sometimes she bought maize, ground it and made yellow makki rotis to break the monotony.

My mother's thick barley rotis, baked on the earthen tawa[44] and on the embers, were perfect. She prided herself on her roti-making

[42]Fireplace

[43]A 'ser' was slightly less than a kilogram

[44]Equivalent of a hot plate

skills and soaked them in home-made ghee. After coming back from school, I polished off a couple of these thick rotis with mashed potato curry made in buttermilk or with green leafy vegetables or daal. Never, in my later life, have I eaten anything more delicious or satiating! Mother packed some rotis for herself and left the more generously buttered ones for the two of us, in the manjoosh gifted by Miru Teli.

After that, she set off to fetch fodder for the cow from the fields. Before leaving, she hollered at us to wake up and reminded us to not be late for school.

◆

During summer months, our school started at seven o'clock. Before sunrise, my brother and I went for ablutions to the nearest well, called Biasry, which was half a kilometre away from our home. This well belonged to some Jat cultivators who lived in settlements nearby. They did not object to our defecating in their fields as it added to soil fertility. We carried two buckets and a rope for drawing water. The well was about 40 feet deep. After bathing, we brought back the buckets filled with water, supplementing Mother's supplies of drinking water.

Quite often, the well was 'running'. The cultivators would be irrigating their fields, drawing water by a charsa. On those days, we were saved the trouble of drawing water. We would just strip down to our underpants and lie down on the stone floor called *dhana*, where the charsa was emptied and cool waves of water would flow over us.

Our breakfast generally consisted of *chhach raabri*, cold barley gruel mixed with buttermilk, which was quite filling. There was no school uniform; we mostly wore a white shirt and khaki shorts stitched by a town tailor—hand-washed and unpressed. The older boys came to school wearing white or striped pajamas. None wore trousers except for a few teachers. For shoes, we had *jutis* made by local cobblers. Father had bought us two briefcase-size tin boxes from Indore to carry our books in to school, which made us mighty proud.

It was my duty, before going to school, to take the cow to the cattle collection point near the railway line and leave her in the custody of the cowherd, Sonu Padhya. He would take the entire town herd to a village pond for day-long grazing and bring it back in the evening at the same point. While returning, the cows hurried to their homes on their own, needing no escort!

◆

While we were at school, Mother worked in the field, mowing or reaping the grass. After a quick break to eat her breakfast rotis, she resumed and continued till she had made a huge pile. She bundled it all up and, with the help of a cowherd, placed the load on her head and started homewards. Two or three times, on the way, she had to take the load off and rest awhile.

My mother would come back sometime later, carrying a headload of fodder. She would eat her lunch and rest awhile. Her schedule was somewhat relaxed in the evening. The only hard task left was to fetch drinking water. After her day-long exhuasting tasks, this was like going on an excursion in the company of the household ladies, the only time she got for chit-chat and update on daily events. She would wear her sequined lehenga and odhani and accompany the other ladies to the well, which lay beyond the railway line, on her way to the fields.

◆

We reached home from school at around 2 p.m. sometime before Mother arrived and greatly relished our lunch of barley rotis soaked in ghee, accompanied by spicy vegetable curries, finishing with a bit of gur[45] for dessert.

---

[45]Jaggery

In summer, dinner was usually a wheat gruel called dalia, made of coarsely ground wheat mixed with moong daal. Once in a while, Mother would also cook a barley dalia, called ghaat, going through the elaborate process of de-husking the barley grains. In winter, she made bajra khichdi for dinner: we ate the khichdi with ghee, along with besan kadhi[46] as an accompaniment.

Once or twice a week, my mother had to perform a very arduous task after returning from the field: chopping dry bajra stalks with a hand chopper, for the cow. The task was as strenuous as it was hazardous. A cloud of tiny straw particles and fine dust engulfed her as she worked, settling on her hair. The after-effects of this were to be far-reaching: years later, when I was in college in Jaipur, she was hospitalized there for tuberculosis.

She was an astonishing bundle of energy. The other ladies in our guwadi marvelled at her—for keeping a cow and feeding her by bringing fodder, so painstakingly gathered, from faraway fields. For them, their usual daily grind was back-breaking enough—grinding flour, fetching drinking water from sweetwater wells outside the town, cooking food, rearing children and doing sundry, never-ending chores!

•◆

Mother once narrated a tale about the dalia. A thrifty housewife had cooked dalia for dinner. But her husband was still sitting in the porch, gossiping with a neighbour over puffs of hookah. She dreaded calling him openly for dinner, lest he invite the neighbour. Therefore by way of giving him a veiled invite she sent her little boy to give him a coded message:

Dalpatsinghji aaya chhen (Dalpatsinghji has come),
Loonkaranji saath chhen (He's accompanied by Loonkaranji),
Milno ho to mil-lyo (If you want to meet them, come quickly),

[46]Gram flour curry cooked in buttermilk

Nahin to ghati utriya jayen chhen (Else they are going down the mountain pass).

Dalpatsingh was none other than the precious dalia, who was accompanied by Loonkaran—the good old '*loon*' (Sanskrit: *lavana,* salt). She obliquely conveyed to her husband that if he did not come in soon to partake of his share of the dalia, she and the children would make short work of it—it would go down their gullet.

◆

Once I had returned from a conference in Calcutta and she asked me how I felt when I was travelling in an aeroplane. I told her that the plane goes sailing over a bed of clouds and that I saw the snow-covered Himalayas to my left when we were flying over Bihar. She was wonderstruck. 'Only Vishnu,' she said, 'could behold such a sight perched on his Garuda. 'You are lucky like the gods!' she had said.

I arranged a joyride for her in a small trainer plane in the Pinjore Flying Club. She boarded the plane with great trepidation but came back wonderstruck and elated.

6

TALES BY FIRESIDE

On cold winter evenings, Mother would tell us many stories, sitting by the chulha, stirring the broth, as we sat in the cozy warmth of thc hearth. Here are some of the stories that I particularly liked.

THE PRINCE WHO KILLED A TIGER

A prince had been exiled from his kingdom by his father, for some reason, and had wandered far into the capital of another kingdom. He had been lodging in an inn, for the night, where he learnt that the king would marry his beautiful daughter to one who, riding the king's wild and impetuous horse and wielding the king's heavy sword, chopped off the nose and ears of a tiger in the forest. The tiger had turned into a man-eater and had become a menace to the people. None dared ride the king's wayward horse nor wield his heavy sword and go into the forest to meet the tiger, so the princess had remained unwed.

The exiled prince took up the challenge. He went to the king's palace in the morning and asked for his sword to slay the tiger. He was given a heavy, double-edged sword, its handle inlaid with gold. Then he proceeded to the king's stable for the king's horse. They took him to a tall black stallion who was impatiently tugging at his reins. The prince patted him, affectionately caressed him and saddled him. Untying his reins, he mounted and went into the forest at a gallop. Many other youths of the town went after him on their own mounts.

After exploring the jungle for a long time, the prince sighted the tiger lurking behind a bush and gave chase. Soon he caught up with him and in a swift maneuver, slayed him with the king's sharp sword. He dismounted, chopped off the tiger's nose and ears, put them in his pocket and rode back. He was weary to the bone after his adventure, tired and thirsty. He, therefore, stopped by a spring to drink water. The horse was thirsty too, so he took him to the water. Exhausted, the prince went to sleep under a shady tree, tying the reins of the king's horse to his toe.

The young men who had come following him, saw the dead tiger lying in the forest and the prince sleeping under a tree. They chopped different parts of the dead tiger and returned to the king's palace, each claiming to have killed the tiger. But none had the tiger's ears and nose.

The king sent his soldiers in search of the young man who had taken the royal steed and the sword. They found him and woke him up. He mounted the royal stallion and rode back to the palace and produced the tiger's nose and ears before the king. The king was overjoyed to meet this handsome and courageous youth and invited him to stay at the palace. Preparations were made for the royal wedding and shortly afterwards, the brave prince was married to the lovely princess. He began to live in the palace as the consort of the princess.

A few months later, in the pleasant month of Shravan, the prince and the princess were sitting in the palace balcony. The sky was overcast and dark clouds came thundering in the eastern skies. There were flashes of lightning and the prince said to the princess, 'Look, dear, the lightning is striking in the direction of our kingdom!' He had not revealed his identity so far and the princess was surprised.

'You have a kingdom?' she asked.

'Yes, dear, my father's kingdom is even larger than your revered sire's.'

'O wow!' The princess exclaimed ecstatically. 'Then let's go home!'

The happy king sent them in his royal chariot along with a posse of soldiers. The prince returned to his kingdom with his pretty bride, to a hero's welcome, and they lived happily ever after.

THE QUEEN'S PLAN

There was a king who was very fond of hunting. One day, he went along a little river and sighted a black buck under a mango tree. He gave chase, even shot an arrow, but the buck escaped.

It was a hot and stuffy day and the king was thirsty. After a while, he came upon a field of corn. A young woman was hoeing the crop, removing the weeds and singing softly to herself. On seeing him she stopped her work and stood looking at him. The king reined in his horse, dismounted and asked for water. She went to a nearby tree, brought a small pitcher lying under it and poured water into his cupped hands. The water tasted like nectar to the thirsty king. As he rode off, the woman resumed her hoeing and her song.

On his return to the palace in the evening, he found his queen reclining under an awning on the terrace; two ladies were fanning her from both sides of her bed. She sat up seeing the king, and remarked: 'What hot and beastly weather, milord! Twice have I bathed but there's no respite.'

The king retorted, 'My dear queen, you should have seen that young woman hoeing her field of corn in the sizzling sun at noon! She was singing to herself while she was hoeing! And here you are! Cribbing and complaining while the chambermaids are fanning you!'

The queen was hurt by the king's taunting remark. She thought of a plan to teach him a lesson. The next morning she called the palace gardeners and told them to stop watering the garden. They were stupefied by her order and told her the plants would die. She dismissed them, saying they were to do as told.

A week later, the king and the queen were sitting on the terrace in the evening when he noticed that his garden was dying; the shrubs and creepers had withered and the trees were shedding their leaves. They were obviously withering for lack of irrigation. He called the gardeners and asked why they had not watered the plants. They told him that the queen had forbidden them. He cast an angry look at her and asked her why.

She smiled and said, 'O my wise lord, look at the trees on the hill yonder. They are green and merrily swaying in the wind. Who waters them, pray? Why can't our garden plants be that way? Why are they wilting and dying?'

'But can't you understand?' The king explained, 'The trees on the hill are not raised in the way our garden plants are. They are different.'

'Exactly, milord! Your queen too was not raised like the lovely lass you saw in the cornfield.'

THE ELEPHANT WHO KILLED HIS MAHOUT

The Rao-Raja of Samod had a majestic elephant. One day, the mahout took him to the pond in the town for drinking water. Leaving the elephant there, he went off. Some boys bought a packet of batasha[47] and threw them before the elephant, one at a time. The elephant picked up the coin-sized batashas with the tip of his long trunk, put them in his mouth and enjoyed them immensely.

---

[47]Fluffy snack made of white sugar

When all the batashas were finished, a boy thought of a prank. He brought a white pebble of the same size and placed it before the elephant, who picked it up and when he crushed it, his teeth broke. He was wild with rage and ran after the kids, who fled. The mahout came back in the meanwhile. He ran after the furious elephant. On seeing his mahout, the enraged elephant picked him up in his trunk and threw him down with a thud on the cobbled road, killing him instantly.

The mahout's wife heard about the elephant having gone berserk and killing her husband. Her world collapsed. She brought her eight-year-old son, made him stand before the elephant and with tears rolling down her cheeks, she told the elephant, 'You have killed his father, now kill him also!' The elephant advanced slowly towards the boy, stood for a moment before him and then lifted him with his trunk and placed him on his back where the mahout sat! 'He is my mahout now,' the elephant apparently told the mahout's distraught wife and walked back to the palace.

TALE OF TWO SISTERS—HALDI AND SOONTH

Mother would also narrate a charming fable about the two sisters, Haldi (turmeric) and Soonth (dried ginger). The two sisters, she said, had different traits. While Haldi was a hard-working girl, Soonth was ease-loving and lazy. Once Haldi had gone to stay at her nani's[48] place. She cheerfully helped her nani with household chores and when she left after a few weeks, her nani gave her many gifts—ornaments and new clothes. Some time later Soonth also went to stay with her nani. Unlike her sister, she lazed around the whole day, never stirring her little finger. When her nani asked her to fetch something or hang her washing on the line, she paid no heed, pretending she hadn't heard. Her nani would get exasperated

[48]Maternal grandmother

and tell her what a wonderful, hard-working girl Haldi was. Soonth would pout and retort with utter disdain:

> *Woh thi koi Haldi-faldi, mein hun sathvan Soonth.*
> *Kaam karoon to mere saal par jaye na!*
>
> That Haldi-faldi is a common and coarse girl, I am special, delicate and refined. If I were to do household chores, I would get aches and cramps in my body.

This fable brought out the distinctive properties of these two condiments. During winter, women ate laddoos made of haldi and soonth to tone the body. While one may continue doing household chores when consuming haldi laddoos, one had to take special precautions when eating soonth laddoos and avoid exposing oneself to the elements and refrain from strenuous physical activity. During winter, when my mother made soonth laddoos for herself and ate them in a week or so, she required our assistance in doing outdoor chores like fetching drinking water from the well; she often used to relate this story then.

FATHER'S TALE OF THE BOY JHOONTHYA

My father, too, used to tell us stories on occasion, when he was at home. I remember his story about this boy Jhoonthya who had once gone to his nanihal[49]. He had to pass through a dense forest, where he met various wild animals on the way, each wanting to eat him up. Jhoonthya told each of them to wait until he returned from his nani's house after eating kheer and malpua every day, adding a lot of fat to his bare bones and becoming mota-jhota[50]. However,

[49]Mother's parental home

[50]Fat and chubby like a calf

on his way back he got a dholki[51] from his nani which was sealed at both ends. He climbed into it and swiftly rolled it down the forest path. When the lion saw the dholki hurtling down, he asked it if it had seen the boy Jhoonthya. The dholki merrily chimed:

Kaisa Jhoonthya, kiski baat?
Chal meri dholki dhamak dhum!

Who is this Jhoonthya? What are you talking about?
Go my dholki—dhamak dhum!

The bear and the wolf got the same answer from the dholki and Jhoonthya reached home in one piece.

MOTHER'S REPERTOIRE OF CEREMONIAL SONGS

My mother had a phenomenal memory for songs sung collectively by ladies on formal occasions, like weddings and festivals. There were different songs for a boy's or a girl's wedding, and for different occasions in the course of the wedding, like the reception of the baraat[52] or the wedding couple going round the sacred fire or at the time of vidai[53]. My mother knew them all and always led the chorus. Maybe it had something to do with her higher rank in the hierarchy; every woman in our extended family addressed her as 'Kakiji'[54].

Her vast repertoire amazed me no end. Now, I only remember the refrain of a song at the bride's vidai:

Lala Sedhu Ramji saal sambhal, Kanhaiyo laadi lai gayo!

O Lala Sedhu Ram, check out the inner rooms;
Kanhaiya has taken the bride away!

[51]A wooden drum
[52]Marriage party
[53]Farewell
[54]Next in rank to the mother-in-law

'Sedhu Ram' is a typical name; the name of the bride's father was substituted in its place. 'Kanhaiya' alluded to Lord Krishna, who had abducted his beloved, Rukmani, from her father's house before the start of the Mahabharata war.

There were songs for different occasions—at the reception of the baraat, during *var-mala*[55] when dinner was being served to the wedding guests, or the most important event—when the wedding couple took seven rounds of the sacred fire. Similarly, there were other songs for kunwar-kalewa (bridegroom's breakfast) next morning, and so on, till the poignant vidai—bidding farewell to the bride.

My mother also had a knack of quoting apt sayings.

Holi paachhe dhablo, maar khasam ke moond!

What use is a colourfully knitted skirt after the Holi festival is over? Throw it on the husband's face!

Aap Missarji katara maare auran ne updesh sunave!

Misraji himself is killing the swarm of locusts and giving a religious lecture to others!

Dekh parai chopri kyun tarsave jeev, rookhi sookhi khai ke thanda paani peev!

Why torment yourself with self-pity seeing others eating buttered bread? Eat your coarse and dry bread and drink cool water!

Kaankh mein chhoro, gaon mein hero!

Holding the child under her arm and looking for him in the village!

---

[55]Garlanding of the bridegroom

Sir par to dheero, tamboo mein barba deejyo!

Carrying a load of dried nettles on his head and wanting to enter into a tent!

A DIALOGUE WITH THEKEDARJI

On a hot summer day, my mother was fetching water from the well beyond the railway line. She was all alone. She was carrying an earthen pitcher on her head with a brass container on top. The rope for drawing water from the well had been folded and was tucked up in her right hand, which she was using simultaneously for balancing the pitcher. In her left hand she carried a water-filled bucket.

As she was passing the sand-filled street in front of Ram Sahai Thekedar's haveli, he was reclining against cushions on a wooden takhta in the veranda of his haveli. On seeing my mother, he struck up a conversation with her, asking about my father and our general well-being. Standing in the middle of the sandy path, with the heavy load on her head, she answered his queries. He asked what the boys were doing. At that time I was studying in class 6 and my brother in class 8. She briefed him accordingly. He then remarked: '*Patelanji, padhai mein kya niklega? Unko koi kaam sikhao*.' (What's the use of schooling? Let them learn some job.) She replied that as they were going to school at present, they couldn't possibly be doing any job and added, '*Padhne ke baad koi naukari kar lenge*.' (They will find a job after finishing their studies.)

'*Sarkari naukari milna aasaan nahi hai, Patelanji*,' he retorted. '*Aur padh kar woh kaunsi Collector ki kursi hi pakrenge?*' (It's not easy to get a government job. In any case, are they going to occupy the Collector's chair after their studies?) He was suggesting that rather than whiling away our time in school, we should start learning chiselling and stone-carving like the other boys of our community, to be able to earn a livelihood. As a matter of fact, government jobs, like a teacher's, were few in those days.

My mother was incensed by his patronizing tone and replied, '*Woh Collector kyon nahin ban sakte, Thekedarji? Collector bhi padhne wale ladke hi bante hain*'. (Why can't they become a Collector? After all, it's only through studies that one becomes a Collector.) The Thekedar was speechless at her curt retort, and she turned to go.

She told us about this conversation when she came home and added, '*Tum man laga kar padho aur iss ghadai-chinai ke chakkar se niklo*.' (You should concentrate on studies to get out of this rut of stone-carving and bricklaying.)

Ram Sahai Thekedar was still around when, after about 14 years of this conversation, the town rejoiced at my entry into the IAS, in 1964—the first boy to make it from Sikar district. My mother lived to see me become Collector of Bhiwani district in the neighbouring state of Haryana, in 1974.

THE YOUNG SADHU WHO ATE GREEN GRASS

My mother was a deeply religious person, yet she was a practical, earthy woman. She had scant regard for saffron-robed miracle men or soothsayers who visited the town occasionally.

A young sadhu came to the town once. His long black hair came down to his bare shoulders and he sported a goatee. He looked emaciated, lean and hungry. He walked barefoot and a small saffron cloth was wrapped around his loins. However, the most amazing thing about him was that although it looked like he was starving, when some women offered him food, he staunchly refused it.

Indeed he accepted neither food nor money. He had let it be known that he only ate green grass, which put him in the rare category of a siddh purush[56] and gave him an aura of being larger

[56]One who had attained *siddhis*—miraculous powers

than life. He was instantly hailed as one who was cognizant of the past and future. People fell at his feet and he went round listening to people's woes, giving monosyllabic, cryptic answers. A trail of town urchins followed him into the lanes of the town. I was among the followers.

He had been going round the town since morning but had eaten nothing the whole day. No one had a grass lawn in the whole town who could offer him green grass to eat. Therefore, in the evening the boys took him outside the town, towards the farmers' fields that were irrigated by wells.

As this procession approached the railway line at the outskirts of the town, my mother happened to be coming down the way with a huge load of green grass on her head. The boys stopped her and told her that the young sadhu wanted to eat grass and asked if she'd give him a handful. She was tired to the bone, her neck was aching under the load and she was impatient to reach home. She was flabbergasted at this strange request; she couldn't believe a man could eat grass. Impulsively, she threw the huge load in front of the young Baba, saying, '*Le, khale dhap ke*!' (Here, eat your bellyful!)

Faced with such irreverence, the Baba took to his heels. He just fled from there, going towards the railway line and was running towards the railway station to the right. The boys too ran after him. No one heard of him ever again.

I was mortified by my mother's behaviour towards the young sadhu. She should have stopped for a minute and let them take a handful of grass for the Baba, but I said nothing to her. I helped her to lift her load and we walked home together.

7

LIFE IN THE TOWN

There were quite a few imposing temples in our town and during festivals like Ram Navami or Krishna Janmashtami, they were beautifully decorated.

During the long summer holidays, the temples were our favourite haunts. My brother and I used to make a daily circuit of the town's main temples in the evening, a kind of 'temple crawling'.

We would start with the Raghunathji temple, which was just two blocks away from the High School. Like all our major temples, it was constructed on the first floor. On entering the temple gate, you had to go up a flight of stairs to emerge on a huge open terrace enclosed by a high latticework wall. Beyond the terrace was a spacious pillared prayer hall, its walls and ceiling painted with frescoes. At the end of the prayer hall was the sanctum sanctorum with three graceful shikharas[57] rising high in the sky.

Some katha (Puranic tale) or pravachan (discourse) by a pundit would be in progress at the open terrace—the pundit would be expatiating on an episode from the Ramayana or the Mahabharata or expounding a religious theme before a congregation of 50-60 people seated cross-legged on cotton floormats. Even in the stifling summer days of June, it was quite pleasant in the temple compounds.

In each temple that we visited, we paid obeisance to the deities ensconced in the sanctum sanctorum. We would then sit for a

---

[57]Cupola

while in the congregation, soak in the ambience and quietly leave.

Further down, in the vicinity of the Garh school, at the crossroads of the school road and the Khandela Bazaar, was the most revered Gopinathji temple. Its construction was initiated by the town's founder Diwan Khushali Ram Bohra himself. Going up the flight of white marble steps, one entered the main temple hall resting on fluted pillars, with ornate paintings on the ceiling. Its gracefully sculpted pillars supported a slanting tiered roof, giving the temple hall the appearance of a vimana[58], setting off to high heaven.

The façade of the sanctum sanctorum, at the end, was studded with gems and coloured stones and was intricately carved. Lord Krishna stood inside, in his romantic pose, playing the flute to his beloved Radha. I never tired of gazing at them.

Some singer would be singing songs about Lord Krishna to the accompaniment of harmonium and tabla. We would sit for a while in the cool air with other devotees and then leave.

Sauntering through the bazaar, we came to the Shiva temple in the centre of the town at aarti time. We would go up the steps and stand around the inner shrine, joining the assembled throng of devotees in zestfully singing the aarti. It was composed by Swami Shivananda, with the refrain, *'Om Har Har Har Mahadeva!'*

The temple hall resounded with the deafening sounds of the musical instruments: drums, gongs, cymbals, khartal and chimta. The priest held a lighted multi-wick lamp in his hand which he moved rhythmically around the lingam in adoration, its flickering flames creating an enchanting spectacle. At the end, he sprinkled holy water from a conch shell on the assembled devotees and then came holding the flaming lamp to the devotees, for them to imbibe its aura. They extended their palms to the fumes of its myriad

---

[58]Sanskrit: aeroplane

flames and touched their forehead and eyes in benediction. The aarti was a soulful experience.

On coming down, we would go behind the Shiva temple and enter the cave-like little Hanuman temple. The vermilion statue of the monkey god was in a niche under the very khejri tree, said to have been planted by the town's founder over two centuries ago. The massive trunk of the wrinkled old tree juts out of the Hanuman temple's ceiling in a huge leafy canopy.

Squatting on the temple's cool tiled floor we recited the 'Hanuman Chalisa', a rhymed poem in 40 stanzas, composed by the great poet Tulsidas and memorized by every child. In childhood, one is more susceptible to fears of ghosts and goblins and the 'Hanuman Chalisa' is supposed to work like a talisman against them.

Tuesday is considered Hanuman's day. A stream of people brought offerings of laddoos or pedas on that day and distributed it to those present in the temple, which made us prolong our stay in the temple on Tuesdays.

The temple of Sita Ramji, also built on a high terrace, is on the periphery of the central chaupar. We would sit a while to listen to the usual 'pravachan' in the open terrace. This temple had organized uninterrupted recitals (akhand paath) of Tulsidas's classic *Ramcharitmanas* in later years and I had participated in it.

Late in the evening, we would return home via the Surani Bazaar, which led to our mohalla. The entire temple circuit would involve a walk of about three kilometres and take a couple of hours to finish.

◆

In our mohalla, there was a Murli Manohar temple, smaller than the grand ones in the town. It was constructed by our mason community and was like a private chapel to us. For a few years during my childhood, I took an active part in the evening aarti at this temple, chanting and vigorously beating the gong or the drum.

During our summer holidays I often repaired to this little temple after my morning meal, to escape the unbearable heat of our tin-roofed house. I would lie down in the temple's airy veranda, looking up at the crudely painted frescos on its arched ceiling and walls.

Next to this temple was our community hall called Nohra, with a huge iron gate which was always kept closed. It was meant primarily for meetings of the community panchayat and was also used to lodge wedding parties.

There was another beautiful temple of Murli Manoharji, which was famous for its special decorations on the occasion of Krishna Janamshtami. It was built on the ground floor, and lay to the west of the chaupar in the Sikar Bazaar. It was off our circuit. We only visited it on Janamshtami to look at the fascinating tableaus (jhanki) set up by the temple.

There was a Bhairon temple at a place called Poladas, about two kilometres away to the north of the town, where an annual fair was held. The small shrine had a rough stone slab for a statue, daubed in vermilion, dedicated to Bhaironji[59]. The way to Poladas was partly sandy and partly along the railway line. My mother gave me a chavanni, a four-anna coin, for the fair. I went to the fair with some school friends. We roamed around at the fair, ate dahi vada from a stall and then had a fizzy orange drink.

My friends had left early but I stayed back, enjoying the balmy evening.

Dusk had fallen when I started my return journey. I was walking on the railway track, stepping on the wooden sleepers, when I overtook a small boy, six or seven years old. He told me that he lived in a small dhani some distance away. A few minutes later, the boy shouted in joy; he had found a one-rupee coin lying near

[59]Bhairava, a gana of Lord Shiva

the railway line! He was overjoyed and showed the coin to me.

I was green with envy. One rupee was no mean sum. Four annas, a quarter of a rupee, had got me a plate of dahi vada and a soft drink. I wanted to snatch the coin from him. It was dark by now and there was no one else around. It seemed so easy to dupe or rob the boy. I told him that the coin was not genuine and took it from him on the pretext of examining it. I could see that it was genuine. As I dilly-dallied in returning it, a man overtook us and the boy complained to him. Reluctantly, I had to return the coin.

The man had walked ahead of us and we were left alone again. But I couldn't figure out how to take the coin from him. Indeed, there was no other way but to snatch it from him and run away. I was contemplating this move and was about to do it when another man suddenly materialized from behind us and I had to abandon the plan. This man also went ahead of us and once again we were left alone.

But I couldn't summon enough courage as the boy would begin howling and I might get caught. It struck me as extraordinary that I could not execute my plan to rob the child on the long lonely walk in darkness. Suddenly the boy turned left and ran towards a small cluster of thatched houses. He had reached home with the rupee coin squeezed in his palm.

I was left alone now on the deserted railway track. I felt as if I had been struck by a thunderbolt! That moment it dawned on me that there was a palpable presence of power in the universe!

◆

Festivals were celebrated in our town with great fervour. Teej was celebrated on the third day of Vaishakh, when the idols of Gangaur were taken out to the high sandy ground near the gau-shala, beyond the Khandela Bazaar. When I was in class 5, at the end of this festival, a film called *Krishna-Arjun Yuddha* was screened. We gaped in wonder at the giant screen under the open sky: it was mind-blowing.

Ganesh Chaturthi was celebrated in Bhadon. The women made cowdung replicas of the elephant-headed god Ganesh in the courtyard of their houses. Dressed in their best, they worshipped it in the evening and placed a lit earthen lamp on the god's belly. According to prevalent custom, this lamp had to be extinguished by the hooves of a cow's calf. Our calf used to be in great demand and I had to take him around to perform this sacred duty. The calf did not like the task assigned to him: I had to hold his foot and bring it down on the earthen lamp. With each lamp that he extinguished, the calf received a small laddoo of choorma[60] and I received a much larger one.

The Dasehra procession was, by far, the most spectacular event in town. Boys dressed as Rama, Lakshman and Sita were driven aound town in a chariot, followed by a joyous throng of people. This moving tableau symbolized Lord Rama's return to Ayodhya after killing Ravana and rescuing Sita. Hanuman was usually in a boistrous mood, roaming around and brandishing his mace. In a clear case of mixing legends, this procession also had Narsimha, the man-lion incarnation of Lord Vishnu, the slayer of Hiranya Kashyapa. Wearing a lion's mask and dressed in dazzling robes, he was the main attraction of this procession, which ended at the large open ground fringed by ancient peepal and banyan trees. A miniature sand castle of Lanka, in the shape of a pyramid, had been made on a raised ground. Beside it was created an enormous sand sculpture of the 10-headed Ravana in a reclining posture, his queen Mandodari by his side.

Sita alighted from the carriage now and was escorted to Lanka—the scene of her abduction was not enacted. She sat near the Lanka pyramid and the priests performed some rituals, uttering

[60]A special sweet dish

Sanskrit mantras. Thereafter the drama of destroying the demon king and his Lanka was enacted. Rama's and Lakshman's arrows pierced Ravana, and Hanuman jumped up on Lanka, razing it to the ground. It was a wild scene of destruction; even Mandodari was not spared. Then, Rama held Sita's hand and brought her back to the chariot. The present-day practice of making giant-size paper effigies to be engulfed in dazzling fireworks was unknown in our town then.

Diwali[61] was, by far, the most enchanting festival. Shops in the main bazaars were lit up by rows of little earthen lamps; candles were rare. Shops selling utensils were a major attraction during Diwali. Shop fronts were decorated with dazzling brass, nickel and silverware, interspersed with twinkling earthen lamps. Facades of houses were also decorated with earthen lamps, which were also placed in niches in the rooms, thresholds and on porches.

After lighting the lamps, my mother would do a little puja in front of a printed calendar of Goddess Lakshmi. She would light a special ghee-filled lamp before the goddess's image, then bow down and pray to her, saying: 'Hey Diwali Mata, *jaisi hamare aai hai, vaisi sabke aana*!' (As you have blessed us by your visit, do bless everyone likewise!)

The standard meal on Diwali day, in all households, was boiled rice topped with powdered brown sugar and a spoonful of ghee, accompanied by moong daal.

Holi, the festival of colours, would begin with Holika Dahan (Immolation of Holika), and was enacted in a couple of places in the town. The venue for our part of the town was the assembly ground for the cows before they were taken to graze. A khejri tree was axed and fixed in the centre of the ground three days before the event. This tree represented the child Prahlad, whom the evil Holika

[61]Sanskrit: Deepavali ('deep' and 'avali' meaning 'an array of lights')

wanted to kill. A high fence of dry thorny bushes, representing Holika, was made around the tree. Housewives prepared tiny dung cakes with a hole. When dry, they strung them into a garland and hung them on the Holi tree. Soon, the tree as well as the fence was laden with these highly inflammable cowdung garlands.

On Holika Dahan day, people assembled around the Holi tree in the evening. Just before sunset, the priests would perform puja. Thereafter, the tree trunk (representing Prahlad) would be eased out, leaving behind the thorny fence with dung garlands which represented Prahlad's evil aunt Holika, in whose lap he was supposedly sitting. Holika was then torched, to the merriment of the crowd of spectators.

It was a towering bonfire. People threw votive offerings in the blazing fire and roasted sheaves of ripening wheat or barley plants in the holy fire and ate the roasted grains.

Talking of roasting grains, I am reminded of a bhadbhuja[62] right in front of the high school building. My mother used to buy barley in bulk when the new crop arrived in the market in May. She would soak about five kilograms of barley overnight and give it to me in the evening to get it roasted. I would take it to the bhadbhuja. The oven had red-hot sand, which was poured over the grains held in a sieve. My mother would also get wheat grains roasted on special occasions. She would then give them a coat of gur to make gur-dhani. Similarly, after the harvesting of the summer crop, she would get gram roasted, which was called bhoongra in the local lingo. On Makar Sankranti, she would roast sesame seeds and make til-ke-laddoo.

'Playing' Holi with colours was done the day after Holika Dahan. An atmosphere of happy revelry prevailed, but as the day progressed, the celebrations veered towards the bawdy and

---

[62]Owner of the oven for baking grains

the bacchanalian, ending with a complete descent into boisterous, licentiousness and rank obscenity.

◆

There were three ashrams in the vicinity of our town: two of them, in the east and south, had been set up by Mahadev Thekedar of our community, while the third, in the west, was established by a renowned freedom fighter, Banshidhar Sharma, who was known to be a friend of Jawaharlal Nehru. None of them had been set up as ashrams; they acquired that aura later on.

Banshidhar Sharma was a true Gandhian; he dressed minimally, and spun his own thread on his charkha.

Gandhi had wanted to identify himself with the common Indian. He, therefore, wore only a homespun dhoti with which he also covered his chest. Banshidhar Sharma did not blindly copy Gandhi. Instead, he wore a short half-sleeve khadi shirt and a kutchha. In his down-to-earth, minimal attire he looked uncommonly impressive and had an aura of grace and simplicity about him. He used to come to our school to talk about the freedom struggle, about Gandhi and Nehru, and about self-improvement and self-help.

He had levelled sand dunes in village Gochhaldi, a few kilometres to the south of the town, and created a sizeable farm from wasteland which he cultivated with the help of his bullocks. He had bored a deep tube well at the entrance of the farm; pucca water channels emanated from it to cover the farmland.

The most distinctive feature, which indeed gave his farm the look of an ashram, were four igloo-shaped cottages, made of bamboo and covered with straw, in the four corners of a spacious mud-plastered platform, about a hundred yards square and two yards high. Two of the cottages served as the family's residence, the third was a library-cum-prayer and spinning hall and the fourth, a guest house. These cottages were minimalistic like a forest dwelling. From afar they looked small but were commodious, comfortable and functional. On a Sunday morning I had gone there with my brother. We washed our clothes in the bathrooms near the pump house, bathed in the flowing water of the open water tank and then went up to the cottages. Banshidhar ji and his son were tilling the land behind the cottages. We greeted him with folded hands and he smiled and stopped the bullocks and chatted with us, telling us to come whenever we wished. He was a true karma-yogi.

A young Swedish woman had come to stay in his ashram once. He brought her to the High School and the boys had an interesting interaction with her. Banshidhar ji himself acted as an interpreter. She wanted to visit households and meet housewives. He had taken her to the large havelis of the seths as well as the hovels of harijans. Her visit had created quite a stir in the town. The ladies in our mohalla, my mother included, worked overtime to give their houses a fresh coat of mud mixed with cowdung.

There was a social service organization in our town, called Mahavir Dal[63]. Its members were ardent devotees of the monkey god, Hanuman, and they organized displays of physical prowess during festivals. Wielding maces like Hanuman, sword play, lathi fights and leaping through fire, were some of the things that entertained the crowds.

Mahavir Dal used to set up drinking-water facilities for pilgrims along pilgrimage routes and at fair grounds, and also provided first-aid services to pilgrims who fell sick.

My brother Bhagirath was an active member, and when I was in class 6, he took me to their honorary president, Sunda Ramji, to enlist me in the Dal. I was given a new set of khaki shorts and shirt, the uniform for volunteers, and participated in the forthcoming

---

[63]Lit. 'The Army of the Great Warrior'—meaning Hanuman

Lohargal yatra[64], probably as its youngest member and soon became a favourite of Sunda ji.

I remember walking through a hilly terrain, setting up wayside stalls for serving drinking water called 'piau' to endless streams of pilgrims during daytime and at night sleeping on open terraces of wayside dharmshalas[65], under star-studded skies, hearing birdsong and the rustling of tree leaves.

During the next day's march, we came upon a blue-green tranquil pool, called the Naag Kund, 50 yards in diameter. Water trickled down into it from a steep cliff, about 20 yards high. Bathing in the pool was strictly prohibited, they told me, adding that a divine serpent lived in its depths, as its name suggested. I drank a few draughts of nectar from the pool.

In the evening, we reached the pilgrimage destination. There was a large lake nestled amidst hillocks covered by thorny shrubs. Rainfall had been scanty that year and the lake had shrunk. People had a holy dip in the shallow lake before offering prayers at the shrine of the deity, who, it was believed, possessed miraculous powers of liberating the faithful from the worldly shackles. It was believed that the iron shackles of the Pandava brothers dissolved when they bathed in the sacred water of this lake, which gave the place its name, Lohargal, the melting of iron.

A month after that, I went on a similar mission to the Zeen Mata fair. Perched on a rugged hill, the goddess of this temple loved to drink country wine. Streams of devotees, the women singing her glory and the men dancing and thrashing themselves with iron chains, offered her bottles of the country brew they had brought.

Generally, the temple priest drew the shrine's curtain after taking the offerings from devotees and presented them to the deity in

---

[64]Sanskrit: journey, expedition

[65]Charity lodging halls

seclusion, as I had seen in Samod. But, probably owing to the heavy rush, he opened the bottle's cork and straightaway put it to the Devi's open lips (which were encrusted with silver foil), drained it in her gullet and returned it. The devotees took the bottle and gleefully sipped the few drops that had remained.

I was curious to know where all that liquor went. My volunteer companions told me that a hole had been drilled in the rock behind the statue of the goddess. The holy liquid was collected in the backyard, and marketed.

•◆

Participating in marriage parties was real fun. I was about eight years old when I was considered eligible to join a marriage party. A boy in our clan was getting married; the baraat was to go to a place called Jharli, about 15 miles away from our town—riding on camels.

After a sumptuous breakfast of halua, poories and subzi, the baratis began mounting the camels. I had thought my brother would take me along with him but he preferred the company of older boys. Three of them got up on top of one camel and sped off.

Soon everyone had mounted the camels and had shot off. Besides me, the bridegroom's father and his elder brother, and our community's head Patel, Ghasiram ji were left. The two brothers mounted one camel and Ghasiram ji asked me to come with him on another camel. He was seated first, in front, and I sat behind him, clutching at his portly midriff, as the camel got up awkwardly.

The other camels had trotted off but Ghasiram ji asked our camel man to go slow. The rider feels comfortable when the camel goes at an easy trot. But if it's moving slowly, the ride is jerky and uncomfortable and becomes a torture. All the fun of being in a wedding party had vanished: I was miserable during the three-hour-long journey. I told my brother, after reaching the bride's village, that on the return journey he had to take me on his camel.

Fortunately, the wedding was fun. We were handed a refreshment of laddoos and namkeen in little bowls made out of tree leaves. Later in the night, a feast was served on the terrace of the bride's father's haveli, in the moonlight, while the wedding rites were being held in the chowk around the sacred fire.

We slept on the terrace of the dharmshala. It was a strange experience. I kept looking at the stars before I dozed off.

The next wedding that I went to was memorable because I travelled in a train for the first time in my life. I had just enough standing space near an open window in a crowded compartment, and I was intrigued because the train seemed to stand still while everything outside rushed past furiously. I then discovered an even more intriguing fact—unlike the nearby trees which were rushing backwards, those in the distance, at the horizon, were moving forward. Indeed, the trees seemed to be doing a circular dance in the reverse direction of the train!

We spent that night at a railway station, sleeping on the terrace of a dharmshala. The next morning we rode to the bride's village on camels and stayed there for two nights. We would sit in rows on jute mats and eat from a 'pattal' (plate made of tree leaves) placed in front of us. A man carrying laddoos would go round saying, '*laddoo lyo ji*! (Please take laddoo!)' while another bringing poories would say, '*poorie lyo ji!* (Please take poorie!)', and so on. They served a special feast of 'sat-varni mithai' (seven types of sweets) on the second day which included jalebi, petha, makkhan-vada[66], etc. While the baraat returned on camels, a bullock cart carried the bride and the bridegroom to the railway station.

[66]Common Indian sweets

The radio came to our town when I was in class 6. Madanji Paanwala had a paan shop near the Shiva temple at the Chaupar. He had bought the first radio in the town which blared film songs from his shop. People would particularly gather around his shop while taking an after-dinner stroll, buy a paan and chew it leisurely while listening to the film songs and exchanging the day's gossip. He also brought the first loudspeaker in the town, which he installed on top of his two-storeyed house. People from nearby villages hired his loudspeaker for weddings.

Our school tailoring teacher, Rameshwar Lal, was the second person to buy a loudspeaker. He was actually the local tailor, who had been hired by the school to teach us tailoring in class 6 and 7. When he rented out the loudspeaker for weddings, he needed someone to go and operate it. Since I was his favourite pupil, he offered to pay me a few rupees to do this job during the summer holidays after I had finished class 7. I loved listening to film songs and I jumped at his offer.

People were usually surprised to see someone so young operate the loudspeaker, but I was able to gauge their mood and play music accordingly. The hosts looked after me well and my first couple of assignments went very well.

The tailoring teacher also asked me to go to Jaipur to buy new records and get the loudspeaker batteries recharged. I had gone there earlier with my mother and stayed in my Mamaji's[67] house in Chandpol Bazaar. This time I had the pleasure of watching the newly released film, *Parineeta*, the first film of my life!

However, my relations with the tailoring teacher soured when I realized that he was trying to shortchange the simple village folk.

What had happened was that, as usual, the bridegroom's father had brought his bullock cart to the tailor-master's shop. I was

---

[67]Maternal uncle

summoned from home and we set off on a sandy path. When we reached in about three hours, the village folk greatly rejoiced at our arrival. The bridegroom's mother marvelled at my expertise as I began playing their choicest songs and she plied me with sweets.

I had played the gramophone records for about an hour when Babu Ram, the tailor-master's associate, arrived at the village, riding a camel. It was an unusual occurrence but I paid no heed and continued with my job. I could see that he was trying to talk to me, alone, but I was surrounded by people and he had no chance. When I stopped the session, he took me aside and said that we had to leave immediately, on another assignment, in another village that night. I was perplexed and asked, 'How can that be? How can we leave these people in the lurch?' I knew that the tailor-master had taken money in advance from the bridegroom's father before sending me with him. 'You don't bother about it,' Babu Ram told me and added, 'When you start playing the record now, you disconnect the battery in the midst of a song and say the machine has developed a fault and it can't start now.'

'I can't do it,' I replied.

'OK, you leave it to me. I'll operate it now.'

It was a sordid affair. Evidently the tailor-master had taken a much higher amount from another man and was cheating this simple man.

Babu Ram now started the record player and when he was playing the third song he slid the needle off the disk which made a screeching sound and the song stopped. Immediately he pulled out its connection with the battery. People collected in the room. Babu Ram was tinkering with the apparatus, apparently trying hard to find what had gone wrong. He restarted the record player but there was no sound. The bridegroom's father arrived and asked what the problem was. Babu Ram was perspiring profusely from his labours. He replied, 'The amplifier has failed. It'll not work now. We have to take it back.'

He took the man aside and was arguing with him. The man was saying: '*Meri izzat tau dhool mein mil gayi.*' (My honour is gone to dust.)' Babu Ram took out some money from his pocket but the man refused to take it. Babu Ram asked the camel man, who had brought him there, to load the trunk on the camel. Before leaving, Babu Ram again went to the man and gave him some money.

It was a moonlit night. Holding the reins, the camel man walked ahead on a sand-filled path; Babu Ram followed him and I trudged behind. We must have walked for a few hours. I was dog-tired but kept pace. The moon was in front of us when we had started, it was behind us now. We spied a little village sleeping in the moonlight and heard the howling of dogs. Some men woke up and opened a room. They placed two charpoys on the ground. I dropped down on one of them and slept like a log. The sun's bright rays woke me up.

Babu Ram played music for some time in the morning and then packed again. We went with the baraat to another village. Babu Ram was playing the music after the bride and the bridegroom had taken their rounds of the sacred fire when it stopped again. This time it was a real glitch—the battery had discharged.

I never associated with the crafty tailor-master again.

8

HIGH SCHOOL

The high school building was a simple two-storey structure. A massive neem tree stood at the gate barring the view of the façade and there were a few kaner plants at the left corner bearing fragrant yellow flowers. It was originally built for a middle school, with only the Headmaster's room on the first floor. Four more classrooms were added on the first floor when it was upgraded to a high school. As a result, there wasn't enough space inside its premises for holding the morning school assembly, so it was held in the dusty public street in front. Even the mandatory Independence Day or Republic Day gatherings were held outside, blocking the thoroughfare for a few hours. Lectures and school debates were, however, held in the privacy of the quadrangle; the teachers sat on chairs and the boys squatted on durries.

The best thing about the high school was that it was quite close to our house, just a few minutes' walk.

The central hall in the front was the school library. It had about a dozen man-size shelves, all full of books, their glass doors locked. Each class had a library period once a week, when boys visited the library and got books issued. The boys had to choose their books from a pile of books taken out by the librarian and laid on his table. The shelves remained locked up. Only the teachers could access them.

Our Headmaster, Vidyadhar Kala was a man of high principles

and a forceful speaker. He encouraged us to debate and often invited eminent speakers to address the school assembly. Our Deputy Headmaster, Surya Narain Rao, was an erudite man besides being a colourful personality. He was witty and taught us debating skills.

Sometime after I joined the High School in July 1951, our primary school headmaster, Tara Chand Sharma, was promoted as a high school teacher and became our librarian. He was asked by the Headmaster to take stock of and classify all the library books and he asked me to assist him in this task after school hours.

All the books were taken out of the shelves, dusted, re-catalogued, reclassified and rearranged, and I discovered and browsed through the ones that interested me. Tara Chand ji, conferred on me the special privilege enjoyed only by teachers: accessing books of my choice from the shelves. This development made me a booklover from an early age and an avid reader.

A new Accession Register was started to enter the new arrivals. Filling up this register to record the newly received books and placing them in the almirahs according to the new classification, remained my job till I left school. It was a thrill, handling the new books. Sometimes, I was the first one in the school to read a newly-received book. I remember I was in class 8 when Vrindavan Lal Varma's great historical novel, *Mrig Nayani*, a fascinating love story of Raja Man Singh of Gwalior and a bewitching Gujjar girl, was received in the library. The book had a captivating picture of a lovely girl on its cover jacket which attracted me. Although it was much above my level of scholarship, Tara Chand ji allowed me to take it home to read and I prided myself at being its first reader in the school.

I can recall reading many other great Hindi novels at that time—Jaishankar Prasad's *Titali* and *Kankaal*, Prem Chand's *Gaban* and *Godaan*, Bhagwati Charan Varma's *Chitralekha*, etc. I also read Maithili Sharan Gupt's epic poem *Saket*, although some of its parts went over my head.

Tara Chand ji allowed me to take books home even during the summer holidays.

When I was in class 8, I participated in a short story competition for school children by the celebrated Hindi weekly, *Bal Sakha* and won the first prize—a princely sum of 11 rupees! My prize-winning story was published in the magazine and when the money order came to the school, Headmaster Vidyadhar Kala congratulated me and patted me fondly on my back.

Our Hindi teachers Jagdish Narain Sharma, Vanshidhar Bhavan and Ram Swaroop Joshi, seeing my love for Hindi literature, encouraged me to write the Prathama and Madhyama examinations conducted by the prestigious Hindi Sahitya Sammelan of Allahabad. Tara Chand ji ordered all the prescribed books for the library and Bhavan ji and Joshi ji gave me free coaching at their homes. I had to go to Moti Katla High School, in Jaipur, to write these examinations when I was in class 8 and 9, and obtained high grades.

One day, Jagdish Narain Sharma told our class about the Indian Administrative Service and said, 'Any BA-pass boy or girl in India can take this examination which is held every year. The 100 boys or girls who secure top marks become Collectors and later occupy the highest positions in the central government.' He planted the seed of ambition in my mind.

•♦

Our school had a strong tradition and high reputation in scouting, mainly thanks to our dedicated Scout Master, Jagannath Puri.

Puriji was very popular with the boys, as he used to regale us with his homely wit and humour in the fortnightly assemblies. He was a genial father figure and had a knack for making everyone laugh; he'd crack jokes even about himself. In the scouting fraternity, he was rated among the best scout masters of Rajasthan. Our school contingent, led by him in the national jamboree of scouts at

Hyderabad in 1953, had distinguished itself; my brother Bhagirath was its patrol leader. I began my scouting career as a member of my brother's patrol. Every year, after the end of the rainy season, Puriji organized a three-day scouting camp in Bhaironji ki Bani[68], about two kilometres from the town to the south. It was a forested area, abounding in khejri and kikar trees. There was a small Bhairon temple in it beside a small natural pond. All the six patrols, comprising eight scouts each, used to participate in the camp. The tents and baggage were carried in bullock carts, while we walked the sandy path going along the railway track.

We would reach the camping site in the Bani by noon time and pitch our tents in a large circle at a place earmarked by the scout master, fetch water from a well near the Bhairon temple and cook our meals of vegetable curry, daal and chapattis. Puriji and the assistant scout master, Rameshwarji, had their tent at the head of the circle. They would go round inspecting the quality of the food cooked by each patrol, as also neatness in the upkeep of the tent and its environs. After we had eaten our dinner in the evening and washed our plates and utensils, there was a campfire in the centre of the ring where songs and skits were presented by different patrols.

During daytime the next day, competitions were held in several scouting activities. Finally, on the third day, prizes were given to the winners of each event and to the best patrol. This outdoor camp was a most exciting and fulfilling experience.

I attended the first two camps as a member of my brother's patrol while I was in class 6 and 7. Puriji made me a patrol leader when I was in class 8 and I led my patrol during the next three camps.

A special three-day inter-school camp was organized in 1954 at Neem Ka Thana which was the sub-divisional headquarter. Each

---

[68]From Sanskrit 'Vana': forest

school was to be represented by one patrol. A unified patrol, headed by my brother Bhagirath, was formed to represent our school, comprising other patrol leaders like Sanwar Mal Khunteta, another outstanding boy of class 10, who was designated deputy patrol leader. I was also included in it. In all, six schools from the sub-division, including Neem Ka Thana, were participating in the camp.

A remarkable event of this camp was a trek to a nearby picturesque spot, Ganesar Hill, which had a natural fountain at its top.

Although everyone had to reach Ganesar Hill, each patrol was given a different route map for approaching it. So our ways did not cross, either going up or coming down. We were required to reach the hilltop with our rucksacks on our backs, walking in single file on footpaths winding through small hamlets, following the directions given in the route map supplied to us. The essence of the whole exercise was to have a picnic at the hilltop—relax a while after arrival, bathe, cook our lunch and eat, wash the utensils and pack and then, following the given route map, return before sunset to the base camp—in all, taking about 20 miles in our stride.

It was essentially a competition in map-reading skills, walking at 'scout pace', (a combination of jogging and brisk walk, done alternately), proficiency in cooking one's food (the food quality to be judged by a team of scout masters on the spot), imbibing team spirit and the ability to act in concert and above all, time management.

It was a memorable experience. To this day I cannot forget the thrill of coming upon that natural wonder—a fountain, about a foot in diameter, gushing out of the bare rocks at the top of Ganesar Hill! I had never seen such a wonderful sight in my life! We instantly stripped and went under this cascade of cool water. Oh, the joy of bathing under it!

The State Scout Commissioner, Mr Dhiman, had come down

from Jaipur for the finale. The first prize was awarded to our Sri Madhopur patrol. Proud as a peacock, my brother received the trophy from Dhiman Sahib, who heartily congratulated our team and eulogized the dedication of our scout master, Jagannath Puri.

A weeklong State-level camp was held two years later, in 1956, at the State Scouting Headquarters at Sanganer near Jaipur, in which scores of schools from all over Rajasthan participated. I was in class 10 then and led the school patrol in winning laurels. During the summer holidays after our high school examinations, I led a school patrol on a 15-day social service (shram daan) camp organized at Sanganer state headquarters. However, this time there were only four patrols, ours being the only one from outside Jaipur. Our deputy scout master Rameshwarji had accompanied us. He was lodged in the guest house while we stayed in tents. All the four patrols worked together for four hours every morning, wielding spades and pickaxes like a labour force and constructed a two-kilometre-long approach road thereby connecting an isolated village to the main road. In the evening, there was a campfire and cultural activities.

The State Scout Commissioner, Dhiman Saheb, awarded certificates to the participants in the valedictory function and showered high praise on our team, which had come from outside Jaipur.

An outstanding achievement of my scouting career was when I was awarded the Bharat Scout badge, originally called the King's Scout badge, the highest award in scouting.

•◆

Our headmaster, Vidyadhar Kala, often invited guest speakers like the freedom fighter, Vanshidhar Sharma, to address the school assembly. Once, Kamal Nayan Bajaj, son of the famous industrialist Jamunalal Bajaj from Sikar, came to speak to us. He was a strikingly handsome man—fair-complexioned with large eyes like lotus buds, justifying his name. He spoke in an informal manner and gave us practical tips about life. I particularly remember his one advice that sent the boys tittering—'*subah savere apna maila dekho*' (early in the morning watch your shit). Undeterred by the response, he elaborated on the theme, saying that if the maila was watery, there was something wrong with your digestive system.

Our deputy headmaster, Surya Narain Rao was witty and his lectures were truly enjoyable. He organized debates and taught us debating skills. When I was in class 10, he sent me and a junior boy, Babulal Chaudhary, to Sikar, to participate in an inter-disrict debate, where we won the second prize.

Rao Sahib used to tease boys by calling them by their literally translated names. For instance, if he had to call Chhote Lal, he'd say, 'Hey Little Ruby, come here'. The word 'lal' means a son as well as a red ruby. There was a chubby boy, Shyam Sunder Tewari, in class 9. By translating his name 'Shyam Sunder', Rao Sahib used to call him 'Black Beauty', although he was fair-complexioned. The word 'shyam' meant black as well as Krishna's name.

•◆

Like my sister Chhoti, my brother Bhagirath too was married early, when he was 16 years old, a student of class 8. Like her, he was married in Khetri, the tiny sub-state whose raja, Ajit Singh, was a friend and admirer of Swami Vivekananda and had sponsored his participation in the World Conference of Religion at Chicago.

Munshi Geeg Ram was a respected member of our community and was called 'munshiji' as he had worked as such in the office of the Raja of Khetri. He came to know about our family after my sister's marriage. One day, he sent his two sons, Suwalal and Prabhu Dayal, to our place. In a brief ceremony, the elder brother drew a tilak on my brother's forehead and gave him a coconut wrapped in a red scarf with a silver coin, as a token of his betrothal to their younger sister. Brother hadn't even seen the girl, nor she him—that wasn't deemed necessary at all. When my sister came to visit some months later, she told him that the girl was pretty; he was happy. The wedding took place a year after the engagement.

My father borrowed money for the marriage expenses and organized a feast for the entire community of over a hundred families, three days before the wedding. About 50 men joined the baraat, all of whom boarded the train going towards Rewari the next day and alighted at Maonda station, next to Neem Ka Thana. A bus was waiting there, courtesy Munshi Geeg Ram, for the journey to Khetri. The bus was a relic of the steam age—it was powered by steam, not diesel or petrol. A huge steam cylinder and a coal-fired boiler were fixed at its back. The driver started the process of generating the steam after the arrival of the baraat. The process took about an hour. Thereafter the bus rolled off on a slender road meandering through a hilly terrain. It did not have enough seats and some men perched themselves on the roof.

After running for an hour or so, it halted midway at a place called Babai, to generate more steam, and then resumed the journey. Finally, we neared Khetri town which nestled in the lap of a towering mountain. The cupolas of the old fort-palace looked like a tiara crowning the mountain peak.

Our two community barbers had accompanied the baraat. They opened their kits as soon as we reached the janvasa, the place of lodgement of the baraat. They began grooming the baraatis, giving them haircuts and shaves, and paring nails. A couple of barbers, from the bride's side, soon joined them to assist in the operation.

Water had been stored in tubs to wash and freshen up. There was hot water in a huge cauldron to mix. Soap cakes were provided for bathing and washing clothes. Besides, there were bottles of Brahmi Amla hair oil: for the hard-working bricklayers, this was five-star luxury! The baraat stayed for three days and feasted on satvarni mithai. At the vidai, each member was gifted a brass tumbler, a handkerchief and a rupee coin.

My brother was in class 10 when his muklava ceremony took place and my Bhabhi came to stay with us. Bhabhi's arrival was a huge relief to my mother, who now had someone to help her with household work.

Brother passed his high school examination in 1954 with distinction, one of the two boys from the school to secure a first division. He got an appointment as a school teacher in a place about 15 miles from our town, at a salary of ₹85 a month. He came home on Saturday evenings and left on Monday morning.

◆

My main problem at that time was that I did not have a place to study in, especially after nightfall. It was impossible to study in the dim light of a tiny wicker lamp. Perforce, I had to finish all my reading in the day, in our thatched verandah. I realized that I needed a proper place to prepare for the crucial class 10 examinations. Indeed, this was a common problem in our town.

My classmate, Ram Gopal Jat, was staying in a small room on the Station Road, quite near our school, courtesy his rich friend Banshidhar Misra. He asked me to stay with him and help him in his studies. That suited me eminently and I moved in with him.

One day Ram Gopal told me that Jagdishji Malpani, who used to be our maths teacher in primary school, had met him and wanted my help in solving some maths problems. He was also appearing for the high school examination, privately, to qualify for promotion as a high-school teacher, but he didn't want to go to the maths teacher in the high school. Ram Gopal added that he would come to our lodging.

I was thrilled. A Hindi idiom came to mind: '*Guru gur hi rah gaye aur chele shakkar ho gaye.*' (The teachers remained jaggery, their deciples turned into sugar.) The wheel had come full circle.

Once when I was in class 5, Jagdishji had asked me to whitewash his house on a Sunday before Diwali. He did not want to engage professional men to do the job and had assumed that I knew how to whitewash, since I came from the Rajmistry community. I had taken my friend Shyol with me and after toiling the whole day, Shyol and I had finished the job.

I told Ram Gopal that I knew Jagdishji's house very well and that he had once taken my help in getting it whitewashed. I would be glad to help him in removing cobwebs from his mind now. I added that Jagdishji didn't have to come to our lodging, I would go to his house. I went to him in the evening and he was overcome with gratitude. I sat with him for about an hour and solved all his problems. Four books of mathematics were recommended in our syllabus; I had done almost all the exercises given in those books.

◆

My brother knew that the date of birth recorded in the High School certificate was considered authentic. His own recorded date was erroneous, making him older by a year and a half. Getting it changed later on was highly cumbersome. He was also aware that like his own date, my date of birth was also recorded incorrectly. Munshiji had recorded my age as seven years on the day I was admitted to school. To ensure that the same fate did not befall me, he sprang into action.

He had changed his job in the meanwhile and was working as a goods clerk in the Western Railways at Jaipur at that time. He took leave from office, came home and enquired from Mother the exact day I was born. He then went to Jagdish Narain Sharma, our Hindi teacher, to ascertain from his panchang[69] the corresponding

---

[69]A Hindu calendar and almanac, which follows traditional units of Hindu timekeeping.

date in the common calendar. Sharmaji made his calculations and told him it was 6 August 1939, while the date recorded in the school register was 5 July 1938. My brother did a smart thing then; he asked Sharmaji to prepare my janmapatri[70] showing my date of birth as 6 August 1940, exactly one year later, to give me the benefit of one year in life.

Armed with this document, he took me to the court of the Sub-Divisional Magistrate (SDM) in Neem Ka Thana, filed an application for correction of the date of birth, produced two witnesses before him and obtained a court order. I applied to the Headmaster for 'correction' of date in school records, submitting a copy of the SDM's order. Hey presto! Instead of being 13 months older than I was, I now became younger by one year!

In those days, high school exams were conducted by Rajputana University. We had to go to the Neem Ka Thana High School to write our examination. Our stay was booked at a dharmshala which had piped water supply and was quite close to the examination centre.

We went there a day in advance, escorted by our deputy headmaster, Surya Narain Rao, stayed in a dharmshala, ate in a dhaba outside and slept on the floor on durries. Next morning, we washed under the common pipe and reported at the examination centre, half an hour before time. Our exams lasted about a week and we gleefully boarded the train back to Sri Madhopur, relieved in body and spirit; it was as if a heavy load had been taken off the head.

My friend Damodar Parwal and I decided to go to Jaipur to check our results on the day of publication itself, in the premises of the Rajputana University rather than see it in newspapers the next day. The University was located then in the elegant Kesar

---

[70]A scroll giving the date of birth

Singh Castle[71]. The University was to change both its habitation and name later on. It became Rajasthan University and moved to its extensive new premises beyond the Moti Doongri.

We were jubilant to see that both of us had passed the exam with flying colours. Six boys from our school, including the two of us, had secured first division. We returned triumphantly to the town in the evening, to broadcast the news. Our marksheets were received in a few days. With 74 per cent marks in the aggregate, I had got the highest marks in the school. The others were way below. I was the toast of the town.

[71]A palatial building on the main road

9

MAHARAJA'S COLLEGE

Very few boys from our town went for higher studies after matriculation—most ended up as school teachers and were deployed in government schools in surrounding villages. Boys from the baniya community were employed by Marwari firms in Kolkata to maintain their account books.

From the last batch, only Prabhu Dayal Vyas had joined Maharaja's College in Jaipur. Vyas wanted to be a doctor and had enrolled himself for Intermediate in Science–Biology despite the fact that he hadn't studied high school level Science–Biology. In our school, we only had Commerce, and he suffered from a handicap.

From our batch, Damodar Parwal and I joined Maharaja's College. Damodar belonged to the trading community but his maternal uncle was a doctor. He therefore had the same dream as P.D. Vyas, of becoming a doctor and had enrolled in Intermediate Science–Biology. My ambition was to make it to the IAS. But in the short run, I wanted to do an MA and become a college lecturer.

Maharaja's College in Jaipur is an imposing edifice with expansive lawns in front. It was the biggest and the best college in Rajasthan at that time, with about 5,000 students on its rolls. Just across the road was Maharani's College, the biggest college for girls in Rajasthan: co-education was unknown then.

I joined Intermediate in Arts, choosing high-scoring optional subjects such as Mathematics, Logic & Psychology and English Literature.

•◆

The Government of India awarded a modest scholarship of ₹40 a month to students belonging to the Scheduled Castes and Tribes (SC & ST) and the Other Backward Classes (OBC) for post-matriculation studies. The caste 'kumhar' was included in the OBC list, which strictly meant the 'potters'. We were not potters. Indeed we felt slighted if someone called us kumhar—in our perception there was a big hierarchical distance between us and them.

But in the perception of the society at large there was hardly any difference between bricklayers and potters. It was taken for granted that at some point in history we had branched out from the original class of potters.

My brother took me to the Tehsildar's court near the Garh School, submitted an application that I was going to Jaipur for higher studies and requested him to issue a certificate of my belonging to the OBC category for getting the scholarship. He produced two witnesses who testified that I belonged to the OBC category. The tehsildar issued the certificate and I attached this valuable document with my admission form to Maharaja's College. In time, I received the sanction from the concerned ministry in the Government of India.

Although the payment of the princely sum of ₹400 (for the 10 months I attended the college) came only after the end of the academic session and fell much short of actual expenses, the scholarship served as a virtual plank in my mind to remain afloat.

Indeed I wouldn't have entertained the notion of being a regular college student without the prospect of receiving the scholarship money. I would have taken a school teacher's job and passed BA as a private candidate, even done a master's, and taken the competitive examinations. However, it wouldn't have been the same thing. It is clear to me, in hindsight, that the prospect of success would have been quite dim. The financial support of the OBC scholarship was crucial in realizing my dream, but all my life I was wary of acknowledging that I belonged to the OBC category.

In fact, my surname, Varma, was adopted to veil my caste identity. Our community had a large presence in our town, and our postal address was 'Chejaron ka Mohalla'. Caste was invariably mentioned in school registers and the morning roll-call went somewhat like this: Kapoor Chand Sunar, Kailash Chand Halwai, Gyarsi Lal Chaudhary, Tara Chand Mali, Mahabir Prasad Rajoria, Mukti Lal Thoiwala, Ram Lakhan Kayal, Ram Sahai Chejara, Ram Deen Sharma, Ram Gopal Jat, Hanuman Balai.

My older cousin, Govind Sahai, had changed all that. He was the first man from our community to step outside the town for higher studies. When he went to high school in Mukundgarh near Sikar, he adopted the amorphous surname 'Varma' and boys from our community followed his lead, trying to rub off the stigma of a lowly family profession. I was overjoyed to discover a tenth-century temple in Chamba in Himachal Pradesh, built by King Sahil Varma!

◆

I lived on campus, in a hostel behind the college building. The room rent was ₹10 per month and the monthly mess charges came to around ₹60. I shared a double-bedded room with a Commerce student for a few months, till Damodar joined the hostel, and we became roommates.

By this time, my father had stopped working in faraway cities and had come to Jaipur. He lived in my Mamaji's house, in a small dark room on the ground floor which barely accommodated his cot, and paid him ₹20 per month as rent. Mamaji worked as a head-mistry, getting ₹10 a day, while my father worked in his team as a mason and got ₹5 a day. He earned about a hundred rupees in a month.

Father had to report for work at 8 a.m. He got up early, while it was still dark, bathed at a public water tap on the road outside, cooked his rotis on charcoal fire in an angithi, ate them with some chutney and left for work at about 7.30 a.m. In the evening, he returned around 7 p.m., brought a bucketful of water from the public tap, cooked his food, ate it all by himself and went to sleep on his cot. There was no fan in his room, not even a light. Flies and mosquitoes abounded. He bore it all stoically, never uttering a word of complaint. He felt uneasy only on days when there was no work and he had a holiday.

At the end of my first year, I tried to give my scholarship money to my father. He refused to accept it and asked me to give it to my mother. She was extremely pleased and told me that she had never seen so much money at a time.

•◆

From a cursory look at the syllabus of the IAS and other all-India Service examinations it was evident that a mastery of, or at least high proficiency in, English was essential for succeeding in the IAS examinations. The dice seemed heavily loaded in its favour. There were three compulsory papers for all candidates: General English, General Knowledge and English Essay. English was the medium of expression for the written examination and the interview. Attaining proficiency in English language and literature appeared essential and became a mission of my life.

The curriculum for Intermediate Arts had General English and General Science as compulsory subjects. Besides these, one had to take three optional subjects. English Literature was my first choice, Mathematics and Logic & Psychology next.

I chose Mathematics as I had always got full marks in it. However, I committed the same mistake as P.D. Vyas and Damodar; I had not studied matric-level higher maths. Our school didn't have Science-Maths or Science-Biology. It had Commerce and Accountancy instead, which we had studied. It took a lot of my time and effort to cover the backlog in maths and yet I never got the kind of marks that I had hoped for.

I chose Logic & Psychology as I was told one got very high marks in it. The aim, after all, was to excel.

Soon after joining college, I saw a notice that a written examination was to be held for selecting cadets for the Air Wing of the NCC. It was open to first-year boys of all faculties. I took the exam along with a whole host of other boys. It was a general knowledge test. Three days later, a list of 30 boys who had scored the highest marks was displayed on the notice board. My name was at the top! I just couldn't contain myself and rushed to the Air NCC office.

Squadron Leader Harrington, who looked and spoke like an Englishman, sized up the boys in the same order. The Air Wing had been started in Jaipur a year ago and there were two vacancies in the first batch. Harrington was pleased to consider me and Arvind Mathur, who was second in the written test, against these vacancies in the first batch, after keeping us under observation for about a month. The promotion to second year was something beyond my expectation.

But there was a price to be paid—of spending more time than I had bargained for, cutting into the time required for my studies. We had to do parade practice and participate in some activities with the first and second years for a few months. The second-year boys had the advantage of a year's prior exposure to Air NCC activities.

My biggest handicap was my inability to speak in English. Almost all the instructors in Air NCC were south Indians, who spoke only English and I couldn't converse with them with ease. Unlike me, Arvind Mathur was from St Xavier's, the top English-medium school in Jaipur, and was fluent in English, and so were most of the other boys. The promotion to second year proved to be a curse in disguise.

We had some distinguished teachers of English Literature. S.J.B. Mathur, a portly gentleman with a resounding voice, taught us poetry and would recite the poems in his sonorous voice. He told us the difference between the stressed and unstressed syllables. We had just about 20 poems in our course—sonnets of Shakespeare and Milton, poems of Wordsworth, Shelley, Keats, Lord Byron, etc. We were told to buy Palgrave's *Golden Treasury* and read the selected poems. This little book contained about 500 poems; it was an inexhaustible treasure! One unwittingly stumbled on unprescribed but beautiful poems from these, and other poets, and was lost in a dale of poesy.

Another professor, P. Lal, a short and stern-looking man, taught us A.G. Gardiner's delightful essays and would bring out the finer points of the author's wit and humour.

The teachers' common room was adjacent to the high-pillared entrance hall of the college. Once a student entered it and went to Professor P. Lal, sitting in a sofa chair, and asked him: 'Sir, are you Mr S.J.B. Mathur?' Now, P. Lal was lean and thin while S.J.B. was stout; it was impossible to mistake the one for the other. Evidently, P. Lal was not amused by the student's query and retorted, 'My dear fellow, you neither know Mr S.J.B. Mathur nor poor Mr P. Lal!'

Our Logic teacher initiated us into deductive and inductive reasoning and introduced us to the fascinating world of syllogisms—

'All men are mortal,

Socrates is a man;

Therefore Socrates is mortal.'

He then went on to elaborate the fallacies one could be trapped in. However, the queen of sciences, mathematics, tormented me. It was also quite a large class but the teacher took many things for granted which I was oblivious to, as I had not studied higher maths in high school.

I could not summon up the courage to take part in English debates but began participating in Hindi debates. Dr Satendra Chaturvedi, a Hindi professor, used to organize the debates. Ramacharya, a fellow student from our class who had Hindi literature as an optional subject, had a gift of speaking chaste Hindi extempore. He was selected to represent the college in some debates. His elder brother, Hari Ramacharya, who was doing his master's in Sanskrit was the best Hindi speaker of the college. An African student studying in BA Final was the best speaker in English and used to win prizes in inter-college debates.

My participation in Hindi debates, however, gave me a positive dividend. Our hostel warden, Dr Sarnam Singh Sharma 'Arun', who was head of the Hindi department and a celebrated Hindi writer and poet, used to preside over the Hindi debates. Because of my participation in Hindi debates, he came to know me and like me. He was also the chief commander of the regular NCC battalion of the college.

In the first year exams, I scored high marks in all subjects except maths: she is said to be a jealous mistress who demands regular attention. I could not give her time mainly due to my involvement in Air NCC activities.

◆

During my second year in college, Air NCC began to take an even heavier toll on my time. I had to take regular flying lessons at the Sanganer Aerodrome. There were two trainer aircrafts at the aerodrome. Mr Bhandarkar was the chief instructor and there were two other instructors besides him, Mr Sharma and Mr Vijay Singh. Bhandarkar had an old station wagon in which he would pick up about a dozen trainees from a few designated places in Jaipur at about 3 p.m. and drive them to the aerodrome. Apart from Air NCC cadets, there were some private pupil pilots who also came for flying. They had to pay a hefty fee for each hour of flying. Unlike the busy airport of the present times, there were no regular flights then and Sanganer aerodrome was a sleepy place.

All of us would wait there for our turn to fly. It was a rare day when every one of us got a chance to fly. Even when both the planes were available and weather conditions were favourable, only about half of us were able to go up before sundown, when the aerodrome closed. Bhandarkar would drop us back at about 8 p.m. It was dinner time already in the hostel mess. I would go for food in my mess and be dog-tired when I came to my room. I could barely attend to the most important college assignments before dropping down in my bed.

Mr Bhandarkar took me on my introductory flight in a Piper super-cruiser aircraft; as we took off, I felt a rare thrill—it was my first time on a plane! However, I had to discontinue flying training later on.

From our batch, only our head boy, called Under Officer Ramesh, was the first to go solo. He had logged 14 hours when he was allowed to do it. Although I found the flying experience most thrilling, my focus was on academic excellence. I had logged only six hours of flying by December and my flying capabilities were below par; there was no prospect of going solo. I had perforce to drop out of flying training in view of the impending university examination of Inter Arts and began to concentrate on my studies.

In the meanwhile, I had participated in a Hindi debate in the college, presided over by Dr Sarnam Singh, in which I was awarded the second prize. He cast admiring glances at me when I went up to him to receive my prize, patted me on the back and said: 'Shabaas!'[72]

One evening when I was returning from college to the hostel, I saw him standing outside his office room in the hostel, chatting with a few senior hostellers. I wished him 'good evening' with folded hands. He gave me a broad admiring smile and by way of introducing me to the boys said, 'He is R.S. Varma, in second year, a good debator. In fact, he is not R.S. Varma; he is R.A.S. Varma,' laying emphasis on the letters 'R.A.S.' He was paying me a compliment by indicating that I was bright enough to clear the RAS (Rajasthan Administrative Service) examination. He had probably surmised that joining the RAS was my aim in life.

I have always been a bit of braggart, so I retorted, 'No, Sir, I'd never take the RAS exam; I would only appear in the IAS.' He was taken aback by my bravado and said, 'Yes! Yes! Why not?' and went inside his room. He used to cite this dialogue to his students after I had joined the IAS in 1964.

I fared well in the Intermediate Arts exam; I was one of the seven students who were placed in the first division in the whole of Rajasthan and the only one from Maharaja's College to have that honour. My friend Damodar also did well in his exams and was admitted to the Medical College.

[72]Bravo!

10

RAJASTHAN COLLEGE

Chief Minister Mohanlal Sukhadia had noticed that although Rajasthan was a big state and had many colleges with a sizeable post-graduate population, very few students were able to clear the All India Services exams. He established a new college called Rajasthan College in 1957, with the express objective of preparing students for competitive examinations.

Dr S.P. Varma, the founder principal of Rajasthan College, created the perfect environment for learning, a space which truly became an alma mater[73] to its students. He assembled a faculty that could be the envy of any great institute of learning in India. The teacher to student ratio was 1:5, ensuring an intimate and informal relationship between them. It was also the first co-educational college of Rajasthan with eight girls in the very first batch. The most prized possession of the college was its library: its shelves were neatly stacked with brand new books on all subjects and, most importantly, the books were not locked away. Students could take out books from the shelves and browse at will. The library remained open beyond college hours, till 9 p.m.

The college started functioning in August 1957. To begin with, it just had first year and third year Arts classes with about 60 students and a dozen teachers. The next year, when I joined college, the number of students in all the four classes had gone up to 135 and

---

[73]Latin: A cherishing or fostering mother

that of teachers to 30. The ratio of girls to boys had also gone up.

My friend P.D. Vyas had joined this college when he failed to secure admission in the Medical College. When elections were held for the Students' Union, he was elected its first president. The setting up of this special college had appeared to me as providential for realizing my dream!

The Kesar Garh Castle, which had earlier housed the University, had become the hostel of Rajasthan College. As it could not accommodate more students, the college had now rented three more buildings in nearby Bapu Nagar for lodging hostel inmates.

I shared a room in the Premnath Building with my classmate Durgesh. Dr Iqbal Narain, professor of political science, was our warden. He made me the prefect of the hostel. When the elections to the Students' Union were held, P.D. Vyas canvassed for me and got me elected general secretary. It was a phenomenal rise for me. I was on cloud nine!

I continued studying the same subjects. In English Literature, besides a large number of poems, right from Milton to T.S. Eliot and varied prose selections, we had to study Shakespeare's *Macbeth* and John Galsworthy's *Loyalties*. In Maths we had Algebra, Trigonometry, Dynamics and Statics, Integral Calculus and Differential Calculus. I also continued with Psychology, but Logic had given way to an all-embracing 'Philosophy', which included Ethics and the Theory of Knowledge.

With great trepidation, I began to participate in English debates besides taking part in Hindi ones, mugging up my speeches and blurting them out on stage. Inevitably, I stumbled mid-speech sometimes and cut a sorry figure, but I persevered undeterred.

Saroj Mehta, of BA Final, was our star performer in English debates. She represented the college in University-level and state-level debates and won laurels everywhere. Once, she participated in a debate organized by Rajasthan University in its new campus.

About 15 teams had come from all over, including Maharaja's College. The Economics Department of the University was represented by Yogendra Alagh, who later became the vice-chancellor of JNU and a minister in the central government. In the debate Saroj and her teammate won the first prize, Alagh and his partner got the second prize. In Hindi debates, my classmate Pratibha Bordia was a consummate speaker with her chaste diction and mellifluous delivery. She and her teammate, Manjula Bhandari, won many trophies for the college.

Saroj and Pratibha also took leading parts in English and Hindi plays staged in the college. Saroj had acted the part of Amelia in *Dear Departed.* The versatile Harsh Bhargava and the ebullient Dinesh Maheshwari had acted as husbands of the two feuding sisters. The play was a roaring success. In Hindi plays, Pratibha took leading roles.

The most remarkable feat of Rajasthan College, in dramatics, was the staging of Kalidas's *Abhigyan Shakuntalam,* in the original Sanskrit, for the annual function of the college. Ananthashayanam Iyengar, Speaker of the Lok Sabha, was the chief guest. Chief Minister Sukhadia, the visionary founder of the college, was there along with many of his cabinet colleagues besides the who's who of Jaipur.

Pratibha acted as Shakuntala. She had laboured hard, for about a month, in rehearsals under the guidance of the professor of Sanskrit, Dr P.L. Bhargava. The play got a thunderous ovation. Dr Iyengar went up on the stage and complimented Pratibha for bringing mythical Shakuntala alive on stage and transporting the audience to the sylvan surroundings of Rishi Kanva's forest cottage and the fabulous court of King Dushyant.

The quality of teaching in the college was unmatched. There were only five students in our Maths class and we had Dr G.C. Patni and Prof. P.D. Verma to teach us. Dr D.C. Mathur taught us Philosophy, and for English language and literature we had a veritable galaxy of emiment teachers including Dr K.N. Bakaya (former Head of English Department, B.R. College, Agra), Prof. Mathews (former Principal, Bikaner College), Prof. P.S. Chauhan and Prof. D.P. Wanchoo. Dr Bakaya got a tape recorder and made us speak a paragraph in it, which he replayed to us and told us the correct pronunciation of words.

The eminent Hindi poet and author Dr Sarnam Singh came from Maharaja's College to head the Hindi department. His book *Bhav Kan* was prescribed in the course of BA Final. It was a rare thrill for his students to be taught by the author himself. He also started an NCC Unit in the college and straightaway made me an under officer.

•◆

My trysts with destiny continued at Rajasthan College, and the next one actually put me in the dock.

On a hot Sunday afternoon, my friend Ashok Agarwal and I saw a young man with a girl on a cycle disappearing into the sandy waste beyond our hostel. It was none of our business, but the whole thing seemed fishy, so we decided to investigate. We followed the cycle tracks and found the cycle lying abandoned, but no trace of the furtive lovers. To teach them a lesson, we walked away with the cycle.

The cycle remained lying in a corner of the hostel for about two months, so one day I decided to get it repaired and use it to save the time I spent walking. When I went to the repairman to collect it after two days, I was arrested for theft! The cycle belonged to a policeman. I was produced before a magistrate and released on bail. Our principal had to explain, 'He is no thief; he is our best student!' The DGP retorted, 'If he is your best student, I fear for the worst one!'

Dr Varma's intervention earned me a reprieve, and once again

I realized how easy it is to slip into the world of crime!

◆

When I started my final year at Rajasthan College in July 1960, I decided to stand for the post of president of the Students' Union. I believed that I had become quite popular and would be a natural choice. Harsh Bhargava, who had worked as joint secretary with me, was also contesting the post of general secretary. We were hopeful of winning but we suffered a crushing defeat. Harsh took it bravely but it was traumatic for me!

After a couple of months, I had a bout of jaundice. I was exhausted in body and spirit and went home. My mother took me to a traditional healer who had a reputation for curing jaundice. He made me sit before him on the ground and gave me a jhara[74], with neem leaves, and presented me a garland of the green pods of the khejri tree, tied with a sacred mauli thread[75]. Mumbling a mantra, he put this garland around my neck and said, 'In a few days, when the garland reaches your navel, the disease will be gone.' He did not charge a single paisa, and I was most sceptical of this mumbo-jumbo.

I had lost my appetite in Jaipur but began relishing the daal-roti cooked by my mother. I reclined on a charpoy in the shade of a young neem tree in our backyard, reading poems from the *Golden Treasury* or dozing off. After a few days, I was amazed to see that the garland had become longer: I realized that the green pods had shrivelled up which tightened the knots, thereby releasing a wee bit of thread! I felt better as well; the confidence trick had worked.

◆

---

[74]Dusting, cleansing

[75]Red-coloured sacred thread used by pundits for tying on the hands of the wedding couple before puja

I lost two weeks of studies because of jaundice. Prof. P.D. Verma spent extra time with me for 2-3 days, patiently doing the maths exercises he had done in the class and brought me up-to-date.

Prof. P.S. Chauhan had covered the whole of Act II of *Macbeth* in my absence. When I met him, he asked me to read it by myself, mark the incomprehensible portions and then meet him, he would explain them to me. I opened the book at Act II. This happens to be the most crucial part of the play—Lady Macbeth and Macbeth murder King Duncan in this Act.

I bravely began to read but was stumped by words I was not familiar with. I opened the dictionary for help. After struggling for an hour I had barely covered two pages.

It dawned on me then that Shakespeare did not intend his plays to be read in this manner—with the book in one hand and the dictionary in the other. He had written them for being acted on stage in a span of 2-3 hours. Indeed, his audience did not even consist of university undergrads like me; they were ordinary townsmen and wayfarers. They did not understand many of his words, but they enjoyed the plays in the flow of acting by the gestures of the players.

I, therefore, thought of reading *Macbeth* in the flow; nay, I began to deliver the dialogues aloud. Sometimes I had to go back and repeat the lines when they went over my head and once in a while I had to open the dictionary, but it began to make sense and I began to enjoy it.

After finishing Act II, I could not stop. In the next 3-4 days, in daily sittings lasting about two hours, I finished the whole play—months before Prof. Chauhan did it in class. No doubt, it was a cursory understanding but enough to sense the beauty and grandeur of the play, which deepened considerably after listening to Prof. Chauhan's lectures in class.

Our librarian, Mr H.D. Sharma, was truly remarkable. He kept the library ship-shape and personally replaced the books taken down by the students from the shelves. His knowledge was phenomenal and he guided the students about books to read for a particular topic. He was a book lover and was always immersed in books.

He started a Book Review Club in the library and encouraged students to choose a book, other than the prescribed text books, and review it before a select gathering of teachers and students. I thought of reading *King Lear* for the book club. I told Sharmaji about it and he scheduled it after a fortnight.

I began reading the play, adopting the same technique of reading it aloud to myself in a flow. It took me several sittings but I was able to finish it in a week. Indeed, it turned out to be a most pleasant surprise; my mother had narrated a similar story to me. The king, in my mother's story, had seven daughters and had asked each of them: *'Tum kiske bhagya ka khati ho?'* (By whose dispensation do you eat?) All of them except the youngest replied: *'Hum aapke bhagya ka khate hain'* (We eat by your dispensation), making the king happy. However, the youngest told him: *'Mein tau apne bhagya ka khati hun!'* (I eat by my own dispensation!) The king married the six girls to princes, gave them jewellery and gifts in dowry. But, in his anger, he married the youngest daughter to a leper and gave her nothing. She went with the leper to live in a mud hut at the outskirts of a village. However, soon the wheel of fortune turned and after bathing in a pool the leper was transformed into a handsome young man. They prospered and lived happily ever after.

Shakespeare's King Lear had asked his three daughters which of them loved him most. His two married daughters replied in superlative terms, vying with each other and claiming they loved him more than anybody else in the world. But the third daughter, Cordelia, who was unmarried, told him she loved him as a daughter should love her father and asked:

> 'Why have my sisters husbands, if they say
> They love you all? Haply, when I shall wed,
> That lord whose hand must take my plight shall carry
> Half my love with him, half my care and duty.
> Sure I shall never marry like my sisters,
> To love my father all.'

Her truthful answer angered Lear and he disinherited her. Lear and Cordelia were imprisoned thereafter by his scheming daughters and sons-in-law, and Cordelia died.

As the play ends, Lear appears carrying dead Cordelia in his arms, saying: 'Why should a dog, a horse, a rat have life, and thou no breath at all?'

It's a heart-rending tragedy. In my presentation in the library, I brought out these points and read out some poignant portions from the play. It was greatly appreciated.

11

ALLAHABAD UNIVERSITY

My performance in the BA examination was disheartening: my aggregate did not reach the first-class mark. Our principal Dr S.P. Varma called me to his house and asked what I intended to do now. I told him that I would go back to Maharaja's College and do a master's in English Literature. He advised me to join Allahabad University because their department of English, according to him, was by far the best in the country.

I took his advice and in early July reached Allahabad. The architectural beauty of the principal buildings of the University left me spellbound. They consisted of the imposing Senate Hall in the centre, the library to its right and the English department building to the left. I was greatly kicked to see that the English department occupied a place of pride in the University.

Behind the Senate Hall, there was an old banyan tree. Its secondary roots reached the ground, transforming into new banyan trees. It was obviously older than the University and was chosen as the insignia of the University. Underneath the insignia was inscribed the motto: '*Quot Rami Tot Arbores*', meaning 'As many branches, as many trees', which pointed to the banyan tree's undying nature, as its Sanskrit name 'akshay vat' also suggested. I understood the motto to mean that the offshoots of the University, including its students, in time became institutions themselves. I easily gained admission to the University, but there was no vacancy in any hostel close by. I finally managed to get a single room in the Jain Hostel in Colonel Gunj: it was a modest building compared to the main hostels. I was quite happy.

I went out for a walk in the evening. Close to the hostel, there was the Company Garden, named after the East India Company, an extensive public park which had the Public Library inside it. The library was a beautiful Renaissance-style building from during the British era, a veritable treasure trove which was still functioning. It had an old-world charm about it. Its central hall served as the reading room, its shelves full of old volumes. I lingered there for a while.

Dusk had fallen when I came out of the library and walked back by a road meandering under the old trees, and came upon a circle with a statue placed in the centre. Due to the semi-darkness I couldn't make out whose statue it was. Upon closer inspection, I found that it was the guru of our revolutionary freedom fighters, Chandra Shekhar Azad, twirling his moustache! I went up the steps of the monument to read the inscription. It read: 'This was the spot where the British soldiers surrounded Azad, where fighting valiantly he killed a few of them and was gunned down.' I had read about this encounter in history books and could vividly visualize the scene—Azad sprawled on the ground, firing from his pistol at British soldiers, who were showering him with bullets from behind the trees! I felt a shiver run down my spine as I looked up at his statue in the gathering darkness and stood for a while in silence, like the old trees which had been mute witness to the gory scene.

On my first night at the hostel, I went to sleep on my bed, covered with a mosquito net, which I had got placed in the central courtyard to escape the summer heat. At midnight, when I was in deep sleep, I was pulled out of bed in pitch darkness by two boys and brought before some boys sitting like inquisitors on chairs in the middle of the quadrangle. All lights had been switched off, making them look like faceless shadowy figures.

I knew that ragging a 'fresher' was customary in hostels, but I was taken aback, as I had not experienced it in the hostels I had lived in, in Jaipur.

They shouted at me, *'Oye Rajasthani oont! Farshi salaam karo.'* (Oye Rajasthani camel! Do the Farshi salaam). I retorted in a jocular tone, 'Farshi salaam? What's that? I'd do it if somebody demonstrated how it was done.'

There was a shower of expletives at me. One of the dark figures got up then, went down on all fours and touched his forehead to the floor before me. I laughed and gave him benediction, *'Ayushman bhav!'*[76] and thereafter knelt down and did a Farshi salaam before them. 'Once more!' they shouted and I did it again.

They were gratified and asked me to sing a song. I gave a comical rendering of a Mohammad Rafi song. They asked for one more. I sang another in a more farcical tone. They asked me to dance and I began to twist, singing *'Aao twist karen'*[77] and caught hold of one of them and began to shake him wildly from his hips. They were rattled by my antics and one of them shouted, *'Murga banja!*[78]*'* I laughed and said, 'Show me how to become a murga and I'd do it.' Another shower of expletives produced some mock laughter from me. They were not enjoying my bonhomie and one of them told me to get lost. Relieved, I went back to my bed.

•◆

There were about 65 students in the MA (Previous) English Literature class, including about 15 girls. It was a kind of revelation for me to know that this class represented the entire strength of Allahabad University, that I had only to compete with this group for a position on the university merit list!

---

[76]Sanskrit: May you live long!

[77]A popular Bollywood number

[78]Be a cock!

Allahabad was a non-affiliating university, unlike Rajasthan University, which had about a dozen post-graduate colleges affiliated to it. A student in Jaipur's Maharaja's College could never know how many brilliant students were there in Jodhpur, Bikaner, Udaipur, Ajmer or elsewhere. In contrast, there were no unknown devils here!

We had to write four papers in MA Previous—on Poetry, Prose, Fiction and Drama. The poetry course started right from Chaucer and covered Shakespeare, Milton, the classicists like Alexander Pope and the Romantic poets. Prof. K.K. Mehrotra, our head of the department, taught us Romantic poetry. I learnt that he had lived a romantic life. He had done his master's from Oxford and had been the 'topper' of the class. The pretty daughter of an Oxford professor had been studying in his class; they fell in love and later married. Unfortunately his knees had let him down and he moved around in a wheelchair. Knee replacement was probably unknown in those days. He had got the driver's seat of his old Morris car removed and drove it to the university, sitting in his wheelchair.

Prof. P.C. Gupta taught us fiction. We had novels of Smollett, Fielding, Thomas Hardy, Jane Austen, Charles Dickens and D.H. Lawrence in our course. Prof. Gupta was a marvellous teacher, engaging and entertaining. He carried an old notebook in which he had stored literary anecdotes and tidbits about the authors and their critics. He would steal a glance at the notebook and regale us with them.

We had a bright student, Khare, in our class. He was a repeater; he had not taken the examinations the previous year as he had been unsure of topping the list. One day Prof. Gupta narrated a witty anecdote that had the entire class in splits but Khare remarked, 'Excuse me, Sir, you had cracked the same joke in this lecture last year also.' Prof. Gupta was unfazed; he promptly retorted, 'That's right, Mr Khare, and you are at liberty not to laugh!'

Mr R.N. Deb, younger brother of the former head of the

department Prof. S.C. Deb, taught us Shakespeare and was superb. One Mr Shukla taught us prose; he was prosaic.

•◆

The University had a great library, but to my dismay I found that many crucial pages were missing from some books; they had been torn off by students who had borrowed the books. I went to Prof. Mehrotra, and showed some of those books to him. He was quite distressed to see the mutilated books and very kindly invited me to visit his personal library and borrow all the books I wanted. I was overwhelmed by his gesture.

I had struck up a deep friendship with a classmate, Ram Pyare Rai. I took him along to Prof. Mehrotra's house in Civil Lines. The orderly took us into the drawing room, where Prof. Mehrotra sat in his wheelchair, near his elegant British wife. He introduced us to his wife, told her we had come to borrow a few books from their library. She stood up and wheeled him to a large adjacent room which had 4-5 shelves full of books. We followed them. 'There you are,' said the professor in his affectionate voice. 'Take a good look. Feel at home and have your pick.' They returned to the drawing room.

We selected four books and came back to the drawing room. I showed the books to the professor and asked him if I may make a note. 'No need at all,' he said and added, 'You are free to come here any time, replace these and take more.'

In the two years that I stayed in Allahabad, I made many forays into his library and borrowed about 30 books. On my later visits, I used to leave a note mentioning the titles I was taking away.

•◆

The English department used to organize lectures by eminent scholars which were attended by teachers and students from other departments as well. Raghupati Sahay 'Firaq', popularly known as Firaq Gorakhpuri, was an iconic Urdu poet and had retired as a Reader in the department. He came dressed informally in kurta-pajama and spoke extempore to a packed hall for about an hour on 'What is Poetry'. He made a profound observation: 'Language *tutlane se banti hai*,' and quoted from Robert Burns.

'My Luve's like a red, red rose
That's newly sprung in June:
My Luve's like the melodie
That's sweetly play'd in tune.'

Scottish language, he said, was created by the peasants of Scotland who could not pronounce English properly. He explained that Brij bhasha was born through the mispronunciation of Hindi and gave us the great poets Surdas and Tulsidas.

As for poetry, he said that it flowed from the heart and was unfettered by form, rules of grammar or language. His words gushed out effortlessly like a nimble spring as he quoted passages from Shakespeare and Wordsworth, and from Urdu poets like Mirza Ghalib, Mir Taqi Mir and himself. The audience was spellbound and he received a thunderous applause at the end.

Apart from his scintillating scholarship, what struck me was his phenomenal memory. It was amazing how he had flawlessly quoted chapter and verse from so many poets without the help of notes.

Although Firaq had retired, he was still living in a University house in the campus. One evening, my friend Ram Pyare Rai and I decided to go to his house to meet him. When I knocked at his door, we heard Firaq's booming voice from inside, 'Who's there?' We peeped in. He was sitting on his bed with a glass in his hand, drinking.

'Sir, we are doing MA in English Literature,' I said. 'We had heard your lecture the other day. It was marvellous!'

Firaq was a loner but considering we were studying English Literature, tolerated our obtrusion. 'Sit down,' he said, pointing at the cane sofa chairs. As we were sitting down, I remarked, 'Sir, we have heard that despite your great erudition you were not promoted to professor. How could it happen?'

His eyes flashed at my question and he replied, 'Because Firaq never sirred (sic) anybody! Never sirred even the Vice Chancellor!' He let that sink and then added, 'Do you know, the Vice Chancellor, A.N. Jha, was my junior? In fact, we were classmates in MA Final, but he dropped that year and I topped the University and became a lecturer. Next year, he topped and became a lecturer. His father was vice chancellor then and later, he too, became vice chancellor. But how could I "sir" my junior? That's the reason.'

He asked us who taught us what, and made terse, even acerbic, comments on some of our teachers and after a while we took his leave.

The next time we went to his house after a few days, we found him in much the same way—sitting with folded legs on his bed, sipping his drink and occasionally lighting a cigarette. He seemed to be pleased with our visit.

Thereafter, Ram Pyare Rai and I became frequent visitors to Firaq's house. He used to regale us with selected verses from his poetry although he was well aware of our limitations in the knowledge of Urdu. He would start by saying, '*Mir ko suniye*' (Listen to Mir), and recite a sher[79] from Mir Taqi Mir. He would then translate it in English to ensure that we had understood it. '*Ab Firaq ko suniye*' (Now listen to Firaq), he would say then, and recite one of his own couplets which expressed a similar idea and proceeded to translate it into English. We could see that Firaq's

[79]A couplet

couplet had greater depth and subtlety.

Besides Mir, he recited verses from other poets like Daag, Momin or Zauk and then recited his own verses as a comparison, simultaneously translating every verse into impeccable English for our benefit. All this was extempore, from his prodigious memory! This would go on for an hour or more, till we would rise and take his leave.

One evening when we entered Firaq's sitting room, he said that his maid hadn't turned up that day. Rai and I used to eat at a restaurant on University Road. At our request he went with us and had a meal with us in the restaurant. As there was no likelihood of his maid turning up the next day, I offered to come to his place and make his morning tea for him. He was astonished at this and asked, 'You make your own tea?'

'Who else will make my tea, Sir?' I retorted. 'I make myself tea early in the morning when I wake up, and again 2-3 times in the night to ward off sleep.'

'And you also wash your own underpants?'

'Of course, I wash my underpants and banian. I polish my shoes too!'

He was shocked and reprimanded me, 'Stop it. Such menial work contaminates the mind.'

The next day was Sunday and early in the morning, I carried my stove to his house. He was pleased to see me. He opened his kitchen and took out tea leaves and sugar from small tin boxes lined up on a wooden rack, after opening their little locks. He told me that he kept the boxes under lock and key as his maid was in the habit of pilfering the stuff. He stood at the door, watching me as I lit the stove. I had brought four eggs with me and made fluffy double omelettes for us. Then I boiled water in a pan and made tea for both of us and poured it through a sieve into the teapot and brought everything to the sitting room. I could see that he liked the omelette immensely. We were sipping tea when the maid came. She said her child had fallen ill and she had taken him to the hospital.

◆

At this time, about a dozen of us, including two girls, Manjari Nanda and Promila Sanyal, had started a weekly discussion group which met in a restaurant. We called it 'Minerva Club'. At its second or third meeting I suggested that we invite Firaq to give us a talk at our next meeting. Everyone agreed, as we had been greatly impressed by his lecture on poetry. I broached the idea to Firaq, who readily accepted the invitation. We did not suggest any topic to him, thinking it would be too presumptuous on our part.

For over 30 minutes, Firaq expounded on gay rights and the irrational bias prevailing in society against gay sex. He said there was nothing unnatural about same sex union. Nature had made some people that way, they were not freaks.

He clarified that he was not talking about paedophilia, which was abominable. He was talking about sex between adults: that was the first precondition for gay sex. Second, it had to be between consenting adults; there should be no element of coercion. Thirdly, it had to be done in a private, not a public place. And lastly, it should not be casual, nor for monetary consideration. Indeed the union should be sanctified like a wedding bond.

No one stirred or spoke a word during his discourse: there was stunned silence. No one uttered a word when he finished. It was customary to serve tea after the talk but I stood up and said we were grateful to Firaq Sahib for enlightening us about this unusual topic. I hailed a rickshaw and escorted him to his house.

The girls quit the Club after this meet and it withered away soon thereafter. Firaq's speech proved to be the swansong of the Minerva Club!

I had great regard for him but I, too, felt scandalized by his talk. I realize, now, how far ahead of his time Firaq was. There has been a sea change in our attitude since then. Gay rights have been acknowledged by several countries in the world and gay marriage has been legalized. In September 2018, the Supreme Court of India passed a landmark judgement, holding that there was nothing abnormal or unnatural about gay sex, just what Firaq had maintained that day.

Firaq used to attend the annual mushaira[80] organized at the Red Fort in Delhi; indeed he was the doyen of Urdu poets. He was also a great admirer of Jawaharlal Nehru. In the mushaira held after Nehru's demise, Firaq sang:

Iss khandhar mein jalte hain kuchh bujhe bujhe se chirag,
Inhi se kaam chalao, bari udaas hai raat!

(In these ruins are flickering a few dim lamps,
Let's be content with them, it's a very sad night!)

Nehru had been succeeded by the diminutive Lal Bahadur Shastri and this is how he felt about the change.

◆

On a Sunday evening in August, Ram Pyare Rai and I decided to go to Suryakant Tripathi Nirala's house to meet him. I had read some of his moving poems like, '*Maine dekha use, Ilahabad ke path par, vah todti patthar!*' (I saw her on the road to Allahabad, she was breaking stones!) We felt that he empathized with the poor and the downtrodden.

We knocked on the door of Nirala's house in Daryagunj, near Sangam, getting no response and seeing that the door was open, we entered. He was fast asleep. But our intrusion had disturbed him.

[80]An evening social gathering at which Urdu poetry is read

He woke up with a start and asked in English, 'Who are you?' and then, roaring in rage, he advanced menacingly upon us. We fled.

We decided to visit the sangam. We walked along the turbulent Ganga and reached the confluence where it mingled with the blue waters of the Yamuna. I drank a handful of the holy water and sprinkled some on my head.

•◆

In the MA (Previous) examination I stood fourth in the order of merit of the University. A quiet girl, Mira Saxena, had topped the list, Khare was second and a boy from Bihar, Debakar Panda, was third. I was crestfallen and resolved to work harder the next year.

After about a fortnight of the opening of the University after the summer vacation, Prof. P.C. Gupta called me to his room and gave me a pleasant surprise. He told me that Prof. Mehrotra was pleased to nominate me as the Secretary of the English Association and I should call on him to thank him for conferring this honour on me.

I was dumbfounded for a moment at this unexpected news. I said in disbelief. 'I don't quite understand, Sir. Don't you know, I'm fourth in the list? It's given to the topper. It should go to Mira Saxena.'

He smiled and said, 'You leave that to us.'

'But it would cause hurt and jealousy, Sir,' I persisted.

'Don't let that bother you. We asked her. She is unwilling to take it as it involves a lot of running around and time.'

I felt greatly relieved but asked him about Khare and Panda.

He told me that Khare is a repeater and Panda's pronunciation left much to be desired.

I thanked him and went to Prof. Mehrotra's chamber. His face lit up with a sweet smile when he saw me. 'Do sit down, Ram Sahai,' he said. 'We have selected you as Secretary of the English Association.'

'Sir, I am grateful to you for this high honour. I hardly deserve it, but I hope to come up to your expectations.'

There were two main functions of the Secretary of the English Association. He is the editor of the University magazine and he has to organize occasional lectures by eminent scholars. He solicits articles from students for the University's annual magazine, edits them and gets it published before the end of the academic session.

The lectures that I organized were very well received. The first lecture was by Prof. S.C. Deb, predecessor of Prof. K.K. Mehrotra. He traced the evoloution of English Literature from Chaucer's *Canterbury Tales* to its flowering in the Elizabethan age when Christopher Marlowe wrote *Doctor Faustus* and Shakespeare produced a series of immortal plays.

The next lecture was on modern poetry by a brilliant senior lecturer of the department, J.S. Saxena. He threw light upon the debt T.S. Eliot and Y.B. Yeats owed to the American poet Ezra Pound, in writing poetry. Saxena observed that when Eliot's poem 'The Love Song of J. Alfred Prufrock' appeared, it created a sensation in the literary world. He also dwelt upon 'The Waste Land' and concluded his lecture by observing that this unique poem reflected the horrors of World War I.

After a couple of months, our favourite teacher Y. Sahay, Firaq Sahib's younger brother, gave a talk on literary appreciation. His oratory was spellbinding and he received a round of loud applause from the audience.

For the University magazine, I had received about a dozen articles; Prof. P.C. Gupta had also contributed a paper on the new trends in English fiction. To these was added a one-page gist of each of the three lectures we had organized. I attempted a draft of my editorial, giving critical comments on the articles, and submitted it to Prof. Gupta for his approval. He made a few corrections in it and I went to the press and gave the entire material to the manager.

In a few days, the manager sent me galley proofs. It was a tedious, time-consuming task to spot the errors and mark corrections. I now realized why Mira Saxena did not want to be Secretary. Our MA Final examinations were to be held after a fortnight. I burnt the proverbial midnight oil and corrected the proofs in 3-4 days.

The printed copies of the magazine were received when we were in the throes of the examinations. I left for home after the examinations were over.

•◆

My brother was working as a Goods Clerk in the Western Railways at Jaipur in May 1962, when I returned from Allahabad after finishing my exams. He had rented a modest three-room house in an unauthorized colony known as Lal Kothi opposite Bapu Nagar on the main Sanganer Road. There was a young neem tree standing in its sandy courtyard, just like the one we had in our backyard at Sri Madhopur. He had brought his wife, two children, Ajay and Vijay, and Mother from home. Besides, he had retired Father from active work and taken him out of the dingy cell in Mamaji's house.

Most people living in the colony belonged to our community of stone masons and bricklayers. Our family was new to Jaipur, but my Mamaji, Prahladrai Samodwale, was a prominent member of our community there. On a festive occasion, when we were dining at Mamaji's house, he told us about Bhonrilalji Khargata, who lived near the Ganesh Temple at the foot of the Moti Doongri Fort Palace. Mamaji said that Bhonrilalji was showing interest in Ram Sahai (me), for his granddaughter, as there was no other boy in our community who had done his MA. His son, Girdhari Lal, was married to Badri Sahayji Photographer's daughter, whose forefathers had been the official photographers and portrait-makers of the royal family of Jaipur. Girdhari Lal, he said, was an architect and had an educated marriageable daughter and they wanted to invite us to see the girl.

My parents and brother were thrilled to hear this and I was not averse to the idea. I had been charmed by girls in my class in Jaipur and Allahabad but they were a class apart. I wanted to marry a homely girl who understood my deep parental debt and shared my dream of looking after my old parents. I welcomed the idea of an arranged marriage within the community.

But I did not like the newfangled custom of going to 'see' the girl. I thought it was a traumatic experience for the girl. She was exhibited like a commodity and mutely suffered rejection. I would not be able to say no if I went for a dekho. I would rather that my mother saw her and talked to her, and if she liked the girl, to perform the *gaud bharo* ceremony, instead of leaving the question of acceptance hanging in the air. I thought that this would convey to the girl the deep bond that I shared with my mother.

•◆

My mother and my Bhabhi went one fine morning to the Khargata haveli, taking Ajay with them. They were cordially received and offered tea. They liked the girl, Savitri, who brought the tea tray, made her sit near them and talked to her. She told them that she had passed High School from Patiala, where they lived. Mother asked her to sit in her lap and blessed her and offered her the sweets and presents she had carried with her. A few days later, a delegation of men, led by Savitri's grandfather and father, came to our rented house in Lal Kothi and sat under the neem tree. Like my father, Savitri's grandfather, Bhonrilalji, wore a safa. He drew a tilak on my forehead and gave me a dry coconut, wrapped ceremoniously, along with a 100-rupee note. I was engaged to a girl I hadn't even seen.

•◆

In June, I received my result from Allahabad University: I was fifth in the order of merit. No one had secured a first division. Prof.

Mehrotra sent me a glowing testimonial, extolling my performance as Secretary of the English Association and praising my qualities of head and heart. I sent him a letter of thanks in gratitude.

I had applied for a post of lecturer in English, in response to an advertisement by the Director of Education, Rajasthan. On a hot summer day in early July, I went walking to the Director's office to find out if I had been selected.

I was sure of getting a lecturership in a government college as there were about 20 vacancies of English lecturers in the state. No interview was required; the selection was to be made on the basis of marks obtained in the MA examination.

At my query, the clerk in the Director's office looked into his papers and stoically handed me a cyclostyled appointment letter for English lecturers. My name figured in the list; I had been appointed a lecturer at the Government College in Churu, in northern Rajasthan. I was supposed to report in a week and my emoluments would be a princely sum of ₹275 a month.

I had also applied for a lecturer's position advertised by the newly created University of Jodhpur. The eligibility for the University job was a good master's degree (which I had) and two years' teaching experience in a college (which I did not have). When I reached home, a telegram was waiting for me, calling me for an interview in Jodhpur in two days. My brother advised me to attend the interview in Jodhpur. Of course they might not take me as I did not possess the minimum qualifications. Then I could proceed to Churu from there.

I reached the Jodhpur University office at SMK College on the designated day. There was a regular crowd of candidates.

My name was at the tail end. It was past five o'clock when I was called. Prof. V.V. John, Director of Education, Rajasthan, was in the chair. Mr Girde, Principal of the Jodhpur Engineering College, sat beside him. I had learnt, while sitting outside, that the vacancies were in the Engineering College, which was a constituent of the new University.

I bowed to them and was about to take my seat when V.V. John shot a question at me, 'But you don't fulfill the eligibilty criteria, why have you come?' 'Because you sent me a telegram, Sir,' I shot back. He cooled down and said, 'Okay, sit down.'

My Allahabad University marksheet showed that I had scored high marks in the poetry paper, so he started with John Donne and came to Romantic poetry. He moved to Shakespeare then, considering we had a full paper on him, and asked a question about the character of Macbeth; I likened him to Raskolnikov, the hero of *Crime and Punishment,* and said that like Raskolnikov, Macbeth, too, could not digest the crimes he had committed. I quoted Macbeth's soliloquy, 'I have forgotten the taste of tears…' They thanked me and asked me to wait outside. I came out, weary and uncertain. I realized then that my interview had lasted over 20 minutes.

I was the first to be called in and a beaming V.V. John told me that they had decided to overlook my ineligibility and were happy to offer me a job as a lecturer at the engineering college of Jodhpur University. I thanked him and he asked when I could join. 'I can join tomorrow morning, Sir!' I said beaming, and added that I would have to dump Churu College, where he had appointed me. He chuckled.

It struck me, as I came out, that I would start on a salary of ₹400 a month. Wow! That's what an IAS officer starts his career with! I couldn't believe my luck!

12

JODHPUR UNIVERSITY

Along with me, three others had also been appointed as lecturers of Jodhpur University at the same time: Mahle, Naithani and Arora.

Mahle was married; he rented an independent house while the three of us who were single, shared rooms in a newly constructed house near the Engineering College, which was some distance away from the main town. Naithani was from Palampur in Himachal Pradesh and he took on the job of cooking for all of us. I remember him, wrapped in a white apron like a professional chef, presiding over the cooking range and talking wistfully of the towering Dhauladhar mountains.

I enjoyed teaching English to the students of the engineering college and introducing them to English poetry. I recall their eager faces as they trooped into my class after a lecture on structural engineering. I loved to recite poems to them that were not even prescribed for them. They enjoyed them as they were so different from their mainstream studies.

The numerical strength of the English faculty in the engineering college had doubled with the addition of four new lecturers. The head of our department, Prof. Ojha, was a merry old soul. In our vacant periods, we used to sit in his room as there was no other staff room for us. He was always spinning quips and puns and used to regale us with his witticisms and wisecracks.

Even after a lapse of more than five decades, I haven't forgotten some of them. He would say, 'People travelling in a bus, when they see men walking on the road comment, "Poor fellows, they are be-bus"[81]!' There was another variant of this quip, 'Men going in a car see people walking on the road and say, "They are be-kar"[82]!' One of his favourites was, '*Aajkal ulta zamana aagaya* (It's a topsy-turvy world nowadays). *Pahle diye taley andhera hota tha* (In olden times it used to be dark under the lamp), *ab diye ke oopar andhera hota hai* (now there is darkness above it—as in a bulb hanging from the ceiling).' Every day he would coin a new one. There was another delightful doggerel that he had composed, in a similar vein:

Pahle ghee se subzi banti thi, ab subzi se ghee banta hai,

In the good old times ghee was used to prepare vegetables, now vegetables are used to prepare ghee—as in Dalda Vanaspati.

Pahle aurat junti thi, ab sara aalam janata hai.

In the old days women delivered babies, now every one, men and women, are 'janata' i.e. common people.

A lecturer in the department, Mr Saxena, invited us to a party on the birthday of his son. Mrs Saxena had prepared several delicacies and had laid a festive table. Standing near the table, she was pointing them out to the guests and inviting them to taste them. The toddler had started walking and was romping around. We had loaded our plates and were savouring the dishes. Saxena went to Prof. Ojha and urged him, 'Sir, try this gulab jamun; it's home-made. Sir, you haven't tasted this barfi; this is also home-made.' Prof. Ojha was a trifle annoyed by his repetition of the

---

[81]Hindi: Helpless; Literally: Without a bus

[82]Hindi: Unemployed, useless; Literally: Without a car

'home-made' blurb. He turned towards him and pointing to the toddler asked, 'Saxena Sahib, tell me this. Is *he* home-made too?' Mrs Saxena turned red in the face and went inside the house; poor Saxena was dumbstruck by the boss' devastating comment, but said nothing.

•◆

Becoming a University lecturer immediately after my MA had been an unexpected stroke of luck. However, I wasn't happy teaching in an engineering college: I wanted to teach students of English Literature and for that I needed a transfer to SMK College.

Prof. V.V. John came to deliver a lecture after a few months. At tea, after the lecture, I went to him, explained my problem and requested him to transfer me to SMK College. I added that one more lecturer, Rastogi, had joined the engineering college and they could easily spare me. He promised to look into the matter and within a few weeks my wish was granted.

SMK College and Jaswant College had a common campus, the latter being the Commerce faculty college. Unlike the Engineering College, they are situated near the city. I rented an accommodation in the large haveli of a senior lecturer from the Commerce department, Satya Prasanna Singh Bhandari.

•◆

After teaching for a few months, I realized that sometimes a wish fulfilled is a dream shattered.

Besides other classes, I taught General English to a BA final year class, the largest class in the University, with more than 70 students. This class, mostly consisting of repeaters, was a remnant of the old four-year Bachelor's degree course and this was their last chance to earn their degree under the old system. Those who did not succeed would have to join a three-year degree course from the first year, thereby losing many years in the process.

The lecture theatre was too small to accommodate this class and many boys would perch themselves on windowsills, to be able to conveniently slip away into the corridor after the roll-call.

Dr Nagarmal Sahal, Head of the English Department, summoned me one day and reprimanded me for permitting the students to leave after the roll-call. He said that I was encouraging indiscipline and instructed me to repeat the roll-call and mark students absent at the end of the class. I tried to explain that the situation had improved since I had taken over, but I was summarily dismissed from his office. I ignored his suggestion about the double roll-call. Next week, the class was taken away from me and given to a senior lecturer who had a better rapport with the students. I was bothered by it, but I was also relieved.

Unexpectedly, the class went on strike, demanding my return and refused to budge from their stand. The Vice Chancellor summoned me, demanding why I was instigating the students; I told him the whole story, adding that, in fact, I had felt relieved when the class was taken away from me and that I would be the last person to instigate them.

I was reinstated and told the boys that they should not slip out if they liked me so much. I became a minor celebrity among fellow lecturers who did not like Dr Sahal's headmasterish ways.

After this incident I began to concentrate on preparing for the IAS and fulfil my boyhood dream.

Unlike the present system of a common examination for All India Services, in those days there was a clear distinction between candidates who wished to compete for the top two Services (Indian Administrative Service and Indian Foreign Service) and the rest. Competing for the IAS or IFS was an altogether different ball game, inasmuch as those aspiring for them, had to write two additional papers of master's level. Serious candidates actually did their master's in two subjects before making an attempt. There were no Prelims in those days.

For the three BA-level compulsory papers, I chose English Literature, British History and European History and for the MA-level optional papers I chose English Literature and British Constitutional History. I borrowed books from the college library and began preparing for the next year's examination.

In a book by Walter Bagehot, I found an irreverent and light-hearted interpretation of the British Constitution. In his inimitable style he opined that England was ruled by a 'double set' of institutions—dignified or theatrical ones like the Queen and the House of Lords and the efficient ones like the House of Commons and the Cabinet. The mystique and pageantry of the former helped to impress and govern the people.

Reading European History seemed to bridge so many gaps in my knowledge and complemented and contrasted with British History. I had read *War and Peace* during the summer holidays after my BA examination. Now I read a couple of books on Napoleon, which brought a large part of European history into clear focus. I seemed to be journeying from singularities towards the whole.

•◆

Sometime after my transfer to the SMK College, Prof. V.V. John's son George John joined the English department as a lecturer. We took an instant liking to each other. George had inherited his father's erudition and dry wit, but unlike him, was quiet and softspoken. We formed a little group with fellow lecturers P.C. Joshi and M.C. Joshi, who exuded warmth and sweetness. After our classes were over, at about 2 p.m., we would cross the railway track and go to the Coffee House on the main road for a leisurely repast of dosa and hot coffee and indulged in what came naturally to lecturers—blah-blah-blah.

The next year, one of my teachers from Allahabad University, J.S. Saxena, who had taught us modern poetry, joined the department as a Reader and became the presiding deity of our Coffee Club. With his coming, the repast became less victual and more intellectual. He was a chain-smoker, literally. The moment he had snuffed out the stub of the cigarette he was smoking, in the ashtray, he would light the next one. Smoke belched out from his nostrils and he remained perpetually enveloped in fumes. His large eyes protruded from their sockets as he peered through smoke curls. He was a compulsive talker and would be expatiating on modern poetry in general and Eliot and Auden in particular. He spoke in a guttural voice and varied the pitch, going down to whispers sometimes, which made the sense even more obscure than it was.

George kept his gaze fixed on J.S. with rapt attention and sat like a devotee before an oracle, silent in adoration.

◆

My mother had come to stay with me. She liked Jodhpur; its lanes did not stink like Jaipur's lanes, where her brother lived. She also liked its soft, courteous speech. She used to go to the Ghantaghar[83] Chowk to buy vegetables. The place was bustling with life like any Indian bazaar—hand carts and carriages, bicycles, rickshaws, horse-drawn tongas, three-wheeler autos, scooters and cars and people exhibiting and selling their wares, squatting on cobblestone pavements. She was used to the hustle-bustle, having been familiar with Jaipur's crowded Chaupars.

She came back one evening and narrated an incident to me. As she was returning home, carrying a bag of vegetables, she heard

---

[83]Clock tower

a tongawallah's insistent call from behind, *'Maa sa*[84] *haallo!', 'Maa sa haallo!'* (Move on, honourable mother!) She hadn't heard his earlier calls in the melee and he was on the verge of losing his patience. But he wouldn't use a harsher phrase. My mother moved away but found the tongawallah's behaviour highly unusual. She told me that in a similar situation, in Jaipur, the man would have hurled invectives at her, like *'Dokri, maregi kya?'* (Old hag, Do you want to die?)

I had also noticed the liberal use of the honourific 'sa' in their speech. As I cycled in the morning to college through the narrow lanes of the old city, little boys playing in the street would ask, *'Kinni vaji sa?'* (What's the time, Sir?) As this was an oft-repeated query, I half-suspected it was their way of teasing such passersby as were wearing a wrist watch. But their sweet, respectful lingo made it so endearing.

•◆

We already had another Reader, Prof. Sequeira. His pretty wife, Rose, was a lecturer in the department. They hosted a dinner one evening; there was beer and whisky to drink. I had started drinking beer occasionally but had never tasted whisky. George was sipping whisky and offered me a glass with a mischievous twinkle in his eye. I took a sip; it tasted like petrol, burning my gullet. With a brave face, I continued sipping with quiet determination.

As I neared the bottom of the glass, the room and guests seemed to start gyrating. I wanted to go to the toilet, but wasn't sure if I could steady myself, so George held my hand and took me to the toilet. Thankfully, when I returned a few seconds later, the room had stopped gyrating.

On another occasion, when Mahle invited George and me to

---

[84]Short for 'Sahab'

a party at his house, the tables were turned. Mahle lived in a new suburb about two kilometres away from the old city and I offered George a ride on my bicycle.

Beer and rum were flowing freely when we arrived, accompanied by hot and crisp vegetable pakoras. I stuck to beer while George tried rum. Two hours and many drinks later, when there was no sign of dinner, we realized that it was a cocktail party. I was a little unsteady, but George had been knocked out cold; the Army rum had proved too potent for him.

We tried to wake him up, but to no avail. Mahle and the others offered to lift George and place him on my bicycle: the first attempt ended in an ignominous tumble. On the second attempt, I managed to balance the still-asleep George on my bicycle. When we came to the main road and took a left turn, the shaky equilibrium gave way and two respectable lecturers of Jodhpur University lay sprawled on the deserted road! As I was scrambling to my feet, I saw a baton-wielding policeman hurrying towards us, taking us to be drunken vagabonds.

I straightened to my full six feet, assumed professorial gravitas, informed him that we had been dining at Professor Mahle's house down the road and had skidded, and asked him to go fetch a tonga for us.

George was still fast asleep and the policeman was eyeing him suspiciously. He had only gone a few paces, when I heard the clip-clop of a tonga coming. I called the policeman back and he helped me put George on the front seat. I took the back seat, holding the bicycle which the policeman placed there.

On reaching George's place, the tongawallah and I lifted George and carried him to his bedroom on the first floor. I paid the tongawalla ₹5 for his services and spread myself on a divan in George's bedroom. He finally woke up at about 4 a.m. and was puzzled to find himself in his bed, and me on the settee. I heaved a sigh of relief, amazed that there was neither a scratch on his person nor the tiniest recollection in his mind!

•◆

There was no occasion to reveal my caste identity in Jodhpur and I was happy in the bliss of anonymity. However, on the first floor of our favourite haunt, the Coffee House, there was a photographer's studio. The owner of the studio turned out to be from the family of Badri Sahaiji photographer of Jaipur, therefore a cousin of my would-be mother-in-law. He came down one day when I was sitting with my friends, introduced himself, and invited me upstairs for tea. I couldn't refuse.

Soon thereafter, a building contractor called Shivlal Tak, a member of the Jodhpur Municipal Corporation, met me and said that he, too, belonged to my community and invited me to tea. I wondered how he had found out my caste and was reluctant to accept his invitation but I liked his suave manners and went.

It transpired that his daughter was my student: she was there to greet me along with her parents. They plied me with delicious home-made goodies and eventually Shivlal ji told me that his daughter was weak in English and requested me to coach her at home. I explained that I was opposed to private coaching on principle, and was too busy preparing for competitive exams. However, his entreaties made me relent and I agreed to come for an hour on two days, every week.

When I went to his house the next time, there were two other girls of her class from the neighbourhood. I became an honorary tutor to these giggling girls. However, they spent most of their time in bringing me tea and fritters.

•◆

I had to go to Jaipur to write the IAS examination in October, as there was no centre in Jodhpur. I took my mother along, who stayed at her brother's house, while I stayed in the Rajasthan College hostel with a friend. When we were returning after a fortnight, Mother told me that there was a rumour in Jaipur that I would be marrying Shivlal Tak's daughter, that he was giving me a car in dowry, that I had almost become a member of his family, spending most of my free time with them on the pretext of coaching his daughter, and that Shivlal Tak was not even from our caste, but a Kumhar.

I was flabbergasted. What yarns people spin! Obviously the studio owner had been keeping track of my activities and was at the root of this nonsense. Mother said, 'I was furious when they told me this. I told those women from the Khargata family that there was no question of breaking the engagement. It was a matter of family honour for us!' She assured me that she had told the 'informer' that 'a man may leave a woman after marriage, but cannot leave his maang[85] unfulfilled.' I was sure that statement wouldn't have mended matters.

◆

When I returned to Jodhpur, I discontinued the coaching; when I saw the girl in college, I told her that she was free to ask me anything in college. The studio owner met me once or twice in the Coffee House and invited me to tea again, but I smiled and made excuses to avoid him. He was a likeable, friendly man but had created bad blood in a very sensitive matter.

None of my colleagues had enquired about my caste. However, an uncomfortable moment developed during a picnic of the university teachers at the picturesque Mandor Gardens on a Sunday. While everyone else sauntered around, an elderly professor, Mr Bhagat, sat in a chair, engrossed in carving a piece

[85]Betrothed

of sea foam with a knife. We knew each other, so I drew close to admire his work: I was amazed by this novel art form. He told me that this was his hobby and offered to show me some pieces he had made.

Suddenly, without taking his eyes off his work, he asked me what kind of Varma I was. My friend, Ram Pyare Rai, had asked me the same question in Allahabad. Varmas were celebrities in Allahabad—Mahadevi Varma, Ram Kumar Varma—but they were Kayastha. So, I couldn't have claimed the same caste. Hoping that he wouldn't know much about the Rajputs, I told him we were a humbler offshoot of the Rajputs. He did not seem convinced, but did not probe further.

Here in Rajasthan, Kayasthas like Prof. S.P. Varma used the same surname. I had taken Prof. Bhagat to be a Brahmin, since the word 'Bhagat' means 'devotee', so I tried to pass myself off as a Kayastha. Without looking up, he immediately demanded, 'Which Kayastha?' I blurted out, 'Bhatnagar,' the only branch I was aware of. Prof. Bhagat looked me straight in the eye and said he was a Kayastha as well. Both of us knew that I was fibbing and I slinked away from him, overwhelmed with guilt and shame. No invitation ever came, and I never saw his creations of sea foam.

Gandhi had said, 'If you tell a lie, you have to concoct a hundred more in its defence.' Somehow, I have never felt comfortable in admitting the harsh truth of my origins, they seem so degrading and dwarfing. I shudder to think how infinitely more painful it must be for people who belong to the Scheduled Castes.

•◆

I had written my IAS examination well and was quite confident of qualifying for the interview, which would be the decisive factor.

I began interacting with people who had gone through the ordeal, to learn the ropes. George had been called for an interview once, but was not selected eventually. S.P.S. Bhandari, in whose house I lived, told me that he too had been called for an interview, but the prize had proved elusive.

I received a telegram in early February, summoning me to the fateful encounter in Delhi on 18 February. I was in a flurry of excitement: the goal seemed near. In those days, there was no reservation for Other Backward Classes; it was only for persons belonging to the Scheduled Castes and Scheduled Tribes. Reservation for OBC was introduced much later in 1980, when Prime Minister V.P. Singh dug up the Mandal Commission report that had been gathering dust and took a sudden decision to implement its recommendations.

The most important question was my attire for the interview. Winters in Jodhpur were mild and most of the lecturers came to the University in shirtsleeves in February. It would be much the same in Delhi, but almost everyone told me to get a new suit stitched for the occasion. A woollen suit might be uncomfortable in February, but a terylene suit was a must, they advised.

I had got a blue terrywool blazer and grey woollen trousers stitched while studying in Jaipur and had been using them in Allahabad and Jodhpur. Getting a new suit stitched seemed too showy and farcical, so I decided to wear my old combination suit. My new friend, Kapoor, from Delhi, who had just joined the department, gifted me a black necktie and taught me how to tie different kind of knots.

I would be visiting the capital for the first time, so George suggested that I could stay with a friend of his, Prem Shankar, who was a lecturer in Ramjas College. He lived in a room in the college hostel, which was not very far from the railway station. I was overjoyed.

Many of my friends came to the station to see me off and it was very heartwarming. The train reached Delhi early in the morning and I took a three-wheeler to Prem Shankar's place. He hugged me like a long-lost friend and took me to Connaught Place by bus in the evening. Napoleon had called the English a nation of shopkeepers, so I was not surprised that they had designed a shopping complex in the same grand classical style as the Parliament House: a trading complex was as sacred to them as the hall of democracy. Prem Shankar was greatly amused by the way I stared shamelessly at the gorgeous girls in the most fashionable dresses I had ever seen.

The next morning, I reached Dholpur House and waited for my turn. There were eight or nine members in the panel, which was chaired by the former ambassador K.P.S. Menon. I have no recollection of the questions asked but I remember answering most with ease. There were two or three which I was clueless about, but it did not bother me unduly. After reaching Jodhpur, I boasted to my friends that I was in.

One breezy April morning when I was invigilating exams, S.P.S. Bhandari showed up in the verandah. He took me aside and said that my name was not in the IAS/IFS list which had come out in the morning paper.

Most candidates mentioned all the Services in their application form, and were happy to be selected even for a Class II Service. I had been choosy: I had only added the Indian Police Service to IAS and IFS in my application form. When the next list came out after a couple of days, my name figured almost at the top of the combined list: I had made it to the IPS. It was a huge relief.

My friends and colleagues heaped fulsome congratulations on me. My brother was jubilant. He wrote a long letter showering praise on me, saying how proud Father, Mamaji and he were. He added that Savitri's grandfather, Bhonrilalji, was insisting on fixing a date for our marriage. After discussing with my mother, I wrote back to say that we could have the marriage in early June, before

I went to join the Academy in Mussoorie. My brother conveyed the news of my selection in the IPS to Savitri's grandfather and uncle and asked them to find an auspicious date for our marriage in June. They were overjoyed; the cloud of uncertainty that hung over their heads had dissolved.

◆

I was required to present myself before Dr P.L. Rishi, F.R.C.S. and Chief Medical Superintendent of Jodhpur Hospital for certifying my physical fitness. He performed some elaborate tests and told me that I was in fine fettle except that my left testicle was hanging a little lower than it should. This indicated the possibility of suffering from dreaded varicose veins later in life, say after 10 years, he said. It might even cause impotency, he added ominously. I was glad to hear that a small operation would solve the problem, and was ready for the procedure.

Unexpectedly, Dr Rishi advised me to appeal against his finding to the Medical Board in Jaipur; his suspicion needed to be confirmed. I was perplexed by his ambiguous stance. I told him that I had no intention of appealing against his judgement and wanted the problem to be removed. However, he asked me to think about it.

Kapoor, who was from Delhi, offered to take me to his father, a senior surgeon in Sir Ganga Ram Hospital, Delhi. All my friends advised me to take a second opinion, but I did not want any unnecessary delay, so I went back to Dr Rishi and asked him to fix a date for the operation.

Dr Rishi operated upon me under local anesthesia, and afterwards, I was moved to a private ward for convalescence. Unluckily, after a week or so, while removing the stitches, he noticed some pus. He told me not to worry: the problem had been solved, and he would send my fitness report in a few days as soon as the stitches healed.

In the hot and sultry weather of Jodhpur, my stitches took much more than a few days to heal, almost the whole of June. I was in an air-conditioned room and a nurse cleaned the stitches twice a day, yet frequent power-cuts meant that I was often bathed in sweat. Uncertainty hovered over my joining the Mussoorie Academy. Besides, plans of my marriage had gone awry: I was supposed to ride a bedecked horse as a bridegroom in June, but I lay in the hospital, nursing the rupture in my abdomen.

•◆

One day, I had an elderly visitor: it was my would-be father-in-law, Shri G.L. Varma. He asked me what the ailment was. I was tongue-tied; it was so embarrassing to talk about testicles. I reassured him that I was hale and hearty, and the operation was to rectify an internal problem that the doctor had noticed while verifying my physical fitness for the police service. My father-in-law looked at my healing stitches and examined the hospital file. He had thought that the whole story of my operation and the prolonged convalescence was a hoax, invented to avoid the marriage. He had therefore decided to investigate the matter personally.

He was working as an Assistant Architect in the government of Punjab and was posted at Patiala. He had taken a month's leave for the marriage and had moved his whole family to Jaipur in the last week. When he asked me to set a date for the marriage, I explained that everything depended on my convalescence and appointment. I noted down his address and gave him my brother's address and told him that my brother would keep him informed.

He left, sullen and downcast. I could sense his pain. I had learnt that he had been deceived once: his daughter's first engagement had been broken off by the groom's family.

•◆

By the time the university reopened in July, Dr Rishi had sent my file to the Ministry in Delhi. I resumed teaching, cycling to and from work in the sizzling heat.

The Mussoorie Academy had already opened its portals to the probationers of the 1964 batch; their training had started. My colleagues and students continuously wondered why I handn't already left: I was too embarrassed to tell them the story of my erring testicle!

Meanwhile, I had applied to re-take the examinations in October. I did not want to be a policeman all my life; I had to strive for the IAS, if not the IFS. I was distracted by the inexplicable delay in the arrival of the appointment letter: it should have come in July, after the fitness report reached the Ministry, or at the latest in August. There was no pleasure left in teaching, nor could I concentrate on revising for the next examination. My frantic letters to the Home Ministry, expressing my anguish at not receiving the appointment letter, had received no response.

In October, I went to Jaipur to write the IAS examination again. I had flu and my performance was below par. Finally, in the last week of October, the letter arrived from the Government of India, asking me to report to the National Academy of Administration, Mussoorie. Hooray! The clouds of suspense and gloom had scattered at last.

I rejoiced with my friends and had a party at George John's place in the evening. Beer was priced at ₹5 a bottle those days; I bought two cartons. As my friends discussed the imminent changes in my life as an IPS officer, George exclaimed that I had actually been appointed to the IAS!

I was so fixated on being appointed to the IPS that I had taken the words 'appointed to the IAS' in a generic sense.

'How can it be?' I queried in disbelief, 'my name never figured in the IAS list.'

'But the letter unequivocally mentions the IAS,' George replied, 'and gives the IAS scales of pay, right upto the post of Cabinet Secretary. There's no mention of IPS anywhere.'

I snatched the letter from his hand and read it. He was right. My heart missed a beat. It was too good to be true!

'Maybe, you were on the borderline,' George explained, 'and someone from the IAS list was disqualified on health grounds or something, and you've been pushed up. That's why it took them so much time to write to you, perhaps.'

His words were followed by another shower of congratulations and we got another carton of beer bottles.

•◆

Armed with laddoos, late in the night I went home to break this news to my mother and said to her, *'Bhagwan ne aapki ichchha poori kardi hai. Aapka beta Collectory ki pariksha mein pass ho gaya!'* (God has granted your wish. Your son has passed the examination to become Collector!) She hugged me to her breast and blessed me.

I called on the Vice Chancellor the next day and requested him to allow me to resign from my job immediately and order my release. He congratulated me and asked me to see the Head of the Department, Dr Sahal. When I met Dr Sahal, he remarked that I had actually been demoted, since I would start on a salary of ₹400, when I was already earning ₹480. I chuckled at his quip and replied that the President of India was oblivious to the great sacrifice I was making for the nation!

•◆

Dr Sahal hosted a dinner in my honour for the entire faculty that evening and showered praise on my 'qualities of head and heart' in his farewell speech. I am probably being cussed and uncharitable, but it seemed that his excessive show of happiness actually said, 'Good riddance!'

13

CHARLES VILLE: THE IAS ACADEMY

Early one morning, I reached Dehradun by train via Jaipur and Delhi. A bus for Mussoorie was waiting; I boarded it. Going up the meandering mountain road, halting at several places, the bus reached the bustling Library Point on Mussoorie's Mall Road, late in the afternoon. It was misty up there; I could feel the caress of the cool mountain air on my face. I was on cloud nine!

I took a rickshaw for the last two kilometres from Library Point to the IAS Academy. It was a lonely narrow road then, winding through pines, oaks and deodars, resonating with birdsong; today, it is a wide road, full of cars and buses hurtling full speed to Kempty Falls and beyond, connecting to Rishikesh and Uttarkashi.

I went directly to the Director's office and signed my joining report on 29 October 1964 at around 4 p.m. Then, I said to myself, 'I am a member of the Indian Administrative Service; I've arrived!'

•◆

I was lodged in a guest house near the Director's office: an orderly took me to my room on the first floor. I was enchanted by the view that greeted me through the wall-size glass panes.

Charles Ville is perched on a cliff: a steep fall leads to a wooded valley, where a slender stream meanders in the distance. The mountains rise in layers of terraced fields, dotted with tiny hamlets, ending in sky-kissing peaks, daubed in the golden glow of a setting sun.

I sat entranced on the sofa, gazing, unblinking, at the view. The orderly brought tea, and I kept sipping it till the kettle was empty. This view has remained etched in my memory ever since.

Soon, I started shivering, even though I was still wearing my terrywool blazer over a full-sleeved sweater, all the warm clothing I possessed, and sitting beside a glowing red-hot heater. My body had never known such bone-chilling cold.

After dinner I got under the blankets. I asked for more blankets, curled into a ball and slept fitfully that first night.

Next morning, I discovered that the Foundation Course for the probationers of all Services was ending. I had missed the military attachment in Kashmir and many other assignments. In two weeks, the probationers from the other Services would leave the Academy to join the training institutes pertaining to their specific branch of the Services. IAS probationers would leave for a two-month 'Bharat Darshan' to avoid the harsh winter of Mussoorie and re-assemble in March. I felt like a child who had arrived at the fair when the rides were being dismantled.

•◆

Most probationers lived in rooms built on terraces along a steep path going down to the Happy Valley Club, which housed tennis courts and a horse-riding court. There were a few rooms in the Club as well, where some probationers lived. A one-room cottage was lying vacant, which was allotted to me. Omesh Saigal, S.S. Suri and Kamal Devgan were my neigbours in the Club. They took me under their wing and co-opted me into their group, which included Maharaj Krishen Kaw, a Kashmiri Pundit, and Ram Naresh Gupta from Punjab. They were among the brightest in the Academy: Omesh was second in the IAS-IFS list and I developed an instant liking for them.

George John had correctly guessed that my entry into the IAS was facilitated by a candidate's physical infirmity. There were 115 probationers in the IAS: 95 in the 'general' category and 20 more in the SC/ST category. Ram Briksh Pathak, who had secured one mark more than me in the aggregate was the 94th and I was 95th. Cadre allotments had already been decided except for these last two slots and there was one vacancy each in the Punjab and Kerala cadres.

My friends in the Club told me that Pathak had gone to Delhi to lobby for his allotment to the Punjab cadre. I was unfazed by the prospect of going to Kerala.

They said, 'Don't be stupid. Your life will be ruined if you get Kerala. You'd have to learn Malayalam, a very difficult language, and be an alien all your life, getting sidey jobs.'

'But it'll be the same in Punjab. I'd have to learn Punjabi, be an alien, as you say, and get sidey jobs. So what's the difference? As it is, I have already won the lottery by getting into the IAS!'

'You don't understand. There is a hell of a difference. North is North, South is South!'

'In any case, I don't care. We are in an All-India Service, after all.'

'Don't be so naive. If you know some MP or minister, you should go to Delhi at once and try and get Punjab.'

'But I don't know anybody, really, and I wouldn't have gone even if I did.'

The next week the cadre allotments came from the Ministry, Pathak was allocated to the Kerala cadre, I got Punjab. My extravagant luck hadn't run out yet.

I got a new woollen jacket and trousers stitched and, in a few days, got used to the cold. Walking to town in the evening and sauntering around the Mall became a daily routine, but nothing gave me greater pleasure than sitting in the main lounge and watching the mountain peaks thrusting into the blue sky. I never tired of gazing at this larger-than-life 'painting' while the lounge resonated with the haunting melodies of Lata Mangeshkar on the record player. Those were moments of sheer bliss!

•◆

Just after my arrival, an eminent intellectual delivered a lecture on 'Ethics in the Civil Service'. I sat with Omesh Saigal and S.S. Suri in the packed hall. After the speaker concluded his discourse, N.K. Singh, our batchmate who heads the Finance Commission nowadays, made some witty observations; S.K. Sharma from the Punjab cadre made a few critical comments; encouraged, I also stood up and gave my reactions.

After the lecture, Omesh accosted me, 'You 95th! You just came here the day before and yet have the audacity to stand up and air your views on the guest lecture! And here I am, second in order of merit; I have been listening to these lectures for the past five months and haven't stood up even once!' He was chiding me for my brashness but there was an element of admiration too. I laughed out and said, 'But I've been doing this for the last two years in Jodhpur—taking potshots at guest speakers!'

As part of the Punjab cadre, I was drawn into a new circle of friends who were going to Punjab. We were 16 in all, probably the largest contingent after UP. I was the only one in the group, from Rajasthan. Our mess manager, the tall and handsome Swaran Singh Boparai, was from Punjab. The mess manager is elected, and is like the Head Boy of the Academy!

Swaran Singh had a great sense of humour. One day, with a mischievous wink, he said to me in Punjabi, '*Oye Varma, hoon tainu Punjabi sikhni chayidi hai.*' (You have to learn Punjabi now.) I replied that I had already started learning it from the librarian, Sharmaji, who taught Punjabi to 'outsiders' like me. Swaran Singh, Ram Naresh Gupta, S.K. Sharma and Darshan Kumar had a hearty laugh at my expense: the word *Sikhni* also meant 'a Sikh girl'! Punjabi is full of *double entendre.*

14

BHARAT DARSHAN

In the first week of December, all IAS probationers went to Delhi. We went to the Rashtrapati Bhavan to call on the President, Dr Radhakrishnan. He was dressed in immaculate white: Carnatic conical headgear, a long muslin kurta and a dhoti with a gold border. I had heard him speak earlier, at Jodhpur University, and was impressed by his command over the English language. This time I was wonderstruck again by his mellifluous flow of words. I don't remember his exact words: perhaps I was paying too much attention to the décor of the Durbar Hall.

The day after that, we called on Prime Minister Lal Bahadur Shastri. He was quite informal and had none of the aura of his legendary predecessor Jawaharlal Nehru. A simple and sincere man, he joined us for tea and freely conversed with us.

We then called on Home Minister Gulzari Lal Nanda in Hyderabad House. He said that we were passing through the most critical years in our history, that the nation was on trial. He looked gaunt in his broad Gandhi cap and tight khadi pajamas. When he had finished, I stood up and agreed with him, that the nation was on trial, but quipped that some people who deserved to be on trial were actually going scot-free and, as a result, we were being seen as a soft state.

A stunned silence followed my remarks; our chaperon and the Joint Director, R.P. Khosla, glared at me and gestured at me to sit down. I realized that the home minister's speech was not like a guest lecture at the Academy which could be freely commented upon; it was a formal address meant to be passively imbibed.

In the next couple of days, we visited the Indian Agricultural Research Institute, popularly called the Pusa Institute, the National Archives and the Okhla Industrial Complex.

Since I belonged to north India and was allocated to a northern state, I was going to South India for Bharat Darshan. Abhimanyu Singh of the Bihar cadre, a stern-looking bespectacled man, was our group leader. Our teacher-in-charge was the professor of linguistics in the Academy, K.S.R. Sarma, a gentle soul who taught Hindi to non-Hindi-speaking probationers. He belonged to Andhra Pradesh and knew South India like the back of his hand, as we realized in the next two months. There were 20 people in our group, including Omesh Saigal, M.K. Kaw, R.N. Gupta, S.S. Suri and Kamal Devgan. A fellow Rajasthani, Chandra Prakash, who was allotted Rajasthan cadre, was also in our group. A first-class coach was reserved for us for the entire length of the tour. This journey gave us time to bond with and get to know each other.

The train steamed off from Delhi at night. We woke up somewhere in Madhya Pradesh, passing through hilly terrain. It was Bharat Darshan in the literal sense as we saw the vastness of India, the diversity of its land and the people.

The immensity of our country dawned on us when we reached Hyderabad after two nights in the train. We went to call on the chief minister of Andhra Pradesh, Brahmananda Reddy, who spoke to us for a few minutes; then, the chief secretary gave a speech eulogizing the chief minister.

We stayed in Hyderabad for a couple of days and explored the old Golconda Fort, which used to be the capital of the Qutb Shahi sultans. When we reached the Baradari at the top of the fort, we were given a demonstration of the old fort's magical acoustics system. A man began to clap standing at the dyodhi (entrance gate) of the fort, which is at a distance of about a mile from the Baradari. The sound reached us on air waves; we could distinctly hear the man's clapping. A wireless system had existed in the sixteenth century to convey messages to the guards at the Baradari, the guide exclaimed! Next, we saw the fabled Charminar and then visited the Salar Jung Museum, which displays the personal collections of the state's former Prime Minister Salar Jung. I remember the beguiling two-in-one statue of Mephistopheles, the devil in the Faust legend. The glass on the wall behind this statue did not reflect the back of Mephistopheles; it showed the beautiful Margaretta! The museum also houses paintings by Raja Ravi Varma and many European masterpieces in marble.

•◆

We reached Madras, now called Chennai, early in the morning. Hawkers called out *'Kaapi! Kaapi!'* instead of the familiar cries of '*Chai, garam Chai!*' They had a special way of pouring the coffee back-and-forth between a steel tumbler and a katori to make it frothy, their hands moving with elegance and precision. I liked this heady concoction, the aroma of freshly ground roasted coffee beans: it was the true taste of the warm South!

During the day, we called on the collector of Chingleput district, Ms Satyabhama and in the evening we headed to the Marina Beach.

We had never seen anything like the rolling thundering sea that was waiting for us at the silvery Marina Beach. The towering waves crashed at our feet in bubbly froth: we threw off our blazers and ties, shoes and socks, rolled up our trousers and frolicked barefoot in the sea. All our frigid inhibitions and air of self importance melted away in the cool spray of the waves and the exhilarating sea breeze. I visited Marina Beach later in life, but never recaptured that exhilaration, that magic: even the sand seemed to have lost its silvery sheen and turned grey.

At dinner that evening, another new experience awaited us: we sat on benches with hundreds of other diners and banana leaves were placed before each of us. One after another, rice, sambar, rasam and various chutneys were served with clockwork precision.

All of us knew sambar and rasam from the food served at the Academy, but this mode and manner of serving and eating was something new. Most of us were used to eating rotis using our fingers and the watery rice-sambar mixture was beyond our skills. When we asked for spoons, the waiters were foxed: they had none. We observed the locals and tried to imitate their technique, but it was not an easy task!

•◆

Prof. Sarma ensured that we visited the great temples of Tamil Nadu, in Kanchipuram, Chidambaram, Tanjavur, Kumbhakonam, Madurai, Tiruchirapalli and many other places, which represent the temple-building traditions of the Pallava, Chola, Pandya and Nayak dynasties.

I was bowled over by the colossal size of the South Indian temples: they were not like the temples I had seen in Sri Madhopur or Jaipur, or even in Delhi.

We visited Kanchipuram first. The magnificent gopuram seemed to touch the sky; life-like statues of gods and goddesses, animals and mythical creatures were carved in stone, painted in bright colours and arranged in horizontal layers all along its length. What imagination! What wondrous craftmanship! What architecture!

I was amazed to discover that the garbha-griha, where the deity resided, was not underneath this magnificent tower, which was not even the central part of the temple as I had presumed. Prof. Sarma explained that each gopuram was a gateway of the temple: the main shrine of Lord Shiva was a few furlongs inside the temple complex!

The Kanchipuram temple is an amazing walled city, enclosed by towering gopuras. In comparison, the temples in the North seemed but meagre tributes to the lord. The South had redefined the idea of a temple: in the North, the deity resided like a king in a grand, gilded mansion; here in the South, the deity presided over a wondrous re-creation of the vastness of the universe!

•◆

Kanchipuram is famous for silk saris; since I was going to be married soon, my friend Chandra Prakash suggested that I buy a Kanjeevaram sari. We had two hours at our disposal, before our departure by train.

We went to a large shop in the market and I chose a stunning parrot-green sari with a bold red border. I bought it after some bargaining and we went straight to the railway station. My friends wanted to see it and they opened its folds: this was fortuitous, for we discovered a long tear down the middle. I was aghast: it was foolish not to have checked it before buying. We decided to go back to the shop and have it exchanged; the train was supposed to leave in half an hour, we still had some time.

When we reached the shop, I told the shopkeeper that he had sold me a damaged piece and showed him the tear. Instead of apologizing, he refused to exchange the sari, insisting that he had not given me a damaged sari. I was beside myself with anger.

'Don't talk nonsense! Give me another sari at once, we'll miss our train!' I shouted at him, at the end of my tether. The shopkeeper's knowledge of English was rudimentary, but the word 'nonsense' stung him to the quick.

'You call me nonsense?' he shouted back in anger. 'You are nonsense!'

I lost my cool and threw the sari at him saying, 'Okay, keep it.' As I was leaving his shop, I added in Hindi, *'Tum chor ho!'* (You are a thief!) He understood that I had hurled an abuse at him in Hindi and was livid with rage.

'What you say?' he demanded.

'I said you are a *chor*, a thief!' I elaborated with some relish.

'Thief? You call me thief?' Other shopkeepers had collected in the meanwhile and were talking agitatedly among themselves in their language.

Luckily for me, Prof. Sarma had sent the Tehsildar to check why we were late. His arrival changed the demeanour of the shopkeepers completely. He whispered to them that we were IAS officers; immediately, the sari was replaced and we rushed back to the station. My sari purchase had delayed the train's departure by ten minutes!

Chandra Prakash related the whole episode to my friends in the train and repeated my words *'Tum chor ho!'* with unconcealed glee. I was ashamed of my unsavoury remarks, but I was sure that the man had thought he could get away with his dishonest intentions. Several factors had helped in the quick resolution of the situation: Kanchipuram was a small town, the market was close to the railway station, the Tehsildar knew where to look for us and the Station Master was considerate enough to hold up the train for us.

•◆

In Mahabalipuram or Mamallapuram, Prof. Sarma first took us to the rock sculpture depicting the descent of the celestial river Ganga to earth.

According to the Puranas, Ganga had descended into the locks of Shiva at Mount Kailash. On the entreaties of King Bhagirath, Shiva released Ganga from his tresses and she flowed down the sheer cliffs of the Himalayas. The sculptors of Mahabalipuram have captured that tumultuous moment: a natural cleft in the rock suggests the river; when it rains, water flows down the cleft. Carved into the rock, on either side of the cleft, are images of the denizens of the forest, animals, birds and mythical beings, all bearing witness to this happening. Age has not withered this wonderful work of human creative genius nor robbed it of its eternal charm.

The remains of the majestic Shore Temple stand nearby: the onslaught of the ocean, sun, wind and rain has reduced it to a fraction of its former glory. Two large and two small temples stand inside a walled compound. Most of the carvings are greyed and weathered, except a host of giant Nandi bulls, Lord Shiva's mount.

The Ratha Temples stand close to the Shore Temple: these monolithic rock-cut temples derive their name from the chariots they resemble. Beautiful statues carved in relief decorate these temples: Vishnu reclines on the folds of the Shesh Naga; a varaha stands guard; Goddess Durga, riding a lion, slays Mahishasura; Shiva and Parvati hold their son Skanda; Krishna lifts the Govardhan Mount. The Tamil sculptors had brought the ancient Indian myths alive!

◆

According to our itinerary, we were supposed to take the train from Mandapam to Rameshwaram, to visit the Rameshwaram Temple. However, a catastrophic cyclone had devastated the coastal areas and destroyed the Pamban Rail Bridge, which connected the Rameshwaram Island with the mainland. Our group decided to skip that stop and proceed to Madurai.

This was not acceptable to my friend Chandra Prakash. Through his queries, we got to know that people were crossing the small sea creek below the damaged Pamban Bridge by boat and then walking to the next railway station to take a train to Rameshwaram. The train wasn't coming to Mandapam now and my friend's enthusiasm was vetoed by the rest of the group.

Chandra Prakash and I planned an escapade. We took a change of clothes and some money, and slipped away from the rest of the group. Walking along the railway track, we reached the collapsed bridge and witnessed the scene of stark devastation caused by the cyclone. We took a small boat and the boatman gave us useful tips in his mixed diction. From the other side of the creek, we walked till the next railway station with a host of local people. While waiting for the train to leave, we bought green coconuts, drank the fresh water and had the seller scoop out the thin crust of coconut cream from inside the shell—it was delicious!

The train reached Rameshwaram and we set off for the temple. The temple's gopuram stood tall and graceful against the blue sky, surrounded by the flattened devastation of habitations. The temple is said to mark the site where Rama, the prince of Ayodhya, had made obeisance to Lord Shiva before going to Lanka to rescue his wife Sita. The present temple is the latest in a chain that goes back to the distant past.

The parikrama[86] of the Rameshwaram Temple is designed in such a way that it seems infinite; many pilgrims were resting there and others were going to Dhanushkodi to see the mythical 'Rama Setu', an outcrop under the sea that connects India to Sri Lanka.

We did not have time to linger and returned to Mandapam, where we enquired from the station master where our coach had gone. He told us that it had crossed Madurai and was on its way to Quilon, now called Kollam, from there. So, from Mandapam, on the East coast, we boarded a train to Madurai, arriving there at about 10 p.m. After a spartan repast of idlis we got into a night train which steamed into Quilon, on the West coast, the next day.

We found our group in a cashew nut factory, sampling fresh cashew nuts. Our arrival caused a flutter of excitement; we

---

[86]Path for ritual circumambulations around the temple

proclaimed triumphantly that we had reached the temple. Prof. Sarma and our group leader Abhimanyu Singh were not amused. After the group's mandatory call on the collector of Quilon, Prof. Sarma gave us a lecture on maintaining discipline and group leader Abhimanyu Singh glowered at us, saying how worried he had been for our safety.

Our adventure to Rameshwaram meant that we missed seeing the great Madurai Meenakshi temple. My friends told me that it had 12 gopurams and was probably the grandest temple in South India.

•◆

On our way to Kanyakumari, we visited the Padmanabha temple at Trivandrum, now called Thiruvananthapuram. The pundits allowed us to enter the temple only after we had swapped our Western apparel for cotton dhotis and bare chests.

More than the temple, people were drawn to Kanyakumari to experience the thrill of being at the southernmost tip of the Indian peninsula, at the confluence of the Arabian Sea, the Bay of Bengal and the Indian Ocean. A huge rock sits some distance away in the ocean, popularly called the Vivekananda Rock. The impressive Vivekananda Memorial had not yet been built at that time. We were told that Swami Vivekananda used to swim to the rock and sit there in meditation. The sea was choppy on that day and I had a vision of the handsome Swami being tossed up and down by the unruly waves.

Kanyakumari is a vantage point for watching the sun rise and set. Standing at the same place, one can watch this breathtaking spectacle in the East or West on a cloudless day.

On that day, a wayward cloud shrouded the sun at sunset, to the great disappointment of the motley crowd which had gathered to watch the spectacle.

15

TEMPLE-CRAWLING IN TAMIL NADU

Prof. Sarma's general plan, as we moved up the peninsula towards Karnataka, seemed to be to visit as many temples as possible, criss-crossing the lean roads of Tamil Nadu.

To kill the tedium of the journey, our batchmate Maharaj Krishen Kaw had devised an excellent antidote. He was a gifted singer and as soon as our bus cleared the city limits, he would initiate the satsang[87] (as we called it) by singing the mukhda (opening line) of a song, like, '*Tohar naam laike, chhoda hai zamana*'[88]. Immediately, the group would jointly repeat it in unison, in the same tone. We had no accompanying musical instruments but we all clapped along to keep the tempo.

Kaw had an astonishing repertoire of old and new hit songs and knew hundreds of them by heart. We fell silent every time the bus came to a halt and as soon as we were back in the bus and it had gathered speed, another singing session began.

We must have visited about a dozen temples during our peregrinations in Tamil Nadu and some stand out in vivid detail in my memory.

The Ranganathaswamy Temple on the banks of River Kaveri in Tiruchirapally is unforgettable. A number of majestic gopurams

---

[87]Community singing of bhajans (religious songs)

[88]'Uttering your name, I have left the world.' A popular Hindi film song

grace the concentric parikramas, and the pillars of this temple are intricately carved with life-like statues of prancing horses and fierce tigers. The Nataraja Temple in Chidambaram, dedicated to the lord of dance, Shiva, is spread over 40 acres. The eastern gateway has a frieze in carved relief, depicting 108 dance postures in the Bharata Natyam style. The sky-kissing gopuram of the Brihadeshwara Temple in Tanjavur is reputed to be the tallest in the world. The lotus-shaped bulbous crown on top of the tower weighs 80 tons and was carved out of a single rock.

I remember another temple, built on a high hill, not for its architectural splendour, but because of the stories about two special winged visitors. Devotees and temple priests claimed that two birds flew all the way from Benaras, now called Varanasi, to feed at the temple every day. Waiting with hundreds of people who had gathered there, we saw two large birds arrive and have their fill of gruel. The faithful remained steadfast in their belief, but in my view, saying that they came from Benaras was priestly licence.

I also remember visiting the Narasimhaswamy Temple at Namakkal because it was the day we finally reached Ooty.

◆

We were expected to reach the Fernhill Palace guest house in Ooty and meet up with another group of probationers at lunchtime but we were delayed as the temple visit had taken more time than expected.

Tired and hungry, we arrived at the impressive portico of our destination. The other group was already sitting around a large mahogany table in the dining hall, being served a four-course lunch by liveried waiters. Carried away by enthusiasm and hunger, we shouted out greetings to them, while simultaneously helping ourselves to whatever was there on their plates. We had been subsisting on rice and rasam and were too impatient to freshen up before sitting down for lunch like gentlemen.

Unfortunately, we hadn't noticed our Deputy Director, R.P. Khosla, having lunch with his pretty wife and daughter: unable to stomach this riotous scene, they left without finishing their meals.

Expectedly, at tea time, Khosla gave us the finest tongue-lashing we had ever received: in immaculate Queen's English, he told us how appalling our behaviour had been.

•◆

Our next stop was Mysore, now called Mysuru, where we stayed at the Administrative Training Institute, learning about Panchayati Raj institutions and decentralized planning.

Legend has it that Mysuru was Mahishasura's city; its name is derived from the mythical demon. Prof. Sarma took us to Chamundi Hill, and we visited the beautiful temple there, its gopuram rising nine storeys into the sky.

After that, we went to see the grand palace of the Maharaja of Wodeyar. I wondered what living in such a magnificent abode would be like, if visiting it is so pleasing and uplifting!

We also visited Tipu Sultan's summer palace, Daria Daulat Bagh. I thought it looked more like a charming villa, nestled amidst a garden by a rippling stream. It's indeed an idyll composed in a dream. However, unlike this well-preserved gem, Tipu's fort was destroyed in the battle with the British forces in 1799. The guide gave a graphic description of the battle and showed us the spot where Tipu fell.

On our way back, we went to see the Brindavan Gardens, imaginatively laid out at the base of the towering retaining wall of the Krishnarajasagar dam.

Krishnarajasagar dam had been acknowledged as a great feat of engineering, executed well before Independence by Chief Engineer Vishveshvarayya, in the employ of the King of Mysore. It was the precursor of the Bhakra dam which Jawaharlal Nehru had hailed as the new temple of modern India. I wish Prof. Sarma had told us how this dam had transformed irrigation and power generation, and effected an increase in agricultural production.

The Brindavan Gardens are designed on the pattern of Mughal gardens, with water channels, fountains and spacious flower-filled green terraces. As night fell, the twinkling lights transformed the garden into a fairyland!

•◆

Over the weekend, we visited Shravanabelagola, where the 57-feet-high monolithic statue of Bahubali Gomateshvara, atop a verdant hillock, is a standing wonder of the world—something that has to be seen to be believed.

This Jain Tirthankar had renounced his kingdom after winning it from his brother, Bharatha, in a fierce battle in the third century C.E. and had found peace by shunning ego and desire, like the Buddha. This monumental statue was sculpted during the reign of King Rachhamal, 700 years after Bahubali's renouncement.

The sculptors had started hewing a solid granite rock at the top of the mountain and came down in a few years to reveal Bahubali's serene human form.

The art of stone-carving reached its zenith in the temples of Halebid and Belur, which we visited soon after. The Hoysala kings built these marvels in stone after their victory over the Cholas. The temple at Halebid was never fully completed despite decades of labour, while Belur remains a functioning temple even today, over 800 years after its completion.

Before going to Bangalore, now called Bengaluru, we went to see the spectacular Jog Falls in the dense forests of the Western Ghats in Shimoga district, where the River Shiravati leaps off a sheer cliff in a cloud of mist. We waded through knee-deep water, trying to go as close to the falls as possible.

Seeing some local boys going up the mountain on a bridle path, I impulsively set off alone after them. I wasn't equipped for a mountain trek; my leather shoes and wet trousers did not help. However, in about 15 minutes, I reached a ridge very close to the falls. I began hollering and waving at my friends down below. They heard my shouts and recognized me and began cheering and waving at me. On an impulse I began to twist on the high rock and came down as they were moving towards the bus.

We stayed at the Woodland hotel in Bangalore for a couple of days. I was impressed by the majestic Vidhan Soudha, built by the great Chief Minister Hanumanthayya in 1956. Hanumanthayya's creation is a happy blend of Indian and Western architectural heritage: the focal point of the Vidhan Soudha is the grand Assembly Hall, proclaiming the supremacy of the Legislature. Its magnificent portal has graceful Greco-Roman pillars, while its enormous dome looks like a lotus. Appropriately, Ashoka's Lion Capital, the emblem of independent India, has been placed on top of the lotus dome.

The next day we went to the Kolar gold mines. Donning safety helmets, we entered the bowels of the earth where miners were digging with pickaxes in dark, airless tunnels. I had expected to see gold nuggets shining inside rocks, but the miners were scratching at black rocks with thin bright lines.

'Where is the gold?' I asked the supervisor. He explained that the mined material would go into a smelter and a minuscule fraction with tiny gold particles would be retrieved from it. I had heard that the Koh-i-noor was mined here, so this was an anti-climax for me.

We took a train from Bangalore to Goa, which was a sleepy, laid-back place at that time. It had joined the republic of India just about three years ago, so our visit was special. We saw the church of Our Lady of Immaculate Conception and the Se Cathedral. Then, we took a leisurely stroll down Miramar beach and sipped beer, sitting in a shack.

◆

One fine morning we reached Bombay, now called Mumbai; its association with filmmaking has always made it seem like a city of romance.

We marvelled at the Victoria Terminus, now called the Chhatrapati Shivaji Terminus, and walked down the cobbled pavement in front of the elegant High Court and the University buildings. The British had designed the exterior of the two railway stations, Victoria Terminal and Bombay Central, in neo-Gothic style. In Allahabad, the University and the Public Library are prime examples of this style, but the effect in Bombay was overwhelming.

We passed the Prince of Wales Museum and came to the Gateway of India, standing tall and proud, complemented by the ornate Taj Mahal Hotel built by the Tatas. The strong sea breeze invigorated us as we strolled down the Marine Drive and ate bhelpuri at Chaupatti.

Chandra Prakash and I went to a restaurant near Flora Fountain late in the evening, to snack on pastries and coffee. The orchestra was playing English tunes and some young couples had taken to the dance floor. We had never seen such openly amorous dancing; we watched, our eyes popping out of their sockets. As we left, Chandra Prakash remarked, 'This is life, yaar!'

Next day, we visited the Aarey Milk Colony on the outskirts of the city. Aarey was a precursor of the Amul Cooperative Milk Federation founded by Dr Kurien at Anand in Gujarat. Dairy farmers maintained a dozen high-quality buffaloes in the campus and their milk was collected, processed hygienically and supplied in bottles to the city. We went to the processing plant and sampled the milk; it was delicious!

The next day, we took a ferry to the Elephanta caves. We passed through a maze of caves with the vandalized remains of beautiful statues and reached a huge cave to see a gigantic rock-cut statue of Shiva's Trimurti.

Next, we went to Jalgaon to see the caves of Ajanta and Ellora. The Ajanta caves were constructed earlier and are entirely Buddhist, unlike the Ellora caves, which have groups of Buddhist, Hindu and Jain caves. Some Ajanta caves date from the pre-Christian era, when the new faith propagated by the Buddha was sweeping across India and the neighbouring countries.

The mind boggles to think that all these caves have been carved out with human effort: an entire township of living chambers and beautiful temples were scooped out of granite rocks by intrepid Buddhist monks, using simple tools like chisels and hammers. Many cave paintings have been lost to time, many disfigured, but one can still see the mastery in the remnants.

The Ellora caves seem to symbolize the death of the Buddhist spirit in India and the revival of Hinduism under the Chalukya and the Rashtrakuta dynasties. The Buddhist and Jain caves are undoubtedly beautiful, but the caves excavated, carved and embellished by Hindu artists excel them by far. The Kailashnatha cave, which is a multi-storeyed temple, remains unrivalled in the world for the grandeur of conception and the beauty of execution.

As our southern sojourn ended, I realized that my knowledge of Indian history had been limited to my school books, which hardly ever mentioned the South Indian kingdoms and empires. This journey gave me new insights into Indian history: I was proud to know that the kings of the South had taken Indian civilization to South East Asia when the Sultanate had subjugated North India.

•◆

Our Bharat Darshan ended in Nagpur; four groups of probationers stayed in a hostel of a central institute for a fortnight, to receive training in civil defence and firefighting.

It was a respite from the daily grind of bus journeys. The climate was pleasant and the city seemed to be the fruit capital of India. Plump and juicy oranges were a dime a dozen!

One evening, Omesh Saigal and I were going to the town, our pockets bulging with oranges. We were taking them out one by one, pealing and eating them, when we saw some probationers coming towards us. Immediately Omesh made an about-turn, telling me to do the same, and began gobbling up the oranges. I followed suit but was perplexed why we were returning. 'Let's finish the oranges,' Omesh said, his large eyes gleaming mischievously, 'else we'll have to share with them.' What a playful, loveable soul Omesh was!

16

BACK TO THE ACADEMY

By the ides of March, we all trooped back to Mussoorie. I had stayed at the Academy only for a fortnight or so before Bharat Darshan, yet my cottage felt like home and we slipped into our old routines easily.

Mussoorie had received quite a bit of snow while we were away: the distant peaks were clad in snow. The nights were cold and the bright morning sun seemed ethereal.

I remember 1 April for a special reason. It was a Sunday and I lounged in my room till noon. It was bright and sunny when I came out. Suddenly, tiny snowflakes began to descend from the clear blue sky. I looked up in amazement. It was miraculous! There had been no hint in the weather, no prediction, no forecast. I had never seen snowfall before and was mesmerized by the snowflakes drifting down ever so softly. There was a strange hush.

I was filled with an irrepressible joy and began shouting at the top of my voice, calling my friends living in the Club cottages. Omesh, Suri, Kaw and Devgan came out and seeing the snowfall, went wild with joy like me. It was entirely unexpected. Snowfall in April was a rare phenomenon in Mussoorie and it transformed the mundane hillside into a picture postcard!

One day, Maharaj Krishen Kaw floated the idea of trekking to the highest peak visible from the Academy. Ram Naresh Gupta and I were willing to join him. We planned to start after breakfast, reach the stream at the base of the mountain by noon and then ascend by the kuccha path. We hoped to reach the peak before sunset and return to the highest village for the night. The next day, we planned to venture to Kempty Falls and return to the Academy by a circuitous route.

Trekking is today an essential part of training for IAS probationers and the Academy provides all necessary gear and infrastructure. It wasn't so in our days. We equipped ourselves as best as we could, with a change of clothes, some packets of biscuits and chocolates, and a few tins of fruit juice. We decided to bunk classes for a couple of days and sneaked out on a Friday morning.

The trek turned out to be much more adventurous than we had imagined. On the way to the stream, we became entangled in some thick thorny bushes and discovered a massive waterfall in the thickets. The peak, which had curiously looked so accessible from the Academy, looked distant and inaccessible from where we stood.

We asked some village folk for help: they were in awe of the probationers from the Academy. They told us that there was a famous Devi temple at the peak and that it wasn't very far.

In reality the ascent was steep and the hot midday sun made it tougher. We managed to reach a small hamlet some time before sunset. Our arrival caused quite a commotion; it was an unprecedented event. Village children escorted us to the Lambardar's house. He welcomed us warmly and wanted us to postpone the climb till the next morning, but we were adamant.

The climb was steeper now and we were tired after the day's trek. The path, partly paved with stones, snaked through a dark and dense deodar forest. Following the Lambardar, we finally reached the diminutive temple at the peak, nestled under tall deodars.

Hundreds of coins had been nailed on the greying wooden walls of the temple by devotees.

We rang a little bell hanging from the sloping temple roof, made obeisance to the goddess, offered a few coins and were euphoric at accomplishing our mission. It had suddenly gone dark: we found the descent even more stressful. The Lambardar had thoughtfully provided us with walking sticks and led the way with a torch. When we emerged from the deodar forest, a pale moon was shining. We were dead tired when we reached his house. His wife had kept the tea kettle boiling.

The Lambardar's house was made of wood, surrounded by a creaking wooden balcony, where woollen rugs were spread out for us to rest the night. In the distance, Charles Ville looked like a castle in the sky and the glimmering lights of Mussoorie mingled with the stars.

We shared our biscuits and chocolates with his children and polished off the leftovers of our packed lunch with the hot tea the Lambardarni made for us. We were tired after the day-long trek and were soon fast asleep in the airy, overhanging balcony.

Before daybreak, the Lambardarni milked her cows and prepared tea for us and we took their leave. We offered them some money for lodging us, but they vehemently refused.

We took our own sweet time coming down the hill, enjoying the landscape, and stopping to talk to men and women working in their little fields. From the stream, we headed for Kempty Falls. The way was longer than we had presumed and we stayed the night in a wayside dhaba: on learning that we were Academy probationers, the owner took extra care in preparing dinner. It was daal, roti and subzi, but with a special tadka[89] of pure ghee. After a hearty meal, we spread ourselves on the woollen blankets that he had spread

[89]Frying or tempering

on hard boards in his tent.

In the morning, the dhabawalla gave us hot water to wash and made us breakfast of 'bread-butter-omelette'. He charged us for dinner and breakfast but refused to take anything for lodging us, which suited us fine.

The Falls were an experience.

We had been to the Kempty Falls on a Sunday afternoon; it was a completely different experience when we reached there after the trek. Gone were the crowds of tourists and probationers. We owned the Falls.

They aren't as high as the Jog Falls, maybe only 100 feet or so, but they have a good volume of water that scatters in a wide area to splash about. However, you can't go under the central stream.

As there was no one around, we threw away our clothes, shed all physical and mental inhibitions, and bathed in pristine nudity—a crude caricature of the Three Graces—frolicking merrily, gesticulating with gay abandon, splashing in the ice-cool water. Ram Naresh Gupta had a small camera and captured our fleeting glimpses in the nude. We ventured nearer and nearer the central fall, but the pool was getting deeper and the hammering harder. With my head under the cataract, I felt like Shiva taking the thundering Ganga in his locks! It was sheer ecstasy! Reluctantly we came out, shivering and freezing, got dressed and walked the last leg of our momentous trek to the Academy on Sunday evening.

The first thing next morning, we got a dressing down from the Director; although as Kaw narrated the details of the trek to him, I could detect a hint of admiration in his eyes.

•◆

In early April, my brother met Savitri's grandfather and requested him to fix a date for our marriage. After talking to his son in Patiala, Savitri's grandfather told my brother about the auspicious lagna of Aakha Teej (Akshay Tritiya) on 5 May.

I called on the Director for leave of absence. He allowed me six days' leave, along with the preceeding and succeeding Sunday. My brother was working as an estimator in the assistant engineer's office of the Western Railways at Alwar. My Bhabhi and other ladies gave me a three-day ceremonial bath to prepare me as a bridegroom. They rubbed a mixture of gram flour, turmeric, curd and oil on my bare body to the accompaniment of traditional songs, before giving me an elaborate bath. My complexion began to glow.

On 5 May, we reached Jaipur. In the evening, I mounted a skinny horse decked in tinsel finery, to lead a baraat of about 50, family and friends. Four men carried petromax lamps on their heads ahead of a measly 10-man brass band in faded maroon livery. It was indeed a lacklustre affair; I was disappointed. When I told my brother that we should have hired a better band, he told me that everything had been arranged by Savitri's tayaji[90], and added that Aakha Teej was the most popular wedding day of the year and bands were hard to come by.

Dressed in a brocade achkan[91], sporting bejewelled headgear and pearl bracelets (all hired by Tayaji from Johari Bazaar), I strode to the gate of the old Khargata haveli, near Moti Doongri Fort Palace, holding a sheathed sword. My mother-in-law welcomed me with a bevy of ladies, singing songs. I touched the ceremonial toran[92] above the gate with my sword and alighted from my horse. Mother-in-law applied tilak on my forehead and did aarti[93], partly in veneration and partly to ward off evil, and then measured my height with a thread. All this while, like the chorus in Greek drama,

[90]Elder brother of one's father

[91]Long buttoned-up coat

[92]Crown

[93]Puja, as performed by the priest before a deity in a temple, holding a wicker lamp in a tray

the ladies continued singing songs.

I was escorted to a place for the varmala ceremony and my brother handed me a garland of red roses. In a few moments, the bride arrived: she advanced demurely, wrapped in sequined silks, holding a garland of red roses in her henna-painted hands. She stood with downcast eyes in front of me, trembling like a flame in the wind. She looked up at me, her eyelids fluttering, before lifting her hands to garland me. We exchanged garlands amidst the showering of rose petals and enthusiastic applause.

No one had a camera, including Savitri's nana[94], who was a well-known photographer and had a photography shop, nor had we thought of hiring a photographer but her image is indelibly etched on my mental screen.

Dinner was served around 11 p.m. and the wedding ceremony began. The priest began with a Vedic hymn in praise of Agni, the fire god, and ignited the sacred fire in the vedi[95]. Then, for the next 30 minutes, he invoked other gods and installed them around the vedi. After that, the bride's parents sat opposite each other across the sacred fire and performed some puja, which involved the mumbling of Sankrit mantras and the offering of ghrita ahuti[96].

All this while, I sat there twiddling my thumbs. Towards midnight, the priest turned to me and tied a sacred thread around my wrist after asking my gotra[97], drew a tilak on my forehead and made me perform a puja of the deities, mumbling shlokas and offering ghrita ahuti in the vedi. Then, he made Savitri's father perform my puja, made him touch my toe in reverence and perform several rituals.

---

[94]Maternal grandfather

[95]Fire altar

[96]Sprinkling ghee on fire

[97]Ancestral lineage

Most people witnessing the marriage were half asleep when he finally called the bride, made her sit on my left and perform puja and offer ghrita ahuti. Then, he asked me to take her right hand in mine and I realized how slender and soft it was. He asked her father to sprinkle sacred water on our joined hands.

For about an hour after this, he recited Sanskrit shlokas, gesticulating like he was conducting an orchestra, made us perform rituals and repeat Sanskrit shlokas we didn't understand. He kept the sacred fire alive by tending to it continuously: the air was smoky from the fumes of the yajna and his voice resounded in the silence of the night.

Finally, the time came for us to go round the sacred fire, the main ritual which has given the name of 'phere' to the Hindu wedding ceremony. Everyone woke up and sat upright. The pundit tied the corner of Savitri's odhni to the sash of my achkan, binding us together for life, and I led her round the fire with slow steps. The ladies burst into a song, drowning out the pundit's shlokas. At the end of the seven rounds, he made Savitri sit on my right, and then made an oration in Hindi, elaborating the solemn vows that the bridegroom and the bride take on this occasion, some of which titillated the audience.

The ceremony of kanya daan[98] began and Savitri's uncles and aunts rose from slumber, arrived in hierarchical order and offered gifts of jewellery or money to her, which were announced to the assembly and meticulously recorded. I was amazed at their unending number; it seemed half of Jaipur was related to her.

The yajna culminated with purna ahuti[99] and the pundit began chanting fervently while everyone present drew near and threw incense into the leaping fire. As smoke rose from the mandap, the

---

[98]Donation to the bride

[99]Offerings on completion of yajna

gods departed after being witness to and having blessed our nuptials.

Dawn was breaking across the eastern sky when we dispersed, weary and groggy-eyed. It was the most elaborate wedding ceremony I had ever seen.

The next day, the ladies made the newlyweds play some games like 'Who'll get the ring from a bowl full of water?' as a ploy to bring us together and to help us shed our shyness. In the evening, there was a banquet in which satvarni mithai were served. The guests sat cross-legged on durries spread out on the floor and were served in pattals[100]. The sweets were accompanied by a pungent jhol (curry) of mashed potatoes and curds, and hot crisp poories were served with pumpkin subzi. The loud belching from guests signified contentment and an occasional flatulence caused great merriment.

On the third day, the bride was given a tearful farewell. Savitri's youngest sister, Gul, accompanied her as we boarded a train to Alwar. When we reached home, my mother, sister and bhabhi along with other ladies from the Railway colony, welcomed us with traditional songs. After lunch they made us perform rituals and play games, and kept us occupied throughout the evening.

The house was cramped with guests and no room could be spared for our suhag raat. We were assigned the open courtyard at the back of the house. At about 11 p.m., when everyone had gone to sleep, my bhabhi signalled me to go into the backyard. I bolted the door behind me. It was a cool, star-studded night. In the dim light from the street lamp, I saw Savitri curled up on the bed, pretending to be fast asleep. I lay down close to her under a starry sky. I covered her with a sheet against the chill of the night. She relaxed and straightened her legs; soon her breathing became even and she fell asleep. I don't know when, gazing at the dazzling stars in the firmament, I too went off to sleep.

---

[100]Plates made of leaves joined together

When I woke up at dawn, Savitri wasn't there, so I went back to sleep. Later that day, two of her cousins came by the morning train (she had no brother, only three younger sisters) to take her home. We walked to the railway station to see her off and the next day I left for Mussoorie.

By the time I returned to the Academy, we had started studying the essentials of Indian criminal and civil law, our administrative, judicial and parliamentary systems and the Indian economy. Besides, we had to learn the language of the state of allocation, which in my case was Punjabi, and acquire matric-level proficiency.

We were examined in these subjects and in horse-riding at the end of our training programme. The marks obtained in these examinations, and the marks of overall assessment given by the Director, were added to our original score in the IAS examination. Our rank in the Service was finally determined by the overall total.

I couldn't possibly go down as I was already at rock bottom; I could only go up! Indeed I improved my rank by about 25 places in the all-India list—quite an achievement for a Johnny-come-lately like me.

17

PUNJAB AND THE CITY BEAUTIFUL

In June 1965, sixteen new IAS recruits descended on India's brave new city Chandigarh, built by Prime Minister Jawaharlal Nehru, and landed up at the imposing Civil Secretariat in Sector 1.

I wasn't greatly impressed by Chandigarh and found nothing particularly beautiful about 'the City Beautiful' as the tourist brochures called it. The Capitol Complex, consisting of the Secretariat, the Vidhan Sabha and the High Court, was situated far away from the city. The main connecting avenue was a sparse and lonely road with huge undeveloped spaces on both sides. The sectors came up later on.

I surmised that this man, Le Corbusier, was a maverick: he was designing a capital city in lieu of Lahore, as it existed then. According to me, he should have placed the Capitol Complex along a canal with fountains.

However, the lake created by an embankment on the Sukhna torrent was a turquoise gem set in the Shivaliks, providing succour to a visitor's eyes.

There had just been a dramatic change in Punjab's political scene: Chief Minister Partap Singh Kairon had been sacked by Nehru after being indicted for corruption by the Das Commission. A political non-entity, Ram Kishen, had been given the reins of the state.

We called on Chief Secretary Kahlon first and then on Chief

Minister Ram Kishen; he was diminutive and unimpressive. Then we called on the Financial Commissioner (Revenue), the flamboyant A.L. Fletcher. He took us to Sukhna Lake for a boat ride and told us that the monsoon rains caused floods in many places in the state. We would be required to go on relief work and access the marooned villages by boat. At the end of the evening, he invited us to his home for dinner.

My friends from Punjab told me that Fletcher was very particular about attire and punctuality. It's impossible to wear a suit in summer, but I did wear the Academy tie and reached his house a few minutes early. Fletcher was waiting at the gate to receive us: what a perfect gentleman! None of us dared to touch the whiskey and instead settled for soft drinks. There was only one lady among us, Kiran Prem. Fletcher sat near her and engaged us in lively conversation.

Savitri's parents had moved to Chandigarh from Patiala and were living in Sector 22, which was a happy development. The day I had arrived at Chandigarh, I had gone to their house in the evening and was warmly received. G.L. Varma and R.P. Varma were brothers-in-law, who were both working as Assistant Architects in the Punjab government. They had lived together in Shimla and Patiala earlier, and had now moved to Chandigarh and were residing in adjacent houses.

Savitri had shed much of her shyness by now. I took her to the lake the next evening and we took a long walk along the embankment, holding hands. In the gathering twilight we sprawled on the unfrequented lawns at the far end, kissing and caressing. When we returned, dinner was served and I was invited to stay the night. It was our suhag raat!

By this time, I had been appointed Assistant Commissioner (Under Training) at Hisar. I was the only one who had been assigned a distant location like Hisar, while all my batchmates had been assigned convenient places like Ambala, Karnal, Patiala, Ludhiana and Jalandhar. I had not realized that postings could be 'managed' by personally approaching the under secretary in the chief secretary's office.

The rail and road connections between Chandigarh and Hisar were inconvenient and slow. A journey by train was comfortable, but there were multiple connections to be made and it was long. Punjab Roadways buses were faster but uncomfortable, since there were no AC buses at that time. I boarded a bus at five in the morning, to reach Hisar after 2 p.m. The roads were in a sorry state, stops were unduly long and there were no restroom facilities for passengers anywhere along the route. It was, indeed, an ordeal.

I had sent a letter about my arrival to the deputy commissioner's office, so a man received me at the bus stop and took me to the rest house.

I was used to the extreme heat of summer in Rajasthan, but Hisar was different. Situated at the edge of the Thar Desert, it was sizzling in the summer sun. Thankfully, the rest house had air-conditioned rooms with thick curtains and a false ceiling which kept the heat at bay.

I was served lunch on arrival and had a siesta, intending to call on the deputy commissioner the next morning. After an hour or so, the chowkidar roused me and brought a tea tray. As I was sipping tea, there was a knock at the door and a smiling young man wearing a turban walked in.

'I am Tirlochan Singh, SDM Hisar,' he said in a gentle voice. 'The deputy commissioner is calling you.'

I came out with him. He had come on his scooter and asked me to sit behind him for a pillion ride. I found it rather odd; I had supposed SDMs had an official jeep. I tucked myself behind him and he whizzed off by a side door to the adjacent district court complex. It took us just about five minutes. The court complex was almost deserted now. He parked the scooter outside the deputy commissioner's court and I followed him in.

Deputy Commissioner S.K. Misra was eight years my senior but looked much younger. He rose and shook hands with me, asked, 'Had a nice journey?'

'It was back-breaking, Sir!' I replied. He laughed heartily and said, 'Don't worry, it'll straighten your backbone.'

I went to Chandigarh on the weekend and brought Savitri from Chandigarh. In her company, the bus journey was anything but tedious and tiring.

I hired a small house in the model town on the Hansi road and wrote to my brother to bring Mother there to stay with Savitri. My mother was very happy to come to Hisar. Her former husband's younger brother, Bilas Rai, had migrated here long ago. By now he had passed away but his family lived in the town. They came and were so happy to meet us.

My brother was still in Hisar when the Superintendent of Police, Mr Luthra came to tea one evening. My brother couldn't contain his pride at this event. After our liveried guest left, he remarked, 'Ram Sahai, you have become a big man; the SP comes to your house on a courtesy call!'

◆

Hisar was the largest district of Punjab at that time; four new districts have been carved out from it since then—Bhiwani, Sirsa, Fatehabad and Dadri. Bordering the Thar Desert, Hisar was a vast sandy tract, barring some areas of Fatehabad and Sirsa sub-divisions which had recently received irrigation from the Bhakra Canal. Rainfall was scanty, and drought and famine were common.

The year I arrived in Hisar, we received less rainfall than normal. Bhiwani sub-division was facing severe drought conditions. SDM Subhash Dua was on a month's leave and the deputy commissioner asked me to go to Bhiwani and carry out the routine work in his absence. I was thrilled.

Every other day the deputy commissioner came to distribute drought-relief material to poor people in the villages. Thousands of men, women and children would collect around a village pond that had a sweetwater well on its edge, and wait for hours to receive a gift of a few kilograms of wheat and rice. It was a kind of poverty alleviation mela!

It pained me to think that nothing had changed in their lives after 18 years of Independence, despite the implementation of three successive Five-Year Plans!

After Dua returned, I returned to Hisar and sat in Tirlochan Singh's courtroom, observing how he conducted his court work. He kept a grave visage and was laconic in his utterances. When police officials entered, he saluted smartly and presented the papers of the men rounded up for apprehension of breach of peace. He would say in his soft voice, '*Suddo*!' (meaning, 'call them', in Punjabi). When the men appeared before him, he would say: '*Dussso!*' (meaning, 'speak'). The men professed their innocence and he signalled his reader to get their personal bonds signed by them. The men were then let off and another set of men brought in, and the same sequence of events followed.

I marvelled at Tirlochan's ability to discharge his magisterial duties with these two magical words in Punjabi!

I also learnt file disposal from Tirlochan. One day while I was sitting with him, his stenographer came in and placed a huge pile of files on his table. Without opening the files and looking at their contents, Tirlochan began to mark his initials on them as the stenographer picked them up one by one. In five minutes, the job was done. I was aghast.

After the steno had taken away the files, I told Tirlochan that he had been most perfunctory in disposing of his files. He smiled gently and explained that those files had come back from the deputy commissioner after he had approved the proposal mooted in the file. These had to be sent for implementation to the office without delay. However, if there was a file in which the DC had disagreed with the office proposal, it had to be detained by him for reconsideration in the light of his orders and resubmitted. He added that his own contribution came only when the file was being sent to the DC.

•◆

An important function carried out by district officers was the inspection of revenue records on field visits, especially the authenticity of girdawari entries recorded by the village-level revenue official, the patwari. These entries are made twice a year with respect to every field under cultivation, for the Kharif summer crop and the Rabi winter crop.

S.K. Misra took me along when he went to check girdawari entries in some far-flung villages of his extensive district. Villages were chosen randomly for inspection and information given a few days in advance. We drove through dusty village lanes to reach the place where people would be waiting. He would walk with them some distance to the fields, enquire directly from the assembled farmers as to who had cultivated a particular field and then verified if the entry made by the patwari in the khasra girdawari register was correct. He then asked the people if they had any complaints and settled them on the spot, issuing a reprimand to erring officials. After inspecting a few sites in a few hours, as evening fell, he told the driver to open the jeep's windshield and climb on a canal bank. He then took out his double barrel gun and shot partridges pecking on canal banks, mixing pleasure with work.

Once, he had spent a whole day in girdawari inspection in Tirlochan Singh's area. Both Tirlochan and I had accompanied him. At dusk when the deputy commissioner shot partridges, Tirlochan and I acted as retrievers. In the evening, we were rewarded with a gala dinner at his residence: a large tray loaded with juicy, lightly braised partridges was the pièce de résistance!

In August 1965, when the Pakistani army crossed the Line of Control, LoC, to seize Kashmir by force, India was down and out. Jawaharlal Nehru had died in 1964, after a severe drubbing in the Indo-Chinese war of 1962. The diminutive Lal Bahadur Shastri had taken over as prime minister.

Pakistan had superior air power and, unlike India, possessed a huge fleet of Patton tanks manufactured in the US. While its forces infiltrated into Kashmir, it attacked our air bases in Punjab and let loose the Patton tanks towards Amritsar.

Hisar also had an airfield and was vulnerable to attacks, therefore a total 'Black Out' was obsevered in town. At night, Misra used to be on patrol and during the day, he organized public rallies in the main towns of the district to boost public morale. People thronged these rallies and donated money for the war effort. Women came to the rallies wearing jewellery, which they then removed and dropped into the donation box.

At that time, the post of district public relations officer (DPRO) was vacant. In his characteristic informal manner, Misra asked me to take over as DPRO. The office had a small van and I began to use it to cover the public rallies, taking some local journalists with me. I issued press notes in the evening, highlighting the donations of money and gold jewellery.

The Tribune was the main English newspaper of Punjab; it was published from Ambala then. It did not have a staff reporter at Hisar, just a stringer, Udmi Ram. Teleprinters did not exist at that time, so he sent his copy by post, which reached Ambala in a couple of days.

To improve matters, I began ringing up the Tribune office and transmitting the news orally. Connections weren't easy; a call had to be booked in advance and then one waited for it to 'mature' when traffic eased, usually after 9 p.m.

The local telephone operator called excitedly, 'Hello, hello, PP[101] holding!'

'Hello Tribune, I am DPRO Hisar!' I shouted, and then read out the press note at the top of my voice to someone at the news desk. A drastically abridged version of my outpourings began to get a measly single column in the newspaper and a double column on a few rare occasions.

This small stint as DPRO changed my career graph. Misra was evidently happy with my performance. Three years later when Bansi Lal became chief minister, he was appointed principal secretary to the CM. He got me appointed me as Director of Public Relations in the fifth year of my service in the IAS, against stiff opposition from Chief Secretary Saroop Krishen, who just couldn't countenance a novice being appointed Head of Department. As a rule, one became HoD after about 15 years of service.

◆

Our batch reassembled at Chandigarh after six months of district training and was admitted to a makeshift Revenue Training School that functioned from a private house, under the tutelage of a retired tehsildar, Ram Kumar.

I hired a two-room apartment near my father-in-law's house and set up a modest household with Savitri and my mother. I cycled

---

[101]Particular person

to school every day. There was no regular faculty; officers of the Punjab government were invited to brief us about the functioning of various departments.

Financial Commissioner Fletcher delivered an initial lecture emphasizing the importance of learning the nitty-gritty of preparing the revenue record. We were taken to the villages contiguous to Chandigarh, taught land survey, measurement and mapping and were required to prepare basic documents like the shajra nasab, masavi, khasra girdavari and jamabandi with respect to the villages we had surveyed.

My batchmate Amar Nath Vidyarthi, who was the first man to enter the IAS from Lahaul and Spiti, had an engineering degree and a penchant for tabulation and chart-making. The two of us were assigned a village at the southern end of the city and were supposed to help each other in preparing the revenue record of the village under the guidance of the local kanungo[102].

Vidyarthi didn't need my help. Holding one end of the zareeb[103] in his hand, the other end held by a helper provided by the kanungo, he'd pace up and down the farmers' fields, recording the field data in the roznamcha[104]. Meanwhile, I sat in the shade of a tree, peeling sugarcane and savouring its juice.

We returned to school in the afternoon and he plotted the data assiduously on the worksheets. We completed our assignment within the stipulated period of two weeks and the documents, duly signed by both Vidyarthi and me, were presented to Principal Ram Kumar, who praised us highly.

Some days later, Fletcher came on a surprise inspection and found four probationers, including S.K. Sharma and me, absent. He upbraided Principal Ram Kumar for condoning such laxity and

---

[102]Revenue officer, superior to the Patwari

[103]Iron chain for field measurement

[104]Daily diary

told him that as punishment, all four of us should be sent to the outlying districts of the state for a month, to dispose of pending mutations. The next day, S.K. Sharma and I were duly asked to go to Mahendragarh district, which was even farther than Hisar. It was verily the driest, poorest, bleakest part of Punjab.

•◆

Early next morning, I boarded a Punjab Roadways bus to Narnaul. Curiously, Mahendragarh was not the headquarters of the Mahendragarh district but of its sub-division. The district headquarters were at Narnaul, which was a larger town. After a day-long gruelling bus ride, I reached Narnaul late in the evening and hired a rickshaw to take me to SDM Tapas Banerji's house. It turned out to be a long, strenuous ride through a dust-filled lane. The rickshaw wheels got stuck in the sand and the poor driver had to get down and move it by pulling hard.

At that time, only the deputy commissioner had an official residence at Narnaul, all other officers, including the SDM, stayed in hired accommodation. Very few houses were available on rent in town: the best available private quarters that Tapas could hire were two tiny rooms on the first floor of a Lala's old haveli in Kath Mandi.[105]

I had brought a hold-all which I spread on the floor of the second room and asked for the toilet. Tapas's young helper, Dharmpal, showed it to me. In a corner of one of the rooms, there was a man-sized cubicle with a hole in the floor; to call it a toilet would be stretching the word. One reached it by stepping on a stone slab projecting from the wall. The faecal matter fell into a receptacle placed on the ground floor, the sound alerting everybody that the toilet would soon be free for the next user.

---

[105]Timber market

The day after, S.K. Sharma also landed there. He came upstairs, calling out to us and embracing us as if after a long separation. It seemed like my arrival had merely cluttered up the rooms, while S.K.'s presence had brought forth effervescence and good humour!

Both Tapas and S.K. had a wonderful sense of humour and a great gift for repartee: they sparred with each other continuously. Their diction was impeccable, pronunciation flawless and they had me in fits of laughter all the time.

•◆

Deputy Commissioner Chaudhary Harphool Singh was a grand old Haryanvi officer; he had been promoted to the IAS from the Punjab Civil Service. He used to tie a safa on his head and smoke a hookah at home. Both his SDMs, Tapas Kumar Banerji at Narnaul and Madhusudan Mukherjee at Mahendragarh, were Bengalis. Tapas was tall and fair, while Madhusudan was short and thin.

Harphool Singh told us a delightful story about Madhusudan. One day, he had been sitting in his court at Narnaul when some villagers from Mahendragarh sub-division appeared before him, complaining about their village patwari's misdemeanour. When Harphool Singh asked them why they hadn't gone to the SDM Mahendragarh, the villagers told him that the SDM was not in his court. The deputy commissioner was taken aback; he had been talking to Madhusudan on the phone in his court. The villagers informed him that they had peeked into the court and seen his chhora sitting in his chair, doing his school work. The DC burst out laughing and told the villagers that they had mistaken the SDM for his son.

Like his simple visitors, Harphool Singh used to call S.K. and me 'chhoras'. Every morning, we went with the revenue officials on our mutation-hunting expeditions to different villages by bus and returned late in the evening. Often, Harphool Singh called

Tapas in the evening and say, 'Arre Tapas, I am getting chicken and kheer made. You pick up a bottle and come with the chhoras here for dinner!' Tapas accordingly bought a bottle of the good old 'Solan No. 1' and the three of us trooped into the DC's house for a rollicking evening.

The Chaudhary regaled us with anecdotes in his Haryanvi lingo, sending us into fits of laughter. The Haryanvi language is most suited for humour; its phraseology has a comical slant. Even a seemingly straight statement is loaded with wry humour. Though a Punjabi, S.K. Sharma too would reel out Haryanvi jokes with a pure Haryanvi accent and ably supplement the Chaudhary's stock.

One evening at dinner, the DC told us that a small band of dacoits had committed robbery in a village in Mahendragarh subdivision and Madhusudan had gone after them in hot pursuit with a posse of police officials. Sure enough, at about 10 p.m. when we were savouring the kheer, Madhusudan landed up and breathlessly narrated his adventure. However, the dacoits had escaped into Rajasthan and he was forced to retrace his steps after instructing the police to go after them. The DC patted him on the back and asked his men to serve him dinner.

•◆

After about 10 days in Narnaul, I sought the Deputy Commissioner's permission to go to Chandigarh. I told him that unlike S.K. and Tapas, I was married and my wife was in Chandigarh. I reassured him that I'd be back in a few days.

The day after my return from Narnaul, Savitri and I went to the Plaza in Sector 17 and were walking towards our favourite haunt, the coffee house, when I saw Mr Fletcher coming towards us. I froze. He looked at me piercingly and said, 'Isn't that Varma? Weren't you supposed to be in Mohindergarh?' (That's how he used to pronounce it).

'Yes, Sir,' I stuttered 'I came last night; my wife was under the weather.' Then, turning towards Savitri, I said, 'Please meet my wife, Savitri, Sir. She is better now.'

The perfect gentleman that Fletcher was, he bowed deeply with a puckish grin on his face.

I was astonished that he had recognized me in the crowd of strollers. After all, I was one of the 16 probationers in the Revenue Training School which he had visited once or twice. He was the top administrator of the state; how extraordinary for him to bother about a probationer in training! In fact, he rang up Harphool Singh next day, who told him that I was on leave with his permission. Tapas sent me a message to return immediately: I boarded the bus to Narnaul the next day.

A day or two after my return, Tapas's batchmate Balu also joined us. An incident from those days remains etched in my memory; it showed me, for the first time, the deep distrust that some people from the South harboured about people from the North.

It all started one morning, when Balu bolted the door of the toilet from outside, with S.K. inside. He opened the door only after S.K. made a terrific din, thumping at the wooden door. The next day was a holiday and S.K. decided to give Balu a taste of his own prank. He bolted the toilet door when Balu was inside. A few minutes later Balu was thumping the door and showering expletives in English; after some time I went and opened the door.

Balu was volcanic with anger: Tapas and I tried to to calm him down, explaining that it was he who had initiated the game, but his tirade became increasingly racial, aimed at 'the dirty, wily, evil Northerners', as he called us. He insisted that the three of us, 'the lordly North Indians' had heaped indignity on a 'lowly South Indian' in retaliation of a momentary, good-humoured prank on his part.

Experiencing this deep distrust firsthand, I understood how

the movement for secession in Tamil Nadu had been sparked by a decision to make Hindi the national language.

•◆

Tapas and I met again in Chandigarh to appear in the Punjabi language examination. At that time, we had to pass departmental exams in civil, criminal and local laws to earn our yearly salary increments. Besides, outsiders like Tapas and I had to pass a Punjabi language exam. These exams were held every six months. Ajit Kumar, the topper of our group, had cleared them within a few months of his arrival from the Academy and had already earned two increments, while I was still at rock bottom, getting ₹400 a month. It pinched a lot, because I had managed to clear all the other papers; I continued working on my Punjabi with Savitri's help, since she was fluent in it.

Like me, Tapas too hadn't cleared the language exam and we were seated in the first row in the exam hall in Chandigarh. We were asked to write an essay on '*Sada Des Punjab*', to sing the glory of Punjab.

I had learnt the Gurumukhi script and could construct written sentences; I could not speak the language but I could understand it. I was determined to pass the exam this time and painstakingly wrote one page. I began by saying that it was wrong to call Punjab a 'des' (country), as it was only a 'prant' (state) of the country; then I went on to clarify that the word 'Punjab' (land of five rivers) had become a misnomer after Partition and it would be more correct to call it 'Doab' (land of two rivers) or 'Triaab' (land of three rivers).

Happy with my introduction, I glanced at Tapas's desk and was dumbstruck. Instead of writing anything, he had drawn a beautiful sketch of a wide river, probably the Hooghly, with fishing boats floating on the waves and birds hovering in the sky. The invigilator caught me staring at my neighbour's paper, sprang to his feet and snatched away my answer sheet, saying it did not behove officers like us to copy from others. I told him I was not copying at all. 'How could I ever copy this masterpiece?' I told him, pointing to Tapas's work. Sheepishly returning my answer sheet, he sternly admonished me to refrain from looking anywhere else except at my own paper.

Tapas and I left the examination hall in some time; neither of us cleared that hurdle.

◆

Little did I know that a bigger blow was in store for me. At the end of the year-long training period, all my fellow batchmates became SDMs; I was the sole exception and was asked to continue as Assistant Commissioner (Under Training) in Jalandhar. Meanwhile, my mother had gone to Alwar to stay with my brother, so Savitri and I rented a room in a house in Civil Lines and began living like honeymooners. Savitri had felt constrained by my mother's presence in Hisar and Chandigarh, and was supremely happy in Jalandhar.

In the evenings, we sauntered to the coffee house or went to see a film. We were often joined by Savitri's old school friend, Veena, and her husband. On weekends, my dear friend Ram Naresh Gupta, who belonged to Jalandhar and was posted as SDM Rewari, joined us with his newly-wedded wife. Looking back, I realize that those were our happiest days—*na fikr, na faka*—no worries, no wants!

My work in the DC's office was light. The DC was an elderly Sikh gentleman who had been promoted from the Punjab Civil Service. Things changed when M.S. Gill, who later became the chief election commissioner and a central minister, arrived as deputy commissioner.

◆

Rampant price rise had been worrying the government of India and as a means of regulating the prices of consumer goods, a scheme was developed to set up 'supermarkets' in some major cities. One such supermarket was functioning in Delhi, with an IAS officer as general manager; consumer goods were being sold there at fair prices by reducing the retailer's margin to the minimum. The concept was proving to be very popular.

The Punjab government decided to set up a similar supermarket in Jalandhar and M.S. Gill chose me to run it: I was appointed General Manager of the (soon to be opened) Cooperative Super Bazar. My appointment was called 'Foreign Service of R.S. Varma, AC (UT)', but the high-flying name did not lead to an increase in my basic salary of ₹400.

The stately Kapurthala House was vacated of sundry government offices and converted into a modern edifice: new display shelves replaced the government-issue old wooden almirahs. Pretty sales girls were hired to man the counters and attract customers.

Governor Dharma Vira was invited to inaugurate the Super Bazar. While he was addressing a distinguished gathering on the lawns, Lala Jagat Narain, Member of Parliament and owner of the influential *Hind Samachar* and *Punjab Kesri*, arrived with a host of his followers. The staff refused him entry into the building and he began shouting, creating a ruckus. I rushed over and saw an elderly man in a Gandhi cap at the head of a crowd. I told him that no one was allowed to enter the premises before the governor cut the ceremonial ribbon. He said that he was a Member of Parliament and was in a hurry to catch a train to Delhi to attend the Parliament session the next day and couldn't wait. However, I stayed firm and he left in a huff.

The next day, his newspapers went to town demanding my scalp for the insult heaped on Lalaji. The Deputy Commissioner called me and asked me what had happened. Eventually, I had to send an apology which was flashed as a banner headline the next day.

Running the Super Bazar was exciting. The sheer novelty of

it attracted huge crowds and we made record sales. R.S. Mann and Swatantra Kumar Alok, from the next batch of the IAS, had arrived in Jalandhar as AC (UT). They told me that they envied my job, bossing around a bevy of pretty girls. However, I did not last long at the Super Bazar. In November 1966, the new state of Haryana was carved out of the Hindi-speaking areas of Punjab. I was allocated to Haryana and appointed as SDM, Rewari replacing R.N. Gupta, who was allocated to Punjab. Proficiency in Punjabi was no longer required, the creation of Haryana healing my twin blows in a single stroke.

18

REWARI TO SIRSA AND BACK

Rewari used to be a small princely state before Independence; its ruler held the title 'Rao'. The former ruler, Rao Birendra Singh, lived in his ancestral haveli in a small town called Rampura, close to Rewari. He used to be a Deputy Minister in Partap Singh Kairon's government but was dismissed because of some differences. After the formation of Haryana, Bhagwat Dayal Sharma, who was president of the Punjab Congress Party, became the first chief minister of Haryana. The notable omissions from his cabinet were Rao Birendra Singh and Chaudhary Devi Lal, who was a prominent leader of the dominant community of Haryana, the Jats.

Soon after I joined as SDM, I was invited to be the chief guest at the annual function of Ahir College, which had been established by Rao Birendra Singh during his rule. In my address, I praised the Rao for setting up the college and promoting the cause of education in a backward region. This was conveyed to him and he rang me up, thanking me for my observations and invited Savitri and me to his house for lunch.

The family of Rao Sahib observed purdah in Rajput style, so his wife did not show up at lunch. Sumira Devi, the daughter of the former ruler Rao Balbir Singh, and the adoptive sister of Rao Birendra Singh, was there. She was a sweet, middle-aged lady, who had remained unmarried. Rao Sahib was tall and handsome, with a high forehead and large expressive eyes; he looked every inch a royal. He charmed us by his graciousness and indulgence. The lunch was a treat, served by the old chefs of the royal gharana.

After lunch, he took us on a walking tour of the estate, called the Ashram. It was a veritable forest, and we learnt why it was called so. It was a mellow November afternoon. Occasional bird calls seemed to deepen the all-pervasive stillness. He showed us a huge square pond filled with lichen-green water. There were cottages nestled in the woods around the pond, meant for hermits who came for a sojourn during chaumasa, the four months of the rainy season, and finally we were taken to a huge hall with a life-size statue of a saint in meditative posture installed in the centre: it was the portrait of the family guru who had made the estate his home in his last days.

After high tea in the ornate hall of the haveli, we took the Rao's leave.

◆

By this time, I had been to Gurgaon to call on the deputy commissioner, Miss Mira Seth. She was an erudite and graceful woman who lived a spartan life, with her mother, in a sprawling old British-era house. The enormous drawing room, with an ornate fireplace, was bereft of all furniture except a three-piece cane sofa with cotton cushions and a cotton duree. She told me that she had locked up all but two rooms of the huge house—the drawing room and the adjacent living room. As we sat there sipping tea, a local lady walked in to socialize with her. A frown seemed to flit across Miss Seth's fair face at her arrival; after a perfunctory nod of acknowledgement, she continued telling me about a book she was planning on Kangra paintings. Suddenly, a black cat materialized from nowhere and perched itself on the sofa beside the lady, making her jump in terror. Miss Seth ignored her and the lady left in a huff, saying that she would visit another day.

◆

Within a fortnight of my arrival in Rewari, I received the Chief Secretary's order, transferring me to Sirsa in Hisar district. I was greatly surprised but shrugged and prepared to leave in a few days.

The news spread in town and reached Rao Birendra Singh: he rang me up and asked if there was a specific reason behind the sudden change. I said that I had no clue whatsoever. Over tea at his place that evening, he told me he had been trying to contact the Chief Secretary, Saroop Krishen, and tell him to let me stay on if possible. I thanked him for the trouble but told him that the transfer did not bother me. He said that it mattered to them, and added, 'I know Saroop Krishen very well; he was secretary of the department of which I was minister.'

When we were having tea, the phone rang and Saroop Krishen came on the line. He listened to Rao Sahib but said he would check up and let him know. Later that night, Rao Sahib rang me up to say that the Chief Secretary told him there was no particular reason but it was not possible to change the orders again. I thanked him for his pains and said it wouldn't be easy to forget his hospitality and kindness.

•◆

I was happy that I was going to serve under S.K. Misra in Hisar district. During my stay in Jalandhar, I had started sporting a moustache. To save him a shock, I wrote to him about this development. When I met him, he chuckled and said good-humouredly that I had done well to warn him: he wouldn't have recognized me with my flourishing handlebars.

Eventually, I learnt that he had been instrumental in getting me transferred to Sirsa with P.H. Vaishnav's help. The earlier incumbent, Hardayal Singh, had left after being allocated to Punjab, and the subdivision had been rudderless for a month or so.

On the day Savitri and I landed at Sirsa, while we were having tea at the rest house, J.P. Rattan, Executive Magistrate 1st Class, told us that Dev Anand's *Guide* was running at a local theatre. We had already seen the film. Rattan sent a message that we were to come to see the last show. We went to Bansal Theatre, owned by the Khajanchi family, and they opened a special box for us. The film had already started, but they stopped it, rewound the reel and began from the beginning, for our benefit. At the interval, the manager plied us with a lavish tea and when I asked him for the tickets, he silenced me, saying, *'Aap to raja hain, huzoor!'* (You are royalty!) I was amazed by my status upgrade in two months; in Jalandhar, we used to buy cinema tickets standing in the queue with the hoi polloi!

Since the British days, the SDM of Sirsa had lived in a sprawling bungalow set amidst several acres of scrub, a little way from the town. The bungalow and the land were owned by the wealthy Khajanchi family, but had been in government possession for quite some time.

However, at that point of time, the bungalow was in a state of decay and its maintenance costs were mounting. My predecessor had given up its possession to the Khajanchis along with the land, in lieu of a new house built by them in a corner of the old property in which the SDM now resided. My orderly, Sohanlal, missed the grandeur of the old bungalow and told me the story of moving into the new house as if he were unravelling a scandal.

◆

SDMs enjoyed the power of collector under Revenue Law and heard appeals against the decisions of Tehsildars; I discovered that court cases had accumulated due to the interregnum. I enjoyed sitting primly in court, hearing the advocates from both sides as they brought out the finer points of law, cited case law in their favour, before finally pronouncing my judgment after weighing both sides.

One day, one of the advocates remarked that court decorum had soared sky-high after my arrival: my predecessor, Hardayal Singh, used to give advocates short shrift and say, *'Han, bako, bako!'* ('Yes, blurt out your nonsense!') He had no patience for old rulings and was free with swear words.

There was a club in Sirsa which I visited once or twice. I was told that my predecessors were regular visitors, but neither Savitri nor I, had any interest in playing cards: we preferred socializing with fellow officers in the evening.

We had struck up a close friendship with the judicial officers O.P. Gupta and Jain, as well as DSP Rajkumar and the CMO Dr Sangwan. One Sunday, we organized an officers' picnic at Ottu Lake, a picturesque place with a rest house on its bank. The lake was teeming with local and migratory ducks. Some ladies sang songs as we sat under the shade of a peepal tree for lunch; I freely imbibed beer and got drunk.

•◆

The first election to the newly constituted 80-member Haryana Vidhan Sabha took place in March 1967; it was Haryana's first general election.

It was also my first election: I was returning officer for the Assembly constituencies in my sub-division, Sirsa, Dabwali, Rori and Ellenabad. In Sirsa constituency, the Congress candidate Sita Ram Bagla was pitted against a Punjabi settler Lachhman Dass Arora, who was from Jana Sangh. Bagla was the sitting MLA of the joint Punjab Assembly; he belonged to the ruling Congress party. His main challenge came from Lachhman Dass Arora. Premsukh Dass of the Khajanchi family was contesting from the Rori constituency on a Congress ticket. Dabwali was a reserved constituency.

Deputy Commissioner S.K. Misra paid a visit to Sirsa before polling day. He inspected the arrangements and asked me to act with strict neutrality and ensure fair play. Like him, I was also an outsider in the state, with no political or social links, and he needn't have worried.

Polling passed off peacefully, with no reports of booth capturing or rigging. Unlike today's paperless electronic election process, voting used to be done with ballot papers which had the names and symbols of candidates printed on them. Voters were required to tick against the symbol of the candidate of their choice and drop the ballot paper into a tin box. These sealed boxes were brought to the returning officer's headquarters after polling and kept under tight security. I heaved a sigh of relief when, at around midnight, Tehsildar Sapra reported that ballot boxes from all the four constituencies had been received. I immediately called the DC to inform him. Counting was supposed to start two days after polling.

The next day, Lachhman Dass Arora came to see me and expressed his apprehension of getting an unfair deal during counting. He thought that the chief minister must have told me to ensure the victory of the Congress candidate and that I would do his bidding. I assured him that nothing of that sort had happened and in any case I would never heed such orders. He was not convinced. He then told me that I was very close to the Congress leader, Premsukh Dass of the Khajanchi family, as I was living in a house built by his family, watched films in their theatre and would obviously favour his Congress rival Sita Ram Bagla. I was stunned by these allegations but realized that they were not altogether unfounded. I told Lachhman Dass Arora that these things did not influence my judgment and he should have no worry at all. While leaving, he said that he was sure of victory if he got justice from me.

The day of reckoning arrived. We began with the counting of the Sirsa constituency. There were about 20 tables under a large shamiana (an Indian ceremonial tent) for the counting of votes. I sat at the main table with the candidates. At each table, candidates could depute one counting agent to keep an eye on the process and raise any objections. No other person was allowed to remain there. I made an announcement on the mike that any person who was not duly authorized to be present should leave at once. Then, I went round each table, ensuring compliance. My PA pointed out a tall man among those who were leaving and whispered that he was Chaudhary Devi Lal. I had never met him. Ten years later, when he became chief minister in 1977, he told me that I had deliberately insulted him on that day by making that announcement, that it had been mainly directed against him, telling him to quit. How people misunderstand!

The counting proceeded briskly; the counting officers referred doubtful votes to my decision. There was one major grey area: in many cases, the mark made by the voter on the ballot paper crossed into the area of another candidate, making the ballot liable for rejection. There were thousands of such ballot papers. I ruled that we could not blindly reject them, for that would be a miscarriage of justice. We had to read the intention of the voter by seeing where the mark started, and count it in that person's favour. They observed me as I demonstrated how to follow the principle strictly, allotting the votes to the rightful candidate, and were satisfied. As a result, we had minimum rejections.

The election was finely poised between Sita Ram Bagla and Lachhman Dass Arora till the end; the contest was close. Every single vote made a difference and the decision in doubtful votes was crucial. I had the pleasure of announcing Lachhman Dass Arora as the winner by a margin of about 700 votes. When I congratulated him, he was overcome by emotion. Eyes brimming with tears, he bent forward and touched my feet. He was a regular visitor to the Amarnath shrine and in the ensuing years, invariably brought prasad for me.

The counting of the Rori constituency was taken up next.

Premsukh Dass was a clear winner. In Dabwali and Ellenabad also, the Congress candidates won with a good margin. We were able to declare all results that day.

•◆

In the state assembly, the Congress party had secured a comfortable majority of 51 members in a house of 90, under Bhagwat Dayal Sharma's leadership. He was sure of getting a regular term of five years as chief minister.

When the newly constituted Assembly met to elect the Speaker, B.D. Sharma proposed the name of Chaudhary Sarup Singh. To his utter surprise, an MLA from the Congress party proposed the name of Rao Birendra Singh for the post and was duly seconded by another Congress MLA. Rao Birendra Singh carried the day, defeating the official candidate. Thirteen MLAs from the Congress had crossed the floor, so to speak, and voted for him He was elected Speaker. B.D. Sharma didn't know what had hit him—the solid earth he had walked on had caved in! He quit the House in disgrace and tendered his resignation to the governor.

The next day Rao Birendra Singh was sworn in as chief minister. The new state of Haryana had made history of sorts. Haryana eventually came to be dogged by the menace of defection and the state earned the dubious sobriquet of 'the land of Aya Rams and Gaya Rams'.

Rao Birendra Singh formed a new party called the Vishal Haryana Party, comprising the Congress MLAs who had defected and voted for him, along with others who had joined his bandwagon. The man who had masterminded this unprecedented floor show for him was Chaudhary Devi Lal, who apparently harboured some old grudge against the erudite Brahmin politician, B.D. Sharma.

•◆

The office started at 7 a.m. in summer season. Some days after this cataclysmic upheaval in the state, as I was getting ready early in the morning and was still in the bathroom, my orderly announced an unusual and unexpected visitor—Chaudhary Devi Lal. He had given no warning for this visit. He lived in his ancestral village Chautala, the last village on the Rajasthan border, and had dropped in on the way to Chandigarh.

He had the aura of a kingmaker and looked larger than life. For a good half an hour, over a cup of coffee, he told me about his eventful public life—his role in the freedom movement, his post-Independence struggle to secure the rights of the share-cropper despite being the son of a big landlord, getting the land ceiling law and the Security of Land Tenures Act passed in Parliament and the State Legislature, his crucial role in setting up the Das Commission against Partap Singh Kairon and testifying against him, citing cases of corruption, and finally in the creation of Haryana and in the formation of the new government in the state. He was tall, wearing a long buttoned-up coat and a flowing dhoti, had a forceful personality and a booming voice. I had limited knowledge about most of these matters, so I was overawed and heard him with rapt attention.

In the next couple of months, he honoured me with similar visits, dropping in without notice early in the morning before office hours. He talked about the same matters in greater detail, enlightening me about people like Gopi Chand Bhargava and Bhimsen Sachchar, and about the latest moves of the present government, undertaken at his instance.

One summer morning, while I was having a hurried breakfast, the orderly announced the arrival of Chaudhary Devi Lal. I was in no mood for a lecture on political history and I hated being late for court. Nevertheless, I joined him in the drawing room, cheerfully sipping coffee with him. He probably sensed my discomfort and came to the point quickly. He said that an appeal was listed before me, in my court that day, for arguments concerning the devolution of the inheritance of a sizeable holding of an old lady in his family. He gave me its particulars and said that the Tehsildar had been most unfair in his judgment and his order deserved to be quashed. He informed me that he had engaged the most eminent local lawyer, Babu Bajrang Dass, and suggested that I accept the appeal.

I was livid with rage. 'How dare he talk so brazenly about a judicial matter to me?' I fumed within. Just a few days ago, he had been telling me about the problems faced by the people in the past, especially in far-flung areas, and I had been acting on his suggestions. But this was the limit.

I walked the few paces to my court and called the listed cases. I heard the arguments in most cases and reserved my judgment. The case mentioned by Chaudhary Devi Lal was listed at the end. Babu Bajrang Dass, the doyen of Sirsa bar, cited many rulings and made out a strong case for accepting the appeal. A young but sharp lawyer, Mohunta, who later became a judge of the High Court, ably defended the Tehsildar's order and produced rulings that poked holes in the ones quoted by Bajrang Dass. In the end, I turned to the latter and asked if he had anything more to say in rebuttal of Mohunta's pleadings. He spoke for a few minutes, reiterating his earlier pleas. The courtroom was packed and there was an expectant hush: it was common knowledge that Chaudhary Devi Lal had met me in the morning and had put in his word for accepting the appeal. I paused for a few moments and said, 'The appeal is rejected.' A stunned silence greeted my pronouncement. Mohunta gaped at me in disbelief. I rose from my chair and walked back to my residence.

A telegram from the Chief Secretary arrived that evening, directing me to relinquish my charge at Sirsa immediately and take over as SDM Rewari. I chuckled; I was being sent to the chief minister's subdivision as chastisement for my disobedience of the kingmaker.

The next day, I dictated and signed all orders, including the inheritance appeal, announced the ones I had reserved, and then signed the form relinquishing my post and walked home feeling light.

The next evening, the Bar Association gave me a farewell tea party. Chaudhary Devi Lal came from Chandigarh and attended the party, sitting next to me. There were a couple of short speeches lauding my brief tenure of about six months in Sirsa and I thanked them for their sentiments.

As we sat with members of the bar, sipping tea and sampling samosas and sweets, Chaudhary Devi Lal declared in his stentorian voice that he had got me transferred because I used to dine at Chaudhary Sheokaran Singh's house in Dabwali whenever I went there for court work, although numerous cases were pending against him in my court. This was a devastating charge.

Sheokaran Singh was a big landlord from that area and a number of cases were, in fact, going on against him under the Security of Land Tenures Act. I had never shown any partiality to him and had invariably granted proprietary rights to eligible tenants on his extensive landholdings. As a matter of fact, I had expedited the process. I had met his young son, Brij Lal, at Deputy Commissioner S.K. Misra's house, where he told me that they (S.K. and he) used to be together at Allahabad University. He had a sophisticated demeanour and pleasant manners and I liked him, so when he had invited me to lunch at his house after court in Dabwali, I had readily accepted. Chaudhary Devi Lal had also met me in the Dabwali rest house a few times but had never asked me for lunch.

Everyone present at the party knew why Devi Lal had got me transferred, but by publicly accusing me of accepting Chaudhary Sheokaran's hospitality, he was cleverly deflecting the issue. He had hit a soft spot. I smiled at his insinuation and retorted that I might have eaten at Chaudhary Sheokaran's house but had never decided a single case in his favour. Then I turned impudently towards him and said, 'Chaudhary Sahib, you never invited me to your house, though you had met me there several times! Chaudhary Sheokaran's son Brij Lal was the only one who showed the courtesy and I had no reason to refuse.'

The whole gathering burst into laughter at my riposte; Devi Lal's face fell. Recovering his composure, he said that he had come specially to attend my farewell party and had to leave early in the morning for Chandigarh, but his brother Sahib Ram would call me shortly and invite me to dine with him.

Sahib Ram called me later and I took a dusty third-hour ride to village Chautala, on the border of Rajasthan, and had a simple Rajasthani meal with him. He conversd in the Bagri dialect, which is a variant of the Bikaneri lingo and fell softly on my Rajasthani ears.

•◆

By the time I rejoined as SDM Rewari, in a week or so, Chaudhary Devi Lal and Rao Birendra Singh had fallen foul of each other. Newspapers were full of reports of the rift which had developed between the two leaders. Devi Lal had reportedly set about demolishing the edifice of the Rao government, which he had helped erect. He had the reputation of being a formidable foe.

Mira Seth had been appointed to serve in the government of India and Rao Birendra Singh had appointed Lala Munshi Ram, formerly of the Punjab Civil Service, as DC Gurgaon.

Lala Munshi Ram was an old-timer who had been a magistrate in a princely state during British rule. He was a man of simple habits, frugal to a fault. He told me that he washed his crease-proof terylene shirt every night when he changed into kurta-pajamas and wore the same shirt next morning after taking his bath.

He had obtained some breeder's seeds of the new, high-yielding, varieties of wheat from the Hisar Agricultural University and asked the local Block Development Officer (BDO) to grow it on the land around his old house, applying proper doses of fertilizers received, for demonstration at farmers' fields. After harvesting the crop, he got the seed packed in one-kilogram packets, in his presence, and gave them to the BDOs, to be sold to farmers at four times the usual rate. He told me that farmers got a higher yield and there was a great demand in the district for the 'DC farm wheat seed'. He considered this to be his contribution to the national effort in boosting wheat production.

◆

I first met Munshi Ram when he came to Rewari on a weekend to receive the chief minister who was scheduled to arrive for a two-day stay at his house. It was customary for the DC and SP to receive the CM when he visited their district.

Rao Sahib alighted from a gleaming Mercedes flying the tricolour, on the stone-paved compound outside the frescoed gate of his haveli which was filled with people from Rewari and the surrounding villages. He was dressed in a snow-white khadi kurta, churidar pajamas and a Nehru jacket.

'So, you've come back,' he smiled at me and remarked. 'Devi Lal is an obnoxious, worthless fellow.[106] When he told me that he wanted you transferred from there, I didn't even ask why. I had always wanted you to work here. Good riddance for you!'

He then went around meeting the people who had assembled at his haveli, heard their petitions and passed them on to his PA. However, when he met a particular group of people, his demeanour

---

[106] *'Behuda, wahiyat aadmi'* were his exact words.

changed. *'Haan, ab aaye ho. Tab kahan the jab voten pad rahe the?'*[107] he demanded disdainfully. Obviously, their village had not voted for him in the elections. They apologized for their mistake and promised loyalty in future, but he was unrelenting. *'Tab hi aana jab voten daloge,'*[108] he said, refusing to even accept their petitions.

As we were having tea in his spacious drawing room, I told him briefly about the court case which had caused my transfer. 'You did very well. Devi Lal is petty and selfish, and a big bully to boot. One has to stand up to a bully. That's exactly the reason why I've repulsed him. Now, we can work in peace,' he said.

The next day, he went around the town with local officers and pointed out a few things for its development: improvement in water supply and general sanitation, and broadening of the circular road. In particular, he wanted an old pond desilted, its brick-lined steps repaired and the frescoed pavilions at the four corners renovated.

•◆

Since Rewari was close to our part of Rajasthan, I had asked my mother to stay with me. The Tehsildar brought us a cow and arranged for a local Gujjar, Dhan Singh, to bring fodder for the cow. Dhan Singh took good care of the cow and milked her for us. We had fresh, frothing cow's milk, morning and evening, a perk of being the local hakim.

One evening, my old schoolmate from Sri Madhopur, Shiv Dayal, or Shyol as we used to call him, turned up at our house in Rewari. In the morning, after taking his bath, he saw a bottle of yellow shampoo. Taking it to be hair oil, he applied it to his wet hair. He couldn't understand why it was frothing so much and came out bewildered. My mother had a hearty laugh at his antics.

---

[107]Yes, you've come now. Where were you when votes were being cast?

[108]Come when you have voted for me.

◆

That year, we received a lot of rainfall in July, and the River Sahibi was in spate. It had washed away many small settlements and surrounded the village Khalilpur on the Rewari-Delhi main railway line. In fact, the railway line was acting as a dam and the village was being submerged in the resulting rainwater lake.

A large contingent from Khalilpur met the CM in Rewari. He told me to go and inspect the site the next day and said that if there was no other way to save the village from inundation, the railway line should be breached.

The next morning, the village appeared to be floating on water. Some kuccha houses in the periphery had collapsed. The downpour continued unabated and the water was rising continuously. The villagers told me that if the rains did not stop that night, they would have to breach the railway line.

I learnt from the villagers that this was an old problem. They had been demanding the construction of a small bridge near Khalilpur, but the railway administration had been insensitive to their demand. Since there was no other way out, in the dead of night, they made a breach in the railway track. The floodwater gushed out from under the rails and the cut widened in no time; all train services had to be suspended.

I received a call from Mr Sahay, the General Manager of Western Railways, asking me to get the breach plugged and restore train services. I told him that it was not possible to do anything till the rains stopped and the floodwater receded.

He landed at Rewari the next day and was highly vexed that the civil administration had not taken any action against the villagers who had willfully breached the railway line. 'You have, on the contrary, abetted the crime,' he told me and quoted the Railways Act.

I told him that it had been an unprecedented emergency; saving human life was far more important than running trains. At the site, Sahay made me sit with him on a rail trolley, and we were pushed along by men running barefeet on the rails. We went towards Delhi and he showed me how the river had been changing its course over the years and the many bridges that had already been constructed at different sites to let the river pass underneath.

I agreed with him but pointed out that the river had been obstructed at Khalilpur for many years, and the construction of one more bridge had become inevitable. It dawned on me that, perhaps, the railway engineering staff had developed a vested interest in creating an emergency in order to have access to unlimited funds.

I think he had also received a message from the CM about the bridge, and when we returned to Khalilpur, Sahay reprimanded the people for breaching the track, but also assured them that a bridge would be constructed. They were overjoyed.

•◆

One evening, Senior Sub-Judge Inder Mohan Malik, who lived in the adjacent house, dropped in for a visit. Savitri made some crisp pakoras and served them with hot coffee. Malik was a pleasant and witty man. He used to work in Delhi and was narrating a funny story about his experience of taking DTC buses.

Suddenly, a local gentleman entered the room and introduced himself as 'Rao'. I did not like his intrusion at all: I was reminded of Rao Sahib's words, that 'Rao' used to be the title of the rulers of Rewari, but every Ahir had taken to using it as a prefix. But what got my goat was that the man added by way of introduction, 'You must have heard of me; I am the CM's right hand.'

The CM had told me that when he wanted something done, he would speak to me himself. The intrusive visitor wanted me to provide police assistance to take possession of a piece of land that he had bought. This was completely contrary to law; police assistance was provided only to implement a court decree. I cut him short, saying that a man's 'right hand' should always remain with the man, otherwise it becomes lifeless. Malik chuckled at my remark and the man left.

I soon discovered that he had complained about me to the chief minister. On his next visit, Rao Sahib expressed his displeasure in the presence of Munshi Ram, for the slight meted out to his close supporter.

Since the man concerned was there, I narrated what had transpired between him and me in the presence of Judge I.M. Malik—how he had barged into my drawing room, introduced himself as 'CM's right hand' and all the rest of it about giving him police help for possession of some land. Rao Sahib then upbraided the man and he slinked away.

•◆

In the coming months, defeating Bhagwat Dayal Sharma in the Assembly by floor-crossing proved to be a Pyrrhic victory for Rao Birendra Singh. His bold adventure, of seizing power by revolting against his party in cohort with Devi Lal, started rebounding against him.

In the six months that his ministry lasted, Rao Sahib continuously added new ministers to his oversized cabinet, to buy the loyalty of MLAs. However, they quit often and repeatedly, rocking the boat. Hira Nand Arya, from Loharu, changed sides four times in the course of a few days, setting a dubious record. Arya was lodged in a minister's bungalow with armed security guards, but Devi Lal still managed to whisk him away.

The CM came to Rewari the day after this incident and I remarked jocularly, *'Aapne to Devi Lal ki neend haram kar rakhi hai!'*[109] He turned to me in mock anger and retorted, *'Arre, tumko Devi Lal ki padi hai; mera usne khana kharab kar rakha hai!'*[110]

Rao Birendra Singh had brought Hathin's MLA, Gaya Lal, to his side and jubilantly declared, *'Gaya Lal Aaya Ram ho gaya hai.'* However, when he decamped in a few days, Union Home Minister Y.B. Chavan commented in the Lok Sabha, *'Gaya Ram bhi gaya.'* Indeed, it was a sordid drama of secret wooing and open betrayal with plenty of farce thrown in. At one point, Rao Birendra Singh had all his 44 MLAs sworn in as ministers, yet his government could not achieve stability.

In his report to the President, Governor B.N. Chakravarty stated that things had come to such a pass that, at any point of time, it was not possible to say which MLA was on which side. He aptly used the analogy of 'weighing live frogs on a scale' and concluded that the circumstances were not conducive to governance according to the provisions of the Constitution. On the strength of his report, President's Rule was imposed in Haryana.

◆

Rao Birendra Singh's exit was even more inglorious than his predecessor's. Sharma had fallen tragically, like Julius Caesar, stabbed in the back by his fellow councillors; Rao Birendra Singh's dismissal was a farcical tragi-comedy, evoking universal mirth and derision.

When Rao Sahib came to Rewari after demitting office on 2 November 1967, he looked uncommonly relaxed and cheerful. The DC Gurgaon, SP and I received him at his house; there were no crowds.

He narrated a hilarious incident from the day of his sacking. Rao Sahib had settled a deal with an MLA and had called him at

---

[109]You are giving sleepless nights to Devi Lal!

[110]You are bothered about Devi Lal; I haven't had a meal in peace all these days!

2 p.m. to the CM's residence. The MLA was to be paid ₹20,000 in exchange for a written document pledging his loyalty. As Rao Sahib was coming down the flight of stairs to meet him, he heard on AIR that his ministry had been dismissed by the President and the State Assembly dissolved. Rather than being dejected, a strange feeling of elation came over him: he had saved the money in the nick of time! He asked his security men to throw the man out. Over 50 years ago, in 1967, the value of the rupee was about a hundred times higher than at present.

◆

By this time, the Senior Medical Officer, Dr Prem Kumar and his charming wife had become our close friends. Mrs Kumar had stylishly decked up their official residence; Savitri and I were in awe of the décor. In comparison, we just had bare essentials in our house.

During his last visit, Dr Kumar had examined Savitri, who was in an advanced stage of her pregnancy, and reassured her that she was in fine fettle.

On Sharad Purnima in October, my mother had made kheer from the milk of our cow and placed the container in the moonlight to absorb the moon's rays, when Savitri's labour pains began.

I called Dr Kumar; he and his wife arrived within a few minutes and took Savitri away in their car. I wanted to go along but they said that it was unnecessary; the delivery would take a long time and they promised to call me. The baby arrived around 5 a.m. by natural delivery. We named her Renu initially, but later changed it to the more formal Vandana, a prayer! She was fair like the moonlight and tiny as a fae.

19

DESTINATION: STATE SECRETARIAT

In April 1968, our batch was promoted to the senior echelons of the IAS; I was appointed Deputy Secretary, Industries Department and allotted a room overlooking the Vidhan Sabha on the sixth floor of the Secretariat, in Chandigarh.

I also received a promotion in pay: I was paid about ₹1,000 a month, almost double of what I had been paid in Rewari. However, in real terms, it was a demotion. In Rewari, I used to have a rent-free government house with a big lawn in front (though the grass wasn't green) and a sentry at the gate—the insignia of authority. I had thought that as a deputy secretary, I would be allotted government accommodation in the City Beautiful, a city made primarily for civil servants. That proved to be a pipe dream.

The formation of the new state of Haryana and the conversion of Chandigarh into a Union Territory had led to a sudden explosion in the number of babus who required housing. Three governments were now functioning in the city. Indeed, a piquant situation had arisen as the two stakeholders, Punjab and Haryana, were reduced to the status of a tenant.

I was told I didn't stand a chance of getting government accommodation for years. There was a long queue and it would be years before I was allotted something.

I, therefore, rented the half-constructed house of a government employee, the best I could afford with my housing allowance. The

Secretariat was about six kilometres away, so I bought a scooter. I had never driven a scooter before and the inevitable happened—I fell off thrice, luckily getting away with minor bruises and cuts.

•◆

During the time of Partap Singh Kairon, a new Industrial Estate was created in Faridabad, bordering Delhi. Industrial plots were allotted at concessional rates and entrepreneurs were given soft loans to promote industrial growth but the progress was far from satisfactory.

R.I.N. Ahuja, Secretary of Industries, was unhappy with the quarterly reports sent by P.N. Sahni, Director of Industries. Ahuja thought that Sahni was unscrupulous, and was promoting his self-interest rather than the industries. Therefore, Ahuja asked me to visit a few units to have a reality check.

I selected five units at random in the category 'In production or nearing completion'. My inspection results were shocking: the first site was a bare plot with only a boundary wall; the second one had a small room for a chowkidar, in addition to the boundary wall. A small shed existed in the third site with no activity in sight, while about 10 workers were making pesticide at the fourth site. At the last site that I visited, a suave young man from Delhi was supervising the installation of machinery in a shed. I told him that according to the report of the director of industries, his factory was already in production. He admitted that his manager had sent an incorrect report and explained that there were delays in importing machinery. He hoped, however, to start trials in three months. As I turned to leave, he invited me to join him for dinner that evening. I liked the young man and was not entirely unwilling, but explained that I didn't know Delhi at all and wouldn't know where to go. He offered to send his car to the rest house and I agreed.

The young man lived in a posh house in Defence Colony with

his father. Both were drinking at the bar in the drawing room when I reached. The middle-aged father was in a colourful t-shirt and skimpy shorts; I was both shocked and amused. I associated such attire with morning-walkers.

'Will you have a Scotch?' the father asked me. I nodded my assent. 'What's your brand in Scotch?' he asked again. This question annoyed me: either the man was flaunting his collection or testing my knowledge.

I knew Chivas Regal and could have mentioned it. But I was peeved and replied, 'I don't drink regularly, only occasionally, mostly beer, though I have had whisky a few times, and Scotch only once. It was much smoother on the gullet than the local stuff. I think it was Chivas Regal. So you might say that's my brand.'

They were not prepared for this long oration. The son meekly poured from a large bottle of Chivas Regal and we said 'Cheers!' I declined a third drink and the ladies joined us for dinner. Later, father and son saw me off.

◆

Meanwhile, in Haryana, mid-term Assembly elections were held under President's Rule in May 1968. While most of the defectors were humbled at the hustings, Rao Birendra Singh's Vishal Haryana Party won 16 seats. The Congress party again secured a clear majority of 51 in a house of 90. Bhagwat Dayal Sharma tried hard to be chief minister again but Prime Minister Indira Gandhi asked former Home Minister Gulzarilal Nanda and Inder Kumar Gujral to find a consensus candidate. Their choice was Bansi Lal, a relatively young politician from Bhiwani, from the state's major Jat community. He had already completed a six-year term as a member of the Rajya Sabha. Bhagwat Dayal Sharma too came around and the newspapers dubbed him a 'dark horse'.

Bansi Lal had no experience of governance and during the first few months he appeared to be fumbling around. For some time, he publicly acknowledged Nandaji and Pandit Bhagwat Dayal as his gurus. This changed when Bhagwat Dayal Sharma tried to dictate everyday decision-making, trying to rule by proxy.

He faced his first real political test when Bhagwat Dayal Sharma walked away with 15 Congress MLAs and Rao Birendra Singh joined him with his men, along with other fence-sitters. The MLAs were paraded before Governor B.N. Chakravarty.

The governor did not want the new government to go the way of the earlier one, so he told the dissenters to table a no-confidence motion in the forthcoming Assembly session in November and prove their majority in the House. It was a reprieve for Bansi Lal; in the next few weeks, he brought many deserters back to his fold and was able to tide over the storm in the Assembly session.

Bansi Lal had appointed S.K. Misra as his Principal Secretary, having been impressed by Misra's functioning as DC Hisar. However, I had not met Misra after my transfer from Sirsa; I hadn't even gone to congratulate him on becoming the chief minister's principal secretary, for fear of encroaching on his time. So, when R.I.N. Ahuja invited S.K. Misra to lunch one day, and asked me also to join them, I was happy to accept the offer. Neither did Ahuja talk shop at lunch, nor did Misra say a word about his hectic schedule; they just had friendly banter, bursting into guffaws of laughter.

•◆

Bansi Lal visited the innovative Beas Sutlej Link Project soon after taking over as chief minister: he was impressed by the Herculean task. Haryana had a 33 per cent share in this project, which was under construction in the Kullu-Manali region. It was a kind of complement to the Bhakra Nangal hydel project, which Nehru had called 'the new temple of modern India'.

Bansi Lal asked the chief engineer of the project, K.S. Pathak, if something could be done to irrigate the dry lands of Loharu and Mahendragarh. Pathak knew the canal network of Punjab and Haryana like the back of his hand. He understood what the chief minister had in mind: a lift canal to traverse the sand dunes. He forewarned the CM that the project would require enhanced availability of canal water at the base of the lift-canal system at Bhiwani and a robust power back-up. A power breakdown might lead to a reverse flow in the canal, damaging the whole system. It would be like walking a tightrope.

'We will walk the tightrope,' Bansi Lal told him. Pathak was reassigned from the BSL Project to Haryana and asked to create a network of lift canal systems to irrigate south Haryana. Jui Lift Canal was the pilot project, involving the lifting of water at seven stages. It covered a part of Bansi Lal's Tosham constituency, of which his ancestral village Golagarh was a part. Working at breakneck speed, the pilot project was completed in a couple of years.

The success of this initial project led to more ambitious ones. In the next few years, large areas of Bhiwani, Mahendragarh and Rohtak district were brought under the seasonal lift irrigation system. It was a staggering achievement—a revolution in irrigation. If Haryana got its due share of water from Punjab, all these canals could become perennial.

◆

By this time, the new district of Jind had been created and a young IAS officer, M. Kuttappan, was posted there as deputy commissioner. To celebrate Haryana Day on 1 November 1968, he planned a cultural programme of dance and drama by students of the local government college. Simultaneously, Haryana's Director of Public Relations, I.E.N. Chauhan, also decided to hold the state-level Haryana Day function at Jind. The department had a cultural troupe of its own and Chauhan landed there with his entourage. Inevitably, there was a clash.

Kuttappan asked Chauhan to allow at least two dance performances by the college students; they had been practising for a fortnight, and would be heartbroken otherwise. Chauhan refused, saying that they could not match the level of excellence of his professional troupe. Enraged, Kuttappan told Chauhan, 'I am the deputy commissioner. Let me see who stops my boys and girls from performing.'

The spat between the DPR and the deputy commissioner resulted in the transfer of I.E.N. Chauhan. S.K. Misra had me appointed as DPR in the fifth year of my service, bypassing the traditional norms of seniority for appointment as HoD. He had faith in the capabilities of youngsters and encouraged them.

The first thing I did as DPR was to disband the cultural troupe, as it had acquired an unsavoury reputation in the orthodox society of Haryana. I encouraged traditional swang performances, putting up skits and plays for rural audiences. In these dance-dramas, men played female parts as in Shakespearean England.

Since there were no TV channels at that time, the print media was everything. *The Tribune* had moved to Chandigarh from Ambala; its senior correspondent, S.V. Bedi, covered Haryana. All daily newspapers published from Delhi and Jalandhar were represented by senior correspondents. Chief Minister Bansi Lal was press-shy; he had narrowly survived the challenge of the Opposition in the assembly session and avoided meeting the gentlemen of the press.

I was a junior officer and had not completed even one year in the Secretariat at that time; I was an unknown entity to the press. In order to establish a rapport with them, I began following an open-door policy by converting my office room into a kind of drawing room. Press correspondents were welcome to drop in and have tea with me in the forenoon, leaving the afternoon for office work. This arrangement helped me develop friendly ties with the press corps.

Besides, I requested the chief minister to hold regular press conferences, at least once in a fortnight. He used to allow only V.D. Chopra of the *Patriot* and B.K. Chum of *National Herald* to meet him occassionally, who, based on the dope they got from the chief minister, used to file exclusive stories. This had created bad blood among other journalists.

•◆

The Beas Sutlej Link Project was creating a lot of curiosity, so I decided to take a press party on a site visit. My office had suggested that I travel by staff car and let the journalists be escorted by a PRO in the bus. I didn't like the idea of travelling in isolation, but I asked a PRO to come along with us in the bus.

One fine morning, we boarded the departmental minibus and headed towards Kartarpur. From there, took the road for the Gobind Sagar Lake. Stopping for lunch at a wayside restaurant, we reached the project headquarters at Sunder Nagar in the evening and were lodged in a guest house.

In the morning, we were briefed about the project: the Beas waters were diverted into the Sutlej, which had been dammed at Bhakra. The Beas waters were meant to augment this reservoir, the Gobind Sagar Lake, named after the great tenth guru of the Sikhs. In a unique feat of engineering, a waterfall of a thousand feet was being created, to produce an extra 1,000 megawatt of electricity. Water channels were being bored through two mountains as part of this attempt. It was the first project of its kind to be undertaken by Indian engineers.

We took jeeps to the tunnelling site and alighted at the gaping mouth of a mountain. From there, heavy duty trucks took us through slush and flowing water, right up to the point where digging was going on. It was an awe-inspiring sight: a jumbo machine was being used like a battering ram. The debris from the mountain was being collected by workers wearing protective gear and dumped into trucks to be carried outside. It was a hazardous operation; accidents happened quite often, when rocks tumbled down suddenly and water gushed out, resulting in worker casualties.

We returned to Sunder Nagar and reached Manali in the evening. We stayed at the luxurious British-era circuit house there, nestled under stately deodar trees, beyond the market. I was mighty kicked to know that Jawaharlal Nehru had stayed in the circuit house.

•◆

The road from Manali to Rohtang Pass had been constructed by that time, but it had not been opened to civilian traffic. Locals and trekkers went to Rohtang and Lahaul valley by foot. B.K. Chum told us that he had gone up some distance along this road in an army officer's jeep, so we decided to see how far we could go in our ramshackle minibus. The road was partially tarred; the bends were mostly gravelled. Our Sikh driver took up the challenge and we set off on a bright and sunny day.

We went slowly along with the sparkling Beas on our left and met many waterfalls on the way. In about two hours, we reached Marhi, halfway to Rohtang. We stopped for tea and snacks at a roadside shop and the locals warned us against taking our bus beyond that point. There were sharp bends in the road ahead and a treacherous snow-covered stretch, ominously called the khooni nalla.

However, nothing could deter us and we set off after the refreshments. We stopped for a while at a giant monolith by the side of the road; Rohtang shone brightly in the sun, some distance ahead. The khooni nalla was indeed treacherous: the bus had to pass through a steep snow-filled gully and navigate a sharp turn in the middle. It was slushy and slippery but we crossed it safely. That was the last hurdle: the road beyond was covered in snow in some places, but the bends were not very sharp. Finally, we reached the shacks near the top of Rohtang Pass and celebrated our arrival by toasting with cups of tea.

Rohtang Pass connects Kullu valley and Keylong valley, which is a part of Leh-Ladakh. We walked along a small stream and reached its source. The priest of the tiny shrine there told us that it was the source of River Beas. This confused me: I had heard that the Beas Kund, where the river originated, was a huge lake surrounded by snow-clad cliffs. The man explained that the two streams from these two sources merged a few miles above Manali to create the Beas.

•◆

At that time, the Department of Tourism used to be a part of the Public Relations Department, and I was Director of Tourism as well. S.K. Misra, Principal Secretary to the CM, was also Secretary Tourism. The Department used to run cafeterias at important bus stations like Karnal.

Misra was instrumental in setting up an autonomous Tourism Promotion Board under his chairmanship and the Plan provision was raised a hundred times. The total budget for new projects was only ₹5 lakhs.[111]

The first tourism complex was built midway between Chandigarh and Delhi on National Highway No. 1, where the highway crossed the Western Jamuna Canal. It was imaginatively planned by Misra. An artificial lake was created to fill up the huge pits along the embankment of the old canal and the complex was situated on this lake. It was as if an oasis had sprung up on the old grand

---

[111]S.K. Misra, *Flying in High Winds*, Rupa Publications, New Delhi, p. 76.

trunk road! It was an instant success and became a haunt of long-distance travellers.

In the next few years, Misra created about 20 such highway resorts. They were all named after birds: Whistling Teal, Parakeet, Kingfisher, Rosy Pelican, and so on. These birds, perched on the highways passing through Haryana, acquired tremendous popularity and Haryana Tourism became a trendsetter for other states.

•◆

Dr Karan Singh was tourism minister in the Union cabinet at that time. That year, he organized the annual Tourism Development Conference in Darjeeling and S.K. Misra and I were in attendance from Haryana.

We had no idea that our guest house afforded fabulous views of the majestic Kanchenjunga[112], because our evening check-in had kept us in the dark. So, wrapped in woollens against the bitter cold, we reached Tiger Hill at the unearthly hour of 4 a.m. the next morning to view the astonishing sight of the Kanchenjunga peaks blushing at the first kiss of the golden rays of the sun. Along with crowds of tourists, we waited for an hour and a half. Slowly, dawn broke over the snow-covered peaks, turning them crimson. What a magnificent sight!

After the day-long conference, Dr Karan Singh hosted a gala dinner. Informal groups formed over drinks. I joind a group of ladies that had gathered around the vivacious hostess, the former Maharani of Kashmir. She had visited Belgium recently and was marvelling about the Belgian crown jewels, poohpooing her own collection. I was amused to hear her lament that their jewels paled in comparison to these foreign treasures. I realized that no matter how prosperous we are, we never value what we have, continuously pining for more.

---

[112]Literally: golden thighs

The next morning, I woke up before sunrise entirely by chance. A few moments later, I saw the bewitching spectacle again: the snow-clad peaks set on fire by the first rays of the sun. I was back on Tiger Hill, without stirring from my bed!

◆

Next year, the tourism conference was held in Hyderabad. Our tourism minister K.L. Poswal attended it, accompanied by the deputy minister Gordhan Das Chauhan and a young MLA, Surjit Singh Mann from Karnal. Andhra Pradesh used to be a 'dry' state at that time. Poswal asked me to talk to the collector and get two bottles of Scotch and gave me ₹5,000. I had to fill up a form with the particulars of the persons addicted to drinking, so I wrote the names of the three VIPs along with my own. Two bottles of the desired tipple were delivered to me; I took them to the minister's room and we consumed the elixir from Scotland during the two evenings we stayed in Hyderabad.

◆

Back in Chandigarh, Minister Poswal phoned me one day to say that he had invited his friend Col. Gupte, Director of Song and Drama Division. The good Colonel had brought recordings of the legendary Pakistani singer Reshma's songs and would be giving an exclusive rendition at the Pinjore Gardens that night. He invited me to come and enjoy this rare treat.

Apart from being the director of PR and Tourism, I was also Director of Hospitality. I issued a letter declaring Col. Gupte a state guest and reached Pinjore Gardens in the evening, carrying a bottle of the elixir from Scotland.

The Pinjore Gardens were created by Mughul emperor Aurangzeb's cousin Fidai Khan. Its terraces were designed in a descending order; one walks down the rippling central channel to the Rang Mahal, Sheesh Mahal, Jal Mahal and finally reaches the open-air amphitheatre at the end. The imposing three-storeyed Sheesh Mahal is the centrepiece of the garden. Col. Gupte had placed four speakers at the four corners of its wide terrace.

Pinjore Garden is full of the choicest mango trees. The heady fragrance of mango blossoms wafted through the moonlit May night. Minister Poswal, Col. Gupte and I sat in easychairs under the starry sky. A bearer served drinks and Reshma's robust voice resounded in the stillness. I had not heard her before: I was spellbound.

◆

After the conclusion of an Assembly session at the end of March, Poswal asked me to plan a visit to the Jim Corbett Park, to see the Royal Bengal Tiger. The Park authorities advised us to visit in June, as the chances of sighting tigers at waterholes are higher during the summer months. We reached Dhikala in mid-June in the evening and stayed in their guest house.

The next morning, we were greeted by a strange sight outside the guest house: a group of agitated tuskers stood around a female elephant, who was tied to a tree. She had been captured the previous day for domestication by the Park authorities. The tuskers had come to lodge a protest and get her released.

The tuskers dispersed before noon and we rode a majestic elephant and reached a little stream in the forest. A machan had been built on a tree beside the stream. The minister and I climbed up and perched there in silence. We were accompanied by a guide and conversation was strictly forbidden, even in whispers. It was a hot windless day; occasional bird calls shattered the silence of the forest.

After about half an hour, a herd of spotted deer came to slake their thirst, their spotted golden coats shimmering in the sun. It was a heavenly sight. Till 2 p.m., there was no sign of the king of the forest, so we rode the elephant back to the guest house for a late lunch.

Around 5 p.m., we went to the machan again and waited till dusk, but to no avail. The director hosted a dinner in honour of the minister and told him that they would tether a goat under the tree that night. He assured us that we would most probably find the whole family having a meal when we went to the machan the next morning.

As planned, we reached the spot at about 10 a.m.: the goat was merrily grazing under the tree! Finally, the guide took us on a leisurely tour of the sanctuary. We had a spectacular sighting of a large herd of elephants emerging from the thick forest and, on the way back, saw a group of barasinghas romping in tall grass.

20

DIRECTOR OF AGRICULTURE

My appointment as Director of Agriculture in August 1971 came as a huge surprise. I had been expecting a transfer since having a small tiff with Chief Minister Bansi Lal, but this appointment was unusual in many ways. Nowhere in the country had an IAS officer been posted as director of agriculture. Agriculture was a technical department like animal husbandry or fisheries, health or PWD; these departments were invariably headed by technocrats. My appointment was a clear instance of a generalist encroaching on the technocrats' turf.

Since the formation of Haryana, a Sikh officer had been heading the agriculture department. A Jat officer, J.L. Dalal, was next in line. Dalal was a knowledgeable and capable officer; the appointment of an IAS officer was a clear snub to him and a huge surprise for everyone. For Dalal, it was the denial of his lifelong, legitimate aspiration.

I heard that a few days before the change was due, Dalal committed an indiscretion which annoyed the chief minister. Bansi Lal had been in Rohtak for a public engagement, and was staying at the PWD rest house. Dalal reached there early in the morning to meet him, and was told that the CM was scheduled to leave soon and a meeting was impossible. In desperation, Dalal jumped over the back wall of the rest house, landed in front of the CM's bedroom and introduced himself. That proved to be his undoing.

I understood Dalal's pain and accorded him high respect and took all decisions in consultation with him. He had trained as a breeder of groundnut at the Lyallpore College of Agriculture, graduating with distinction. He was erudite and witty; he was abreast of research in plant breeding at the Haryana Agricultural University, and in every branch of agricultural science, and used to have lively interactions with University scientists.

•◆

My appointment as director of agriculture gave me a chance to see Haryana at the grass-roots level. India was experiencing a sharp deficit in production of foodgrains and had been subsisting on shipments of wheat from the US. In 1966, Prime Minister Indira Gandhi had gone to President Lyndon Johnson with a begging bowl, as it were.

The existing varieties of wheat had thin, long stalks which were prone to lodging at the ripening stage, because of the weight of the grains. Luckily for us, Norman Borlaug developed semi-dwarf high-yielding varieties of wheat, Larma Rojo and Sonora, which had shorter, stronger stalks. The introduction of these varieties in India and Pakistan gave an unprecedented boost to wheat production. During the 'Green Revolution', our wheat production nearly doubled, from 12 million tonnes in 1965 to 20 million tonnes in 1970, vastly improving the country's food security. There was a sense of euphoria in the agricultural world.

The problem in rice production was of a different kind. Rice seeds are sown in nurseries before the onset of rains and one-month-old seedlings are transplanted in fields flooded with water. It's a labour-intensive, back-breaking operation performed by hired labour. Accompanied by a university expert, I went on field inspection when transplanting was in full swing in the Karnal-Kurukshetra area.

A young girl was planting seedlings in a field. After watching her for a few minutes, the expert told me that in order to finish her job quickly, she was planting seedlings far apart from each other; this led to a decrease in the plant population, which in turn caused a loss in production. I asked him to show her the correct spacing.

He removed his shoes, pulled up his trousers, entered the field and showed her how close they had to be planted. She watched him for a few moments, then pouted her lips in disdain and said to me, '*Yo to kaseeda sa kaadh rahya sai!*' (He is doing some kind of cross-stitch), and continued with her task as before. This incident demonstrated the conflict of interest: she was paid according to the number of acres she covered per day. At her current pace, she covered 3-4 acres in a day; if she followed the expert, she would cover much less and would lose money.

The university expert showed me the prototype of a motorized seedling planter which they had developed; it was calibrated to plant seedlings with the requisite spacing. He hoped that in a few years these mechanical planters would be produced commercially, reducing dependence on manual transplantation and help us achieve a breakthrough in rice production.

Unfortunately, after over four decades, mechanical planters are a rarity anywhere. Even now, rice fields in Punjab and Haryana are mostly sown by Bihari labourers using the same, old methods.

•◆

South Haryana, adjoining Rajasthan, had a sizeable area under bajra (pearl millet) cultivation at that time. The introduction of a hybrid variety had worked wonders for production. A field of ripe hybrid bajra was a fascinating sight to behold; stalks waving jocundly in the air, their long spikes studded with tiny 'pearls'!

However, the area under bajra cultivation was declining after the introduction of lift irrigation in south Haryana; even gram cultivation had gone down. On the other hand, rice cultivation was increasing: it was not confined to the Karnal-Kurukshetra area any more, but was spilling over into Jind and Sonipat districts. I even saw some rice fields a few miles short of Bhiwani. The entire agricultural topography of Haryana was changing.

The agriculture department had schemes for laying out demonstration plots of various crops in the fields of different farmers. Our agriculture inspectors were required to lay out these demo plots; however, few of them ever took the trouble of actually going to the fields. They generally passed on the inputs—bags of improved seeds and chemical fertilizers—to farmers they were friendly with.

While touring Mahendragarh district one day in May 1974, I asked an agriculture inspector where he had laid out the demo plots of an improved variety of moong. He mentioned the name of a village with four demo plots. 'Let me see them,' I told him.

The BDO and I went in my car; the inspector led the way in the BDO's jeep. Even after half an hour on the village roads, he could not find the plots. It was clear that he had neither come to the village nor laid out the demo plots; he had just given the inputs to some farmers who visited him in the BDO's office. Finally, he halted the jeep, all of us stepped out of our vehicles, and he confessed that he hadn't seen the plots.

I lost my temper and slapped him across the face. I consider myself a cool-headed person and had never felt such rage before. I told the BDO to send me a report about this inspector and asked him to inspect the demo plots laid out by the other three inspectors working in his office and send me a detailed report. Then, I turned homewards.

Evening had fallen by the time I reached the new Chakravarty Lake tourist complex on G.T. road. My car was not air-conditioned and I was drenched in perspiration. It was like coming to an oasis. Sitting on a cane chair in the open quadrangle, I was munching a sandwich, when Chief Minister Bansi Lal arrived.

I stood up and joined my hands in salutation. He was on his way to Delhi. '*Kahan ghoom-gham rahe ho*[113], Varmaji?' he asked me good humouredly. I told him about my futile search for a demonstration plot of moong in Narnaul area and my slapping the inspector. He had a hearty laugh at my anecdote.

As he was leaving after a quick cup of tea, he asked me, 'Would you like to go to Bhiwani as deputy commissioner? Devasahayam has to be transferred from there.'

'Certainly, sir, with pleasure!' I answered. 'It's high time I went to a district.' I was the only one from our batch who hadn't done a district yet, although I was head of a department.

[113]Where are you loitering?

21

BHIWANI DISTRICT

Bhiwani sub-division of the sprawling Hisar district had been upgraded by Bansi Lal into a district a few years ago; Devasahayam was its first deputy commissioner. He was admitted to the IAS after his release from the Army. Recently, there was some controversy about rounding up a man and his sister by the police in a village called Rewasa and locking them up for the night in a cell in the police station. There was public outrage because of this and some police officers and the deputy commissioner were transferred to assuage public sentiment.

Bhiwani is an old town on the trade route from Punjab to Rajasthan. Chief Minister Bansi Lal had widened the road which circled the town, built pavements for pedestrians and created colourful fountains at the main crossings. An underground drainage system had been laid and disposal works created outside the town. A new waterworks had been commissioned, to meet the additional requirement of drinking water. An officers' colony and a new PWD rest house had been constructed. A milk processing plant and a government college had started functioning. A new administrative complex, a 300-bed civil hospital and a public library were under construction. When I reached Bhiwani, numerous public buildings were mushrooming all over the town.

My transfer to Bhiwani provided some respite to Savitri. The deputy commissioner's new house was being built, so we moved into an old government bungalow, which had been occupied by Devasahayam, and she heaved a huge sigh of relief.

About eight months ago, we had welcomed our third child. Nurturing a newborn, getting two little girls ready for school, cooking for the family and coping with her never-ending household chores had become very difficult for Savitri. All that changed dramatically. She was served morning tea in bed, evening tea on the lawns under a garden umbrella, and lunch and dinner on a mahogany table! Besides all that, she enjoyed occasionally hosting parties as the first lady of the district. She finally had some time for herself and enrolled in the government college for her BA degree.

•◆

My parents had also never felt at home in Chandigarh; they had no one to talk to and they disliked living a life of idleness. They were used to hard toil and hankered after a piece of land to call their own. At their insistence, I had bought six acres of agricultural land in Kalka tehsil, at the foothills of the Shivaliks near the border of Himachal Pradesh. A few months before I was transferred to Bhiwani, my father had started developing a mango orchard there. When they heard about my transfer to Bhiwani, they said that they would stay at the farm.

'But there is no place to stay at the farm,' I told them. Father smiled and said, 'Don't you remember the little hut of sarkanda I made and slept in at harvesting time in our village? You don't bother about us, I'll make a hut there and your mother and I will happily live in it.'

I got a tent pitched under the old mango trees for them to stay in, and hired the son of a pandit living in the village to serve as their helper and left for Bhiwani, my heart quivering in trepidation.

After a fortnight, when I went to Chandigarh to attend a meeting, I went to meet them. Their initial euphoria had evaporated, but they were settling into their new habitation.

After another fortnight, when I was back in Bhiwani, I received a police message that my mother was unwell. I reached the farm in the evening; she was lying in bed, her speech was slurred. I took her to the government hospital in Chandigarh. Dr B.R. Varma, chief medical superintendent, examined her and diagnosed a mild stroke.

I called my brother Bhagirath from Jaipur and sister Chhoti from Khetri. Seeing them, Mother sat up slowly and placed her hands on their head in blessing. The next day she passed away, barely four days after being admitted to the hospital.

My mother had been a devout woman. *'Heh Bhagwan, chatka ki chaal deeje, patka ki maut deeje,'*[114] she used to pray. She had told me that she wanted to be cremated in Sri Madhopur, so we travelled all night and reached our hometown early in the morning the next day. Her body was laid out in the tin-roofed house that she had entered as a bride; the room resounded with the mourning chants of our kinswomen.

A huge funeral procession of our kinsmen took the same sandy path that my mother used to take every day to fetch water from a well across the railway line. My brother lit the pyre and we sat under an old banyan tree, watching the flames.

In our community, there was a tradition of observing 11 days of mourning, followed by a 'birathery' (community) feast on the twelfth day. Mother had told me that she had been supping at these 'birathery' feasts all her life, but there had been no occasion in her life to invite the birathery to a feast in our house. 'After my demise, you call the whole birathery to a feast, my son,' she had instructed me.

In the evenings, we invited local singers to sing bhajans by Kabir, Mira Bai, Surdas and others. The singers wanted nothing

---

[114] O God, give me a brisk gait and a quick demise.

in return for their labours, except a cup of tea. To honour our mother's wish, we organized a feast for the entire community of about 500 people.

•◆

Being a deputy commissioner was a unique experience. I felt the weight of authority: the deputy commissioner was verily the kingpin of the administration, the leader of the officers posted in the district. My car flew a flag embossed with the state emblem and the magic letters, DC.

People flocked to the court in the morning with their petitions: the water supply standpost in the village had been damaged; someone was erecting a wall encroaching on the village lane; the only teacher posted in the school had been absent for a month; no nurse had been posted in the Block hospital; urea was not available in the fertilizer depot; the police was torturing an innocent man for a crime he hadn't commited, and so on.

Many officers, particularly in the engineering departments, despite their seniority, were answerable to the DC about public complaints against their departments. People flocked to the deputy commissioner to express grievances against any department or officer in the district. The complaints received by the DC were forwarded to the concerned departmental head in the district for immediate redressal. Every month on a fixed day, there was a meeting of the District Grievances Committee, presided over by the deputy commissioner, where complaints were discussed and the concerned officers reported about the action taken. It was a powerful forum and an effective mechanism for grievance redressal.

•◆

My offices were functioning temporarily from some makeshift rooms at that time. The CM had asked me to tour the villages and ensure that they were connected to the network of roads, electricity and drinking water. One day, he made a whirlwind tour of the villages in his own Assembly constituency, Tosham. Instead of making speeches from a podium, Bansi Lal sat on a chair and talked to the villagers; they sat around him on durries. I was struck by his bonhomie with them; he seemed to know everyone by name. Women stood in a cluster around the men's circle, partly veiling their faces.

The CM made me sit beside him on a chair and handed me the petitions he received from the assembled men. Since the stopover lasted just about 10 minutes, his accompanying officers sat in their Jeeps.

For the other Assembly constituencies in the district, he organized regular meetings under a proper shamiana and addressed the gathering from a podium. His address was preceded by speeches of the local MLAs; the distict officers sat on chairs near the stage but he invariably made me sit near him and handed me all the petitions.

•◆

As DC, I received numerous visitors. One fine day, a local seth arrived: he used to live in Mumbai and offered a wristwatch for my wife. He had built a charitable eye hospital in town and wanted me to inaugurate a special eye treatment camp that he was organizing there. The doctor who had accompanied him claimed that he had performed a record number of eye operations.

I went to the hospital the next morning. Hundreds of people were lying in beds, waiting for treatment. They had all been prepared for the operation. The doctor went from patient to patient, deftly removing cataracts, using the same scalpel for all patients, never stopping to clean or disinfect his operating tool. An attendant followed, dressing the eye of each patient. Each operation took hardly more than a minute. I was amazed by the doctor's skill but I had apprehensions about the poor patients. This swift and summary treatment did not augur well for their recovery.

Another day I had a royal visitor, Nawab Aminuddin of Loharu. He had joined politics and was chairman of the Rajasthan Agro-Industries Corporation and lived in Loharu House in Jaipur. He told me that he was on a brief visit to his native riyasat[115] and invited me to dinner the next day. I was pleased to see him and readily accepted his invitation.

The next evening, the Superintendent of Police Y.S. Nakai and I set off for Loharu in our cars; he had also been invited by the Nawab. When we reached, we discovered that there were only a few other guests. Drinks were served, and the Nawab regaled us with anecdotes. When he asked his bearer to offer a second round of drinks, the man sheepishly showed him the almost-empty bottle; in all probability, his men had been imbibing earlier. I told the Nawab that I had vowed not to drink at all when I came to Bhiwani, in deference to the teetotaller chief minister; I declined a second drink. Instead, I asked him to serve dinner.

A huge bowl of chicken curry was placed on the table, along with a few vegetarian dishes. The chicken curry was the *pièce de résistance*. I fished out a small piece of chicken and moved on; Nakai also did the same. The Nawab goaded him, *'Chicken aur leejiye, S.P. Sahib!'* (Please have some more chicken, S.P. Sahib). He was oblivious to the fact that the bowl hardly had any chicken in it; it was full of hot watery gravy. It seemed like the khansama had bought just one chicken to make snacks as well as the curry.

Later, when I related this incident to Chief Minister Bansi Lal and B.D. Gupta, the then Speaker of the Vidhan Sabha, they had a hearty laugh. Gupta said that the Nawab was known for his

---

[115]Domain

tangdusti[116] and kadki[117]; his riyasat was barren. He narrated an anecdote about a seth from Loharu who had settled in Kolkata.

The seth had come to Loharu on a short visit after some years, when he was summoned to the Nawab's court. When he presented himself, he was promptly fined a hundred rupees. A hundred rupees in those days was an enormous sum.

The man was shell-shocked and asked, *'Lekin maine kya zurm kiya hai, Huzoor?'* (But what crime have I committed, Milord?)

'Tum zurm tau zindagi bhar nahin karoge, us-se kya? Tumko zurmana bharna padega.' (You may not commit a crime in your whole life, so what? You'll have to pay the fine.)

Gupta also had another anecdote, about a man who had constructed a chabutara[118] in front of his house in the village. The Nawab summoned him and told him to pay ₹50 as fine. The man apologized for his mistake and promised to demolish the chabutara.

'In that case, you'll have to pay ₹40 as fine!' the Nawab declared.

◆

Among my many visitors, there was Surendra Singh, the younger son of Chief Minister Bansi Lal. He was a handsome young man with smiling eyes and a dimple in his cheek.

One day, he suggested that we should organize a 'Star Night' in Bhiwani to generate funds for a children's train in the newly constructed Bal Bhawan, like the one that had been built in Delhi. The idea seemed far-fetched to me; I wondered which film star would want to visit Bhiwani, but Surendra Singh was confident.

Indeed, the 'Star Night' proved to be a roaring success: Hema Malini came, who was at the top of her popularity at the time, Sunil Dutt and other leading stars came. The melodious songs of

116 Miserliness

117 Poverty

118 Platform

Mukesh enthralled the overflowing audience well into the night. It was a rare treat for the people of Bhiwani.

We collected thousands of rupees for the district Red Cross and built a children's train in Bal Bhawan. Two more 'Star Nights' were organized in the successive years and the Red Cross Society of Bhiwani district received a special commendation from the President of India for all the funds it managed to gather.

Around that time, the construction of the deputy commissioner's new house was completed, and I moved in with my family. Designed by Chief Architect Dhamija, the house was built around a central fountain.

After we moved in, Dhamija came to inspect the house one evening. My little daughters had filled the walls of the gallery around the fountain with quaint graffiti—birds, flowers, letters of the alphabet, and childish scrawls and squiggles. I was apprehensive that Dhamija would reproach me for it, but thankfully he let it pass without comment.

He was not happy with the colour scheme of the rooms but ruled out repainting because of cost considerations; however, he was particularly keen to paint the ceiling of the drawing room black. I thought the idea was bizarre, but I was happy to humour him.

Most of my visitors would look askance at the black ceiling but I got used to it after a while. I wondered about sleeping under a ceiling painted black, showing the bright stars of the great Hunter's Belt constellation. One would then have the soothing sensation of sleeping under the sky's vault.

Sometime after we moved into the new house, the district forest officer R.S. Hooda brought a wonderful gift for my daughters: a little golden fawn with black stripes and spots. She was a beauty and we named her 'Shobhna'. She skipped and scampered and romped freely in the large compound; little Upasana was forever running after her.

A peon named Chiranji Lal was particularly attached to Upasana; she used to call him 'Chilanjilal'. He used to carry her around on his shoulders and take her to the water channel running through the colony. One day, he left her there, asking the gardener to keep an eye on her. Upasana walked up and down the channel for a few minutes and then jumped right into the haudi[119]. The gardener rushed to pull her out; Chiranji Lal materialized and brought her back home for a change of clothes.

◆

Taking advantage of the five-day work week in government offices, I took three days of leave and, accompanied by R.S. Hooda and his family, we set off for Kanha National Park. Hooda had suggested the trip; he told us that we would be able to see tigers in the sanctuary and had made reservations for our stay.

We reached Agra in the afternoon and went to see the Taj Mahal: we had never seen it before. As we entered through the huge gate, I stopped in my tracks, spellbound by the world's most beautiful love poem in marble! There was something ethereal about it—a pearl shimmering in the sky's vault!

The majestic white dome, framed by the four graceful minarets, was shining in the mellow sunlight. We sat on the marble benches and took photographs. Then, we walked up the marble steps and entered the mausoleum: peace and silence reigned inside. Going round the intricately chiselled and ornately inlaid jalis we came under the vaulted dome and reached the tombs of Mumtaz Mahal and

---

[119]Water junction

Shah Jahan. I told the kids in whispers that the king and queen were buried under the tombs. Their eyes widened in wonder and awe.

After driving the whole day, we reached the Kanha forest sanctuary late in the evening. Next morning, we ventured inside the forest with a forest guard. When we came across a herd of elephants, the children were delighted to see the baby elephants, holding their mother's tail in their little trunks. A herd of spotted deer thrilled little Upasana, who was very happy to see so many Shobhnas!

22

SECOND DAWN OF FREEDOM

In June 1975, Justice Sinha of the Allahabad High Court accepted Raj Narain's petition and unseated Prime Minister Indira Gandhi for a couple of minor technical flaws in her election campaign. At the same time, Sarvodaya leader Jai Prakash Narayan's mass movement, calling for 'total revolution', was causing unprecedented fomentation in the country.

On 26 June 1975, two weeks after Justice Sinha's judgement was passed, debarring her from functioning as a Member of Parliament, Indira Gandhi imposed internal Emergency in the country on the pretext of the JP movement. Thousands of opposition leaders and others were jailed without trial, including JP himself.

I was woken up after midnight of 25 June by a telephone call from Haryana's Inspector General of Police, Bajwa. He informed me about the promulgation of Emergency in the country and read out the names of 18 men from Bhiwani district who had to be arrested immediately for anti-national activities. I told him to give the names to the Superintendent of Police, Nakai and ask him to take action. They were picked up on that fateful night.

In the morning, Nakai brought identical cyclostyled orders for my signature and I signed on the dotted line, validating the dark deed done the previous night.

Indira Gandhi's younger son Sanjay launched a country-wide campaign to enforce family planning for those with three or more children, and gave stringent targets to chief ministers. State governments issued instructions enforcing the family planning norm among public servants; those who did not adopt the norm were to be deprived of their salary.

I received Health Secretary V.P. Johar's communication for implementation of family planning norms in all departments of the district. We already had three children; I told Savitri that, being the first citizen of the district, I should be the first to undergo vasectomy. She agreed and accompanied me to the hospital next morning, where Dr Prem Kumar operated upon me.

Bansi Lal had been the country's top performer in major development parameters like rural electrification, roads to every village and extension of irrigation; in family planning, his performance proved to be outstanding as well. In December 1975, Indira Gandhi inducted him into the Union cabinet and gave him the prestigious portfolio of defence minister. Bansi Lal, in turn, crowned his old friend Banarasi Das Gupta the chief minister of Haryana.

•◆

When he left Bhiwani for Delhi, there were two unfinished items on Bansi Lal's agenda. The first item was clearing the town's circular road of encroachments. Two-thirds of this job was complete, one-third remained to be done. The second item was the removal of encroachments around Ghanta Ghar at Loharu Gate; some shops owned by Lala Manoharlal were encroaching on the public road by a yard or two.

Incidentally, Manoharlal was an old friend of Bansi Lal and B.D. Gupta and the two had promised him a grant from the Improvement Trust, to ensure that he suffered no financial loss by this rearrangement. He had agreed to demolish the shops and vacate the public space. However, he reneged on the agreement and alleging mala fide intent against the chief minister, obtained a stay order from the High Court.

The High Court vacated the stay order after the imposition of Emergency in 1975 and Bansi Lal asked his successor B.D. Gupta to have the whole property acquired by the Improvement Trust and create a public park in its place after razing Ghanta Ghar to the ground.

Gupta was beholden to Bansi Lal for making him chief minister; he could not say no to him. The chairman of Bhiwani Improvement Trust, Chamaria, was Gupta's crony. He promptly got a scheme of the Trust prepared accordingly and notified it. The assessed value of the Ghanta Ghar property was about ₹66 lakh. Lala Manoharlal refused to take the money and Chamaria deposited it in his account. The Ghanta Ghar became the property of the Trust.

Chamaria then wrote a letter to me, to provide police protection at the site when Ghanta Ghar was being demolished. He also told Bansi Lal about it, who called me to act on the letter. In turn, I directed the SP to take necessary action and the task of demolition of this signature building of Bhiwani was completed in three days.

Once this was accomplished, Bansi Lal asked me to get the remaining sections of the circular road also cleared of all encroachments. I asked PWD officers to mark the original alignment of the road and delineate the encroachments. Thereafter, accompanied by SDM Singla, I walked down the road and told the residents to voluntarily remove the encroachments within a week and added that if they failed to comply, they would be removed by the authorities.

When the new chief minister, B.D. Gupta, heard about this development in his constituency, he was alarmed. His aides told SDM Singla that the chief minister was upset about this ultimatum and intended to visit the site the next day.

I talked to Guptaji on the phone and reassured him that the

residents were demolishing unauthorized structures of their own volition, without any coercion whatsoever. I requested him to postpone his visit by a week; he said nothing but changed his programme.

In fact, there was a lot of resentment among the residents, but they finally cleared the road in a few days and it was restored to its original condition with a new coat of tar.

•◆

Meanwhile, good sense finally prevailed on Indira Gandhi and on 18 January 1977, she revoked the Emergency. Over 30,000 political leaders and others were released from captivity and elections to Parliament were announced.

There were two main candidates for Bhiwani parliamentary constituency, former chief minister Bansi Lal and Ms Chandravati, a former Congress MLA from Charkhi Dadri. Chandravati was a child widow and a firebrand politician who had hoped to be a minister but was ignored by Bansi Lal. She had joined the Janata Party, the newly formed combine of all opposition parties. Indira Gandhi came to address a public meeting in Bhiwani, canvassing for Bansi Lal.

After polling, the process of counting votes started early in the morning and over half a million ballot papers were scrutinized and counted at the four sub-divisional headquarters. Around midnight, I received the results from all four sub-divisions and handed Chandravati the certificate of victory. The people had voted en masse against the Congress; Chandravati polled over 3,00,000 votes, defeating Bansi Lal by more than 1,65,000 votes.

The election results were cataclysmic. Indira Gandhi, her heir apparent Sanjay and almost all her ministers received a sound drubbing from the people. It was a democratic and bloodless version of qatl-e-aam[120]. The Janata Party won 330 seats in the Lok Sabha while the Congress got 154, mainly from the southern states. It appeared that after breaking the thrall of Emergency, India had awakened into a second dawn of freedom.

Following this, I requested Chief Minister B.D. Gupta to transfer me from Bhiwani. He appointed me director of Public Relations again and I rejoined my old office in the Secretariat in Chandigarh.

There were three contenders from the Janata Party for the prime minister's post—Morarji Desai, Charan Singh and Jagjiwan Ram. In 1947, Mahatma Gandhi had decided in favour of Jawaharlal Nehru and Vallabhbhai Patel had gracefully acquiesced. Now Jaiprakash Narain and J.B. Kripalani chose Morarji Desai, but Charan Singh remained disgruntled.

The new Janata government dismissed the nine state governments ruled by the Congress and brought them under President's rule. Following this development, I requested Governor Jaisukhlal Hathi to transfer me from PR, being a sensitive position, to which I had been appointed by the former chief minister, and he appointed me MD Haryana Seeds Corporation.

Fresh elections were held in these nine states and Congress leaders were swept away into oblivion. It might not have been the 'total revolution' that JP was dreaming of, but there was a total change of guard at the political level. In Haryana, the Janata party won 75 seats in a house of 90 and Devi Lal became chief minister.

Commissions of Enquiry were constituted by the Union government to probe the misdeeds of central and state governments during the

---

[120]Mass slaughter

Emergency period. These Commissions were reminiscent of the Inquisition in the Middle Ages; leaders of the Congress party and IAS officers were arraigned before the Commissions like criminals.

In Haryana, the Devi Lal government registered numerous criminal cases against Bansi Lal and had him arrested and lodged in Bhiwani jail for a night. The next morning, he was paraded in handcuffs through his hometown's bazaar.

In his first press conference in Delhi, Devi Lal had even threatened to put Bansi Lal's competent principal secretary S.K. Misra behind bars.[121] Devi Lal harboured animosity against me too, believing that I was Bansi Lal's favourite officer, and had got a criminal case registered against me in Bhiwani, for acquisition of illegal wealth and corruption. My colleague Prem Prashant, who was deputy commissioner of Hisar at that time, tipped me off about it, and I took anticipatory bail from the High Court.

I was summoned for interrogation by DSP Vigilance, Bhiwani. He accused me of pocketing the proceeds of the three Star Nights which had been organized at Bhiwani during my tenure as deputy commissioner. I told him that the entire proceeds had been donated to the Red Cross Society of the district and a mini railway for children had been built in the Bal Bhawan, besides other projects.

Next, the DSP told me that I had misused the services of the mali[122] of the DC's residence, and had sent him to my farm near Pinjore. That was true: I had sent Ram Adhar for a couple of months to my farm, when my father had been unwell. This was an offence, the DSP said, and I was under arrest. I was saved from humiliation because I had already secured preemptive bail.

Devi Lal was hell-bent on instituting a criminal case against Bansi Lal for demolition of Ghanta Ghar in Bhiwani. However,

[121]S.K. Misra, *Flying in High Winds*, Rupa Publications, p. 86.
[122]Gardener

Bansi Lal had been defence minister at that time, and was not present at the scene when Ghanta Ghar was demolished. Therefore, he could not be made an accused, so I became the convenient replacement.

◆

Justice Jaganmohan Reddy headed a commission to enquire into the demolition of Ghanta Ghar at Bhiwani. The proceedings began in December 1977; I was summoned as the principal accused and my hearing lasted for three days.

After a few preliminaries, Justice Reddy said, 'There is a charge against you, that Ghanta Ghar was demolished on your orders.' I replied that the property had been acquired by the Improvement Trust of Bhiwani for creating a public park and it was the Improvement Trust that had demolished it.

'Following your orders, a large contingent of armed police had been deployed around Ghanta Ghar and you had personally supervised the demolition operation,' Justice Reddy continued.

'The Chairman of the Improvement Trust, Shri Chamaria, had sent me a letter, saying that the Trust had to demolish Ghanta Ghar. He had requested the deployment of police forces at the site, for maintaining public order. I had forwarded his letter to the SP for necessary action and, on the first day of the demolition, I had gone to the site in the company of the SP,' I responded.

'Did you take orders from the chief minister before deputing the police force and beginning the demolition?'

'I did not. The CM's permission was not required. This was a local matter and it was within my competence to depute the police force.'

'Did Defence Minister Bansi Lal ask you to demolish Ghanta Ghar?'

'No, he did not ask me to demolish it. I had received a

phone call from him, informing me that the chairman of the Improvement Trust had sent me a request to deploy police at the site and that I should do as asked. Probably, the chairman had requested him to do it. I had told the defence minister that the letter was received that morning and necessary action was being taken.'

Justice Reddy then showed me a photograph in which a few men were standing on the first floor of Ghanta Ghar during the demolition. Pointing to a man in the photograph, he asked if it was me. I looked at the man; I was not in that photograph and I denied the suggestion.

'But some local officials from Bhiwani have testified that it is you,' Justice Reddy persisted.

'Sir, that is not my picture. You may have me photographed now and get the matter examined by experts. The fact is that I don't feature in this photograph. However, I am not denying that I visited the place. I had gone there in the SP's company while the demolition was going on.'

Justice Reddy also asked me if Bansi Lal had any animosity towards the owner of Ghanta Ghar. I replied that, as far as my knowledge went, both Bansi Lal and his successor B.D. Gupta were good friends of the owner.

Justice Reddy called the chairman of the Improvement Trust a few days later; in my absence. He had nullified all written record and testified that the demolition of Ghanta Ghar was undertaken not on his orders but on the orders of R.S. Varma, DC Bhiwani.

Next, former chief minister B.D. Gupta appeared before Justice Reddy. His government had been dismissed after the Janata party's thundering victory in 1977, and he had turned turtle. In order to save his skin, he was willing to depose against Bansi Lal and everyone associated with him.

Gupta deposed on oath that it was I who, at Bansi Lal's behest, had ordered the demolition and that I never consulted him. He claimed that despite being chief minister, he had to take permission from me before entering Bhiwani.

Justice Reddy did not deem it necessary to call me to cross-examine these witnesses who had made such preposterous allegations against me in my absence. He believed them; he also ruled that contrary to my denial, I was in the photograph that had been shown to me.

Justice Reddy sent a voluminous report to the state government, holding me guilty of demolishing Ghanta Ghar. Such rank injustice from a former judge of the Supreme Court was unthinkable.

•◆

Armed with Justice Reddy's report, the Haryana government registered a criminal case againt me and dangled the sword of suspension over my head. The intention was to browbeat me into submission and compel me to testify against Bansi Lal.

However, when Chief Secretary S.D. Bhambri received the file containing the chief minister's orders to place me under suspension, he called me and asked me to meet the CM personally and explain the matter to him. Devi Lal was camping at Haryana Bhawan in Delhi at that time and I went to meet him reluctantly.

Instead of going into the complexities of the argument about the Improvement Trust acquiring the property, I told Devi Lal that Ghanta Ghar was demolished in compliance of a government scheme and I could not be blamed for it. I used a metaphor to explain my argument: I said that the two-storeyed Haryana Bhawan had been constructed by Bansi Lal, but if he, Devi Lal, ordered me to construct a seven-storeyed Haryana Bhawan in its place, I would demolish it and get the new building constructed.

The logic appealed to Devi Lal; he withheld my suspension orders, but on 23 June 1978, I was transferred from Haryana Seeds

Corporation to a sinecure post of Officer on Special Duty (OSD) Administrative Reforms.

•◆

Next, I was summoned by the Shah Commission and questioned for ordering the arrest of 18 persons in my district under the draconian law, Maintenance of Internal Security Act (MISA), which was passed by Parliament during the Indira Gandhi regime.

Patiala House was packed to capacity with media people and spectatators. I stood in an enclosure, facing the government advocate P.N. Lekhi in an enclosure opposite me.

Justice Shah glared at me and asked, 'Were these 18 people arrested on your orders? What proof did you have against them?'

'I had received a report from the SP,' I replied.

'Did you check its veracity from an independent source?'

'I had received a telephone call from the Inspector General of State Police Bajwa after midnight, informing me that internal Emergency had been imposed and that these 18 persons had to be arrested for being involved in anti-national activities. I told him to give their names to the SP and instruct him to take action. There was no question of checking the veracity of the charges as I had no independent source of information.'

'But they were arrested long before you signed the detention orders?'

'That is probably true, sir. But for that you have to question the S.P.' I pointed him out sitting in the audience. Nakai rose in his seat and bowed to Justice Shah, who shifted his stern gaze to him and gestured at him to sit down.

Lekhi asked me if Defence Minister Bansi Lal had told me to arrest those people. I replied that I had already disclosed who had told me to arrest them.

That was my first appearance; much more was to follow.

Out of the 18 cases from Bhiwani district, two cases of detention in particular, relating to M.D. Dalmia and Pitamber Lal Goyal, received special attention from the Shah Commission.

Dalmia was the head of the Technological Institute of Textiles (TIT) as well as of a textile mill set up by the industrialist K.K. Birla at Bhiwani. R.C.D. Kaushik was the principal of TIT. Kaushik used to indulge in local politics of Bhiwani which was not to the liking of Bansi Lal. He apparently wanted Dalmia to transfer Kaushik from there. Dalmia's failure to do that cost him the detention under MISA.

On 1 June 1978, Dalmia narrated his tale of woe before the Shah Commission, of being lodged in jail for 18 months like a common criminal for no fault of his. K.K. Birla then deposed that he had gone to Shri Bansi Lal 3-4 times to plead before him and soften him but to no avail. Dabriwal, another industrialist who had acted as go-between, then testified that all Bansi Lal had wanted was that Principal Kaushik of TIT should be transferred as he was indulging in local politics. Kaushik was examined thereafter but nobody asked him if he was indulging in local politics. Bansi Lal's lawyer had appeared at the start of the proceedings and had requested for an adjournment on account of the short notice and indisposition of his client. Justice Shah had turned down the request for adjournment and the lawyer had quit.

Superintendent of Police Y.S. Nakai was called then. He made a clean confession that there was no incriminating material against Dalmia in police record and the CID report implicating him in activities prejudicial to the security of India was fabricated at his insistence. CID Inspector Permanand then owned up to the fabrication of the police record.

It was my turn to depose now. Justice Shah grilled me, asking me again and again whether I was personally satisfied that the allegations made against Dalmia were correct and if not, why did I not satisfy myself about their correctness as the law clearly required.

I replied that he was arrested under state government orders after the imposition of Emergency on identical allegations in all the eighteen cases and the report was submitted to me in the morning by the SP in my office after Dalmia and others had already been put behind bars. In the circumstances there was no question of my satisfaction regarding the correctness of allegations, although technically they were arrested under my orders.

Government counsel Lekhi then asked me what kind of a person Bansi Lal's son Surendra Singh was. I asked Justice Shah if the question was relevant; he asked me to reply to it. I thought of parrying the question by saying that Surendra Singh was a public man and did not need any testimonial from me, but I simply said, 'Surendra Singh is a nice person.'

I was allowed to leave after that: I was crestfallen and slightly unnerved.

•◆•

Pitamber Goyal's case was taken up next. Goyal had cleared the examination for entry into the Haryana State Judicial Service in October 1974. A police report of unblemished character was required to be submitted by the SHO concerned, for Goyal to be appointed. However, SHO Harnam Singh had made some adverse entries in the police roznamcha about Goyal's character and his appointment as a judicial officer was stalled.

Harnam Singh appeared before Justice Shah and submitted an affidavit, saying that he had spoiled Goyal's record at my behest. He further alleged that I had asked him to harass Goyal's family members in order to find out his whereabouts, and that he had detained Goyal's father and grandfather at my bidding. This was a bombshell; I was appalled.

Justice Shah asked me to respond to Harnam Singh's deposition. 'That's a lie, sir. I went to inspect Harnam Singh's thana once; that is the only occasion when I met this gentleman, never before or after,' I responded.

The hearing was adjourned for the day at this point and I went to Haryana Bhawan, where I saw Nakai and Harnam Singh together. I accosted Singh immediately; he replied that I had asked him to foul up Goyal's record in the presence of 'SP saab', pointing towards Nakai. I looked at Nakai questioningly and he denied I had ever told him this in his (Nakai's) presence. Singh slinked away.

I had expected to be called by Justice Shah the next day, 7 June. However, he summoned Haryana Chief Secretary S.D. Bhambri that day, for changing the rules with respect to people detained under MISA, so as to debar them from appearing in competitive examinations.

Bhambri stated that Chief Minister B.D. Gupta had instructed him to do so. So, B.D. Gupta was called next. He denied having issued such instructions to the chief secretary and insinuated that Bhambri had probably received direct instructions from Bansi Lal.

Bhambri returned to the witness box, insisting that Gupta was deposing incorrectly; he added that he used to see Bansi Lal only at the behest of Chief Minister Gupta. However, Gupta doggedly stuck to his version and the whole thing became extremely unseemly. At the end of it, Gupta came out as a thoroughly unprincipled and self-serving politician.

At the end of that day, Justice Shah adjourned the Commission for summer recess till 3 July. After a few days, I received a show-cause notice from the Commission about the Pitamber Goyal case.

◆

My next appearance before the Shah Commission was scheduled for 6 July 1978, and I wanted to be well-prepared for it.

I had called for the police record of Pitamber Goyal's case from the SP of Bhiwani. The next day, SHO Sadar, Bhiwani brought the record to me. I also wanted to ascertain the date on which I had inspected Harnam Singh's thana; my former reader Devi Dayal and steno, Hansraj, brought me the necessary records. Hansraj also told me that the task of concocting Pitamber Goyal's adverse report had been masterminded by an officer in the police headquarters at Chandigarh, who had called Harnam Singh there.

I reached Delhi on 4 July and Nakai met me at Haryana Bhawan. He told me that DIG, CID Kalyan Rudra was pressurizing him to support Harnam Singh's version. 'But is it the correct version?' I asked him. 'How can you support it?' He had no answer.

On the day of the hearing, my cross-examination of Harnam Singh went somewhat like this:

'Was there anyone else present when I told you to spoil Pitamber Goyal's record?'

'Jenab, you said it in the presence of S.P. Nakai Sahib Bahadur,' Singh replied.

When I asked Nakai for confirmation, he gave a non-committal answer, 'I don't remember.'

I reverted to Harnam Singh and said, 'My DC office record shows that I had gone to inspect your thana in March 1975.' Singh assented.

'I had never seen you before that,' I continued. Singh assented again.

'However, you made the roznamcha entry regarding Pitamber Goyal in October 1974,' I delivered the clincher. Singh was speechless.

'Sometime later, you were called to Chandigarh by the DIG, CID about this matter, and your statement was recorded there,' I said. Singh agreed.

'But you did not mention anything about me in your statement there,' I declared. Singh was speechless again.

After Singh, I examined Y.S. Nakai and Kalyan Rudra; they

were equivocal in their statements. However, the point had clearly been driven home. Justice Shah mumbled, 'We should have given the notice to the SHO, not him,' and adjourned the proceedings for the day.

Early next morning, I set about writing the arguments I wanted to present before the Commission about this case that had caused such a mental turmoil to me.

I started with Gandhiji's dictum, that to sustain one lie, a person had to invent a hundred others and eventually became trapped in the process, as truth had the uncanny ability of revealing itself. I also intended to quote Justice Shah: 'Written word does not lie; people may.'

It was an effective piece of oratory that culminated with the words: 'The epithets "naxalite" and "communist minded" that chased Pitamber Goyal like fell hounds and barred his entry to the portals of Judiciary, were born in the dark caverns of SHO Harnam Singh's diabolical mind.'

However, I was in for a disappointment: when I rose to present my arguments, Justice Shah looked at me and said in an exhausted voice, 'I don't think we need to trouble you.'

I sat down with the dull pain of stillborn oratory in my heart.

•◆

A few days after my last deposition, on 7 July 1978, I was exonerated by the Shah Commission, after a rigorous and fair enquiry.

I heaved a sigh of relief. That one year, from the time Devi Lal took over as chief minister in June 1977, had been a time of extreme mental turmoil for me. The clouds of gloom finally seemed to scatter.

I contemplated going on the Amarnath yatra. I thought that a pilgrimage would soothe my nerves. The stunning vistas of the snow-bound Amarnath cave in a film I had seen had always haunted me.

Every year in August, the government of Kashmir organized an annual pilgrimage to this Himalayan shrine. I broached my plan to Savitri; she was more than willing to join me. She, too, had been under intense mental pressure because of my persecution and welcomed the idea. She suggested that we visit Vaishno Devi on the way, before undertaking the Amarnath yatra. She had gone to Vaishno Devi as a child, with her parents, and cherished the memory.

Savitri's parents lived in Chandigarh. Leaving our daughters in their care, we boarded the overnight train to Jammu. A bus from Jammu took us to Katra, from where the climb to Vaishno Devi hill begins. There was a huge congregation of people at Katra, devotees who had gathered for the Mata's darshan.

We left our holdall at the Tourist Centre and climbed at a brisk pace, rejoicing in the crisp mountain air. The winding road was overflowing with pilgrims—young and old, men, women and children. There was gaiety and playful bonhomie among the devotees. A young man led a group with his exuberant shouts, exalting the goddess and raising the morale of his group. Savitri joined their group, cheerfully shouting back the refrain.

At Ardhkuwari, there is a narrow circular aperture in a rock which barely allows a man to pass through. Savitri guided me through that dark and claustrophobic space and gave me a look of triumph when we came out on the other side.

We reached Vaishno Devi at nightfall. Just before the Mata's cave, there was a spout of ice-cold water. One had to take a mandatory bath under it and wear new clothes before entering the holy cave. I stripped down to my underpants and ducked under the cold water. When I emerged, I was numb. As I got into my new clothes, my body experienced a hitherto unknown warmth. Savitri also took a quick bath under the spout, her teeth chattering, and went into a cubicle to change into new clothes.

Late at night, we joined the queue of devotees, standing in a knee-deep ice-cold stream coming from the holy cave. The queue seemed to be unending; the path through the tunnel twisted and turned, and the wait seemed interminable. Mata Vaishno Devi was testing the limits of endurance of her devotees—and the depths of their faith.

At last, we reached the end of the queue; we were waiting to enter the small niche for darshan, when a seth arrived, dripping in gold, escorted by a pujari through the exit tunnel. I censured the pujari who claimed that the man was a heart patient; the man in question looked sheepish, and it was obvious that he had bribed his way in.

Savitri and I entered the sanctum sanctorum: water oozed from the rock walls, perennially washing the three egg-shaped white marble stones protruding from the rock. These were the manifestations of the goddess. A couple of priests sat cross-legged. They accepted our gifts with alacrity, tied the sacred thread around our wrists, drew a vermilion mark on our foreheads, sprinkled holy water and gestured us to move on and make way for others. Savitri got down, but I moved to my left, making room for other pilgrims. I continued sitting for a few more minutes, bowing my head in quiet reverence.

It was past midnight when we exited the cave. We ate at a restaurant and came to our room. Wrapping ourselves in smelly blankets, we slept in each other's arms.

The next day, we went up a steep footpath to a shrine dedicated to Bhairon or Bhairav. I had taken a packet of peanuts and baked gram to munch on the way, but it was an ordeal for Savitri: it was Friday, her day of weekly fasting.

It started raining as we began our descent; the gentle droplets soon turned into a downpour. Despite our raincoats, we were drenched and shivering. At about 2 p.m. we reached the Tourist Centre in Katra. Savitri bathed and read the *Vrat Katha* while I freshened up. She finally ate some cold poories after that, and we went to the government restaurant for tea.

The next morning, getting tickets to Srinagar seemed difficult. I had to reveal my identity to the man at the Tourist Reception Centre, who managed to get us the front seat beside the driver.

•◆

The driver was a friendly sort; he talked as he drove, telling us about the beauty of the Kashmir valley and Srinagar's Mughal gardens and the lovely Dal Lake! I had been to Srinagar earlier in a Chief Ministers' Conference, and had seen them all, but did not want to dampen his spirits by disclosing it.

As we approached the Banihal Tunnel, he told us that before the tunnel was constructed, one had to cross the Banihal Pass, which was a narrow road with sharp bends. During winter, it was covered in snow and the valley was cut off from the rest of the world. He added that Jawaharlal Nehru had got the tunnel made in five years, from 1953 to 1958. Savitri was greatly fascinated when we entered the Banihal Tunnel, lit up in pale yellow light.

As we were coming out of the tunnel, the driver veered off the main road to the right, because he wanted to show us the most beautiful part of the Kashmir Valley, Veri Nag, the natural spring and pool from where River Jhelum originates. The Mughal emperor Jahangir had given the natural spring an octagonal shape and created a channel for the stream. A host of multicoloured dahlias swayed along the banks of the rippling channel. The Valley was spread out before us like a green carpet, stretching up to the distant horizon.

We reached Srinagar late in the evening. I took Savitri to a Khalsa dhaba for a meal and then we went to a restaurant in Lal Chowk for Kashmiri cuisine. On a previous visit for a Chief Ministers' Conference, I had sampled a Kashmiri meat dish called gushtaba at that restaurant, which takes a whole day to prepare.

I ordered the same dish, accompanied by rice pulao. It was a superb meal.

After dinner, I coaxed Savitri to have a paan[123]; she had always declined to taste it, but today was special.

The next day, we went on a shikara ride on the Jhelum, but the water was muddy and faeces floated in it. We went downstream to the Maharaja's palace that served as the Assembly Hall. It was a Sunday and the Hall was closed, so we visited the private temple of the Maharaja. The deities were ensconced on gold and silver thrones; Savitri was impressed.

I was fascinated by the rows of old-world houses along the riverbank. There were hundreds of houseboats which served as mobile ration shops.

The journey upstream was tough for the shikara man. He rowed near the bank where the current was not so swift, but there was an awful stink as all lavatories opened into the river. All the romance of boating on the Jhelum thus vanished.

After lunch, we visited Shalimar Garden, which was full of holiday revellers. From there, we went to Nishat Gardens but its water channel had dried up, so we took a shikara ride to Nehru Park, a tiny island on Dal Lake.

The next day, we took a bus to Pahalgam and reached around 2 p.m. There were thousands of pilgrims; the tourist reception centre was full, but I managed to reserve a tent at the Pahalgam Club for the night.

For the three night halts on the Amarnath yatra—Chandanwari[124], Sheshnag and Panjtarani—the government provided accommodation in tents. We had to walk about two miles to book the accommodation. We reached just in time; we were allotted the two last places. I heaved

---

[123]Betel leaf

[124]Chandanwari has since been connected by road

a sigh of relief—Bhole Nath, it seemed, was taking care of us!

Next, we hired a porter to carry our holdall during the yatra. Asif Wani, a lean, boyish-looking man, offered his services.

•◆

Early next morning, we handed over our baggage to Asif at 4 a.m. and set off an hour later. We were part of a river of humanity—thousands of pilgrims and sadhus were on the march. Surrounded by pristine Himalayan landscapes, lofty deodars, gurgling streams and clouds drifting over the mountaintops, it was the most beautiful trek I had ever been on!

We reached Chandanwari in the afternoon and waited for our porter. Apart from his name, we knew nothing about him. I hadn't even asked him his address. Two hours passed; there were fewer pilgrims now, and our anxiety knew no bounds. Suddenly, I saw his lean figure in the distance! Reassured, we headed to the tent colony by the river: I had left the tent reservation paper in the holdall!

We made friends with our tent-mates: the Goenkas from Ahmedabad and the elderly Venkateshwarlu and his wife from Secunderabad. We ate together and went to bed.

There were no toilets for pilgrims, so early in the morning we relieved ourselves in the open like everyone else. Asif arrived at 5 a.m. and we set off.

We climbed steeply for a few miles. Savitri's feet were aching and she walked very slowly, but we did not rest till we had reached the top of Pissu Ghati in about two hours. I realized that we had crossed the tree line, but the hills were covered in green grass and there were tiny flowers blooming on shrubs. Walking slowly but determinedly for a few hours, we reached the emerald green Sheshnag Lake. It stretched till the horizon and reflected the snowy peaks.

The tent colony was a short distance away. The Goenkas were already there and the Venkateshwarlus arrived soon afterwards. We ate at the dhaba of a Sardarji, and as soon as Asif arrived, we spread our bedding and retired for the day.

Chandanwari was at a height of 9,500 feet from sea level and Sheshnag was at 11,730 feet. The next morning, we set off for the Mahaguna Pass, which was at 14,000 feet, and our last camp at Panjtarani.

Savitri was tired after two days of hard trekking: she was out of breath often, and we proceeded with short breaks. Her left foot was bruised and she was limping. We rested for a while at Warbal top, enjoying the magnificent view before us.

The uphill trek to Mahaguna Pass was arduous, but the view from the top was breathtaking, literally and figuratively. Miraculously, there was no wind and the sun was shining brightly. Contrary to my expectation, we did not find snow at the pass.

By the time we reached Panjtarani, the weather had turned menacing. Rumbling clouds had gathered over the pretty spot, where five small glacial streams merge into River Amravati. Thunder, lightning and rain followed, and we huddled with our companions in the tent, sharing whatever food we had carried.

Savitri had fallen asleep; I listened to the news at 9 p.m. on my mini transistor. Chandra Shekhar had decided to step down as president of the Janata Party, in favour of Charan Singh; the warring factions of the Janata Party seemed to have patched up.

•◆

I woke up Savitri at about 1 a.m. and we started for the cave an hour later; we realized that people had started leaving after midnight. The 4-mile-long road to the cave gleamed in moonlight. Walking slowly, we reached Amar Ganga in about two hours and stopped for an icy dip. Then, we changed into new clothes.

After many hours of steep climb, we finally saw the 'cave' after sunrise. The 'cave' was actually a rock formation at the top of a snow-covered cliff, far from our expectation of a hollow beneath the earth's surface; it was a colossal natural wonder.

The 'shrine' was an enormous rectangular space; its ceiling was a gigantic slab of rock with numerous stalactites. Heaps of frozen snow lay on the floor, and stalagmites had formed in many places. We removed our shoes before entering the cave and left our bags outside. As I looked up at the high ceiling, a drop fell on my forehead: it seemed like Lord Shiva had anointed me!

The cave was choc-a-bloc with pilgrims; we were jostled from all sides and carried forward in a crush of people. We couldn't see the Shivling which had formed at the far end of the cave; it had melted and diminished in size as people had been bathing it with the water they had carried from Amar Ganga. We prayed before what remained of the Shivling. Savitri gave the offerings and money to a pujari, who pocketed the money with alacrity and threw the offerings in a huge heap.

We retreated from the cave, wore our shoes, picked up our things and departed. For Savitri, going down the steep slopes was harder than climbing up. Despite moving slow, we reached our tent by noon. It happened to be Friday, Savitri's day of fasting. I sat listening to her katha in the tent. After that, we went out and ate at a dhaba.

The Goenkas and Venkateshwarlus returned after a few hours. They were sorely disappointed, as the Shivling had melted away completely by the time they had reached the cave.

The next morning, the descent began. We walked slowly; our mission had been accomplished. Savitri's face reflected the peace she felt within. By noon, we crossed Mahaguna Pass and reached Sheshnag in the evening.

We faced inclement weather the next day, on the last leg of our adventure. It drizzled continuously, making the descent treacherous. I held Savitri's hand, but she slipped a few times and was miserable.

I could not bear to look at her face, contorted in pain: she had undergone this ordeal for me, in the hope of placating the gods during this stressful phase of my life.

When we reached Chandanwari, we found to our dismay that the tents had been removed. The prospect of walking another 20 miles to Pahalgam was dreadful even to me. Ponies were available on hire, but Savitri was unwilling to take one because it went against her concept of a pilgrimage.

We had plenty of time and the road was even. After a quick rest, we trudged on. Shortly before Pahalgam Club, a charitable organization was offering wholesome, delectable food. We were famished and it seemed like a godsend.

We reached Pahalgam Club by 7 p.m. Asif was already there with our bags, and we paid him his dues. We rented a room at the Club and ordered tea and snacks.

We were in no hurry to return home and stayed another day at the Club, wallowing in the luxury of fulfillment. The Venkateshwarlus were also staying there, and they took us to a Gujrati hotel, where we ate South Indian idlis!

The next day, we went to the Transport Office to reclaim our things; ours was the only baggage still lying there. We took a bus to Jammu, which reached at 11 in the night. After an uncomfortable night at the bus stand, we took another bus to Chandigarh. Thankfully, it was a fast bus and we reached Chandigarh by 3 p.m. We went straight to Savitri's parents' house. The girls had just returned from school; our happiness knew no bounds at being reunited with them.

◆

My persecution had continued unabated in my absence. Police officials inquired into the corruption case registered against me in Bhiwani and the chief minister's advisers continuously pestered me to become an approver in the Ghanta Ghar case and say that it had been demolished on Bansi Lal's orders.

I insisted that I would testify truthfully in court, narrating incidents exactly as they had happened. I refused to become an approver, because that was tantamount to accepting commission of a crime. I was prepared to contest the Reddy Commission's conclusions without giving me a chance to cross-examine Chamaria and B.D Gupta. I was sick of the harassment and desperately wanted to escape this suffocating environment.

I had never availed my Leave Travel Concession (LTC) in 14 years of service, though I was entitled to it once in every four years. I contemplated going on an extended tour of India with the children, during their forthcoming Christmas holidays in 1978.

•◆

My Fiat car, which I had bought when I was director of agriculture, was still brand new; it had run only about 8,000 kilometres in five years. I called my old driver Bahadur from the Agriculture Deparment to take us on an all-India road trip.

The children were thrilled. Vandana was 11 at that time, Jyotsana, 10 and Upasana, 5. I planned a month-long tour, travelling south through central India and returning along the western coast, via Bombay. I wrote letters to district collectors, indicating our approximate dates of arrival and requesting reservations in government rest houses. Savitri packed a kerosene stove, and wheat flour, rice and daal in canisters.

Setting of from Haryana Bhawan one fine morning, we saw the beautiful Deeg Palace, its trellised jharokhas reflected in a lovely lake. Then, we revisited the Taj Mahal in Agra, staring spellbound at the loveliest tribute to Love.

We reached Gwalior, where we visited the imposing ancient fort and saw the beautiful Man Mandir built by Raja Man Singh Tomer.

Our guide also showed us the dark chamber where Aurangzeb's brothers Murad and Dara Shikoh had been imprisoned. Next, we reached Jhansi and saw the ramparts of the fort from where Rani Laxmi Bai had jumped off on horseback, her four-year-old stepson tied to her back.

I had written a letter to Vinoba Bhave's secretary Nirmala Deshpande to meet this greatest disciple of Mahatma Gandhi at Wardha ashram. The gracious lady lodged us in the same room where Indira Gandhi had stayed a few days back! The next morning, we spent an hour with Saint Vinoba. He was keeping a vow of silence that day, but he placed little Upasana in his lap and played with her like a child. Our silent communion was worth a million words.

Our next stop was Secunderabad, where we met our Amarnath yatra friends, the Venkateshwarlus. Our friendship was just a few months old, but it seemed like we had known each other for ages. I was impressed by their simple lifestyle; Venkateshwarlu had retired as a high-ranking officer in the Railways, but his afternoon siesta used to be on a cane mattress on a cemented floor under a fan. They had no air conditioners. We enjoyed a lovely meal with this gracious couple.

We went to Caddapah on the way to Madras, now Chennai. My map had depicted the road as a thoroughfare, but we discovered that it was actually a single road, and that too not in a good condition. As a precaution, I asked a bus driver if the road was motorable. He understood my question but since he did not speak Hindi, he replied laconically in English, 'Express route! Through!'

After driving for a couple of hours, we realized that a stream was flowing across the road. It was a shallow one, meant to be crossed. Unfortunately, just as our car reached the middle of the stream, its petrol tank hit a boulder and the petrol started to leak. The car stalled in midstream and the children panicked. Bahadur and I helped the children and Savitri out of the car, and we waded to safety.

The village folk had reached the scene by then and they helped Bahadur push the car out of the water.

The office of a rural bank was nearby; it had closed for the day. The villagers spread a durrie on the floor of its veranda and invited us to sit. They offered us water and tried to communicate with us, but it was difficult as we did not understand their language and they knew very little Hindi. However, they managed to convey to us that a bus would be passing through in half an hour and the driver should take the petrol tank to the next town for repairs.

Savitri asked Bahadur to bring the stove and the ration canister from the car and she began to prepare dinner. The bus arrived after a while and Bahadur went off with the petrol tank. The news spread and the village folk came in hordes to giggle at us as if we were visitors from another planet!

The weather was pleasant and there were no mosquitoes or flies. Darkness fell, but thankfully there was a light bulb in the verandah. Savitri gave us a royal feast of halwa, parathas and daal. It was 9 p.m. by then, but Bahadur had not returned. Our anxiety was mounting. The village folk assured us that the bus from Madras was yet to arrive. Sure enough, after some time, Bahadur arrived with the repaired and refilled tank. Savitri offered him dinner; then, she held the girls close and within minutes they were fast asleep.

The next morning, the villagers walked ahead of the car through the stream. After a safe crossing, I stepped out and stood before them with folded hands, speechless in gratitude.

We reached Madras by noon, a day or two behind schedule. Luckily, the officer at the circuit house gave us a plush air-conditioned suite. From a veranda to a VIP chamber!

In the evening we frolicked on Marina Beach and Savitri and the girls saw the sea for the first time. The next day, we visited the sky-kissing towers of the Kanchipuram temple and the shore temple at Mamallapuram, as well as the rock carving which depicted the descent of River Ganga. After that, we reached the Sri Aurobindo Ashram in Pondicherry, now Puducherry, where we met the revered Mother. Wearing a white cotton sari, she sat on a takht like Vinoba Bhave. Aurobindo Ghosh had died by then and the dreamworld of Auroville was still gestating in her imagination.

Two or three days later, we reached Kanyakumari, India's southern tip where the Indian Ocean merges with the Bay of Bengal and the Arabian Sea. Half of our pan-India safari was over.

Now, we set off northwards; our first stop was Thiruvananthapuram. Next, we reached Mysore via Ernakulam. In Mysore, we went up a hill to see the Hidimba temple and the giant statue of the demon Mysuru, who had given the city its name. We also visited a zoo where we saw a Royal Bengal tiger catching fish in a water-filled trench.

The next day, we were on the Pune-Bombay road, when suddenly, a bunch of hooligans armed with lathis stopped us. We were on the outskirts of Davangere and they said that we couldn't go further as there was 'galata'[125] in the town. They had blocked the road by placing huge stones and logs on the road. Indira Gandhi had been arrested in Delhi: Davangere was in the Chikmagalur parliamentary constituency, which had elected her after her defeat in Rae Bareli.

I asked Bahadur to enter a house on the left. A hefty man in a lungi stood at the gate. Gesturing to signal my helplessness, I uttered the word 'galata' and he opened the gate. He took us inside his house and asked his wife to fetch water. She hesitated and looking at me said, 'Muslim.' I understood her quandary and said in Hindi, *'Koi baat nahin,'* gesturing that it was okay for us.

She brought water in steel tumblers and a plate of roasted groundnuts; a little later she offered tea to me and Savitri. After we finished our tea, her husband offered to sit in the front seat of our

---

[125]Total ban on traffic

car beside the driver, and escort us through the town. He happened to be the local pehelwan[126]. I wanted to offer some money to his wife but he said, 'You guest,' in English and refused it.

He sat beside Bahadur and all of us squeezed into the back. We were stopped at a few places, but he shouted at the men and shooed them away. He got down at the last checkpoint outside the town and waved us goodbye.

Our next stop was Kohlapur. From there, we started early the next morning and made it to Bombay, now Mumbai, late at night. We had reserved a stay in a multi-storeyed government guest house. Seth Kishori Lal from Bhiwani lived there; one of his sons was married to B.D. Gupta's daughter. Over the next two days, he took us around Bombay: we saw the Gateway of India, Juhu beach, Nariman Point, Chaupatti. He lived by the sea, very close to our guest house, and we really enjoyed his hospitality.

We went to Ahmedabad next, and after checking into a rest house, went to meet the Goenkas, our Amarnath yatra friends. They were delighted to see us and showed us around town the next day. I particularly remember visiting an old mosque that had short 'jhoolti'[127] minarets. The maulvi asked me to enter the minaret on the right. I squeezed myself through its narrow entrance, went up the few circular steps and looked out of its small windows. The maulvi went to the minaret on the left and began shaking it gently with his hands. Wonder of wonders, I could feel my minaret shaking!

We then headed to Udaipur and stayed in a guest house beside the lake. We took a boat to see the dainty Jal Mahal palace, floating in the placid Pichola Lake. The palace hadn't been turned into a hotel at that time.

The next day, we drove straight to Delhi, bypassing Jaipur. Our

---

[126]Muscleman

[127]Swaying

momentous pan-India sojourn had ended. After one month on the road, Haryana Bhawan seemed dearer than home.

•◆

The world of politics had been in constant turmoil, through the length of my persecution and our travels.

Within a few months of coming to power, the Janata Party had developed internal fissures. Charan Singh had not reconciled to playing second fiddle; he wanted to become prime minister. In the realignment of forces, the Jan Sangh faction supported Morarji Desai, while the socialists sided with Charan Singh. In Uttar Pradesh and Haryana, the Jan Sangh ministers were shown the door, while in Bihar, Jan Sangh ousted Chief Minister Karpoori Thakur. Charan Singh levelled allegations of corruption against Morarji's son Kanti and, in June 1978, Morarji sacked Charan Singh. Six months later, Charan Singh stormed Delhi on his birthday, on 23 December 1978, with millions of his supporters from UP and Haryana, who swarmed Rajpath like locusts. Morarji had to eat humble pie; he reinstated Charan Singh and his government became a joke.

There was also a corresponding schism in Haryana. The Janata Party had won an overwhelming majority of 75 members in a house of 90. Despite that, before the Assembly session of January 1978, 43 Janata legislators submitted a memorandum to the party high command, expressing 'no confidence' in Devi Lal. He managed to weather that storm and the subsequent one in May 1978. The third 'Operation Topple' was masterminded by Bhajan Lal in June 1979, with the blessing of Prime Minister Morarji Desai. A fortnight before the Assembly session was due to start, he took the rebel MLAs on a kind of Bharat Darshan to undisclosed destinations. Devi Lal was left high and dry. He resigned on 25 June, one day before the session. Bhajan Lal made a triumphant return with the supporting legistators and was sworn in as Chief Minister on 28 June 1979.

My persecution came to an end with the departure of Devi Lal. I was allotted government accommodation in Sector 16, adjacent to the Rose Garden. I think Le Corbusier was inspired by the famous Hyde Park of London, and placed the Rose Garden in the centre of Chandigarh. Or he might have taken the idea from Central Park of New York. The Rose Garden was the fragrant heart of the town. We began living just a few steps away from paradise.

23

UPS AND DOWNS IN THE BHAJAN LAL REGIME

Bhajan Lal again appointed me director of PR, Tourism and Cultural Affairs, taking me out of the dumps that Devi Lal had thrown me into. Immediately after taking oath, Bhajan Lal went to Bombay to call on JP, who was residing with the press baron, Ramnath Goenka, in his penthouse at the top of Express Towers. Bhajan Lal took me along and I had the opportunity of meeting the great man. He was sick, looking crumpled and crestfallen. Bhajan Lal touched his feet and was at pains to explain why it was necessary to oust Devi Lal. JP heard him in silence and said in a feeble voice, 'Unity *banaye rakhiye.*'[128] It was a cry from a bleeding heart.

Just after a fortnight of the fall of the Devi Lal government, on 15 July 1979, the Morarji Desai government fell on a no-confidence motion tabled in Parliament by the Congress. It was Charan Singh's retort to Morarji for having ousted Devi Lal. Indira Gandhi propped up Charan Singh, fulfilling the Jat leader's lifelong ambition of becoming the prime minister. On 15 August 1979, Charan Singh addressed the nation from the ramparts of the Red Fort. However, five days after that, Indira Gandhi withdrew the crutches and he fell like Humpty Dumpty. Finally, she had the last laugh.

[128]Maintain unity

This time my journalist friends asked me to take them on a tour of Goa. That was unusual; I had been taking them to Kullu and Manali on the pretext of visiting the Sutlej-Beas Link Project, but Goa did not fit in. I asked them to make a personal request to the chief minister: He was an obliging man, surely he wouldn't refuse.

Bhajan Lal instructed me to take the press team on a week's trip to Goa. I asked him to speak to the Lt. Governor of Goa, Col. Partap Singh, a Chandigarh native and a friend of his. He spoke to him and our contingent of about 12 members stayed in the guest house of the picturesque Raj Bhawan at the mouth of the Mandovi.

We explored Panaji the day after our arrival, and in the evening we went to Colva beach. Some of them had never been to a beach before and went wild with joy as the waves crashed at their feet. We frolicked in the silvery sand, going up and down with the waves. At sunset, a golden glow spread on the sea and the sky and we watched the scene mesmerized as the sun's golden orb dipped in the heaving ocean.

The next day, we went to Calangute beach, which was even more picturesque. Many people were swimming in the sea and about six of us jumped in. Swimming is easier and very pleasurable in seawater. I had asked my friends to stay close to the shore, but the waves carried them away. I went after them, gesticulating frantically at them to return to shore; soon, I was in the same predicament, inexorably pulled inwards. Fortunately, we were able to return to shore after about 10 minutes of vigorous swimming.

On their return, the gentlemen of the press thanked Bhajan Lal profusely. The tenor of their despatches about his government's functioning changed radically; it was now marked by a eulogistic flavour.

Mid-term elections to Parliament were held in January 1980 and Indira Gandhi returned with a thumping majority. The wheel had come full circle.

The resurgence of Indira Gandhi sounded the death knell for Bhajan Lal. He was in Delhi when the election results were announced; I was sitting with him. He turned to me and said, *'Yeh to bada jhamela ho gaya, Varmaji; ab kya karen?'*[129]

'Sir, you should go and present a grand bouquet of roses to her on her grand victory,' I replied. 'She is very fond of roses.' He was almost the first to congratulate her in person.

After she had taken over as prime minister, Bhajan Lal took his cabinet colleagues and his party MLAs to Indira Gandhi's residence, carrying a bigger bouquet of roses. Presenting the bouquet to her, he said, '*Madam, hum apne ghar wapas aa gaye hain.*'[130] She beamed a radiant smile and was happy to accept his 'gift'.

Indira Gandhi was contemplating the dismissal of all the 10 Janata state governments in the country. She did not have to go to the trouble of dismissing the Haryana state government and holding fresh elections there: the government had changed colour and become a Congress government! Till then, only individual MPs or MLAs had defected, now a state government had done the same.

All the cases against IAS officers, initiated on the basis of the reports of the Shah and Reddy Commissions, were closed by Bhajan Lal. As regards the corruption case registered against me, the chief secretary got it enquired and I was asked to deposit an amount equivalent to two months' salary of the mali who had stayed at my farm. Thereafter, the case was closed.

One day in June 1980, the Superintendent of Police of Karnal district, Nirmal Singh, called on Bhajan Lal to show him evidence

---

[129]'This is a big mess. What should we do now?'

[130]'Madam, we have come back to our home.'

of petty corruption on the part of DC Karnal, Pius Pandarwani. The SP wanted to register an FIR against the deputy commissioner.

Bhajan Lal called me and showed me the evidence, which was the personal diary of the contractor of a Red Cross fair. It had two hand-written entries showing payments made to the deputy commissioner's wife. I advised the CM against registering an FIR, as the reputation of the DC and the state government would be tarnished. I advised him to remove Pandarwani from his post and give him an oral dressing down.

That evening, as I was about to leave for home, the CM summoned me again. He told me that he had accepted my advice and was transferring me in Pandarwani's place.

This was a bolt from the blue: I had already completed 16 years in the IAS and our batch was up for promotion to the grade of Commissioner.

•◆

Karnal used to be a large district in those days. The three districts of Panipat, Kurukshetra and Kaithal have since been carved out of it.

It is the most fertile part of Haryana and was selected for the introduction of high-yielding varieties in the initial days of the Green Revolution.

The day after my arrival in Karnal, I convened a meeting of the officers posted at Karnal, mainly to acquaint myself with them. SP Nirmal Singh gave me a broad smile.

The PWD rest house near the DC's residence in Karnal became my new office-cum-residence. I had asked my PA in Chandigarh to send a message to Pandarwani, asking him to take his time in vacating the house.

A couple of days later, in the dead of night, there was desperate knocking at the door of the first-floor room where I was sleeping. When I opened the door, I saw a horrific sight of a blood-splattered young man lying on the floor. He had bullet wounds on his body. He told me that dacoits from across the Yamuna had entered their house, in a village near the river's bank. They had killed his father and decamped with money and jewellery. I asked my security guards to take the man to the SP's house across the road and request the SP to talk to me.

Nirmal Singh called me in a few minutes, to say that he was taking the man to his village and would have to go to UP in pursuit of the dacoits. I told him to let these johnnies have a taste of the mettle of the Karnal police. He came back three days later, after tracking down and capturing the desperadoes.

Eventually, I moved into the DC's residence when the Pandarwanis left. I had visited the house before, when Sukhdev Prasad and H.D. Goswami had been deputy commissioners. It was a comfortable British-era house; Savitri and the girls enjoyed visiting it on weekends.

◆

Rains had started some time after my arrival in Karnal. There was good rainfall in July and August, and it continued unabated till the end of September, causing floods in large areas around Asandh. Paddy fields became inundated, damaging the crop. Fortunately, we did not need to evacuate people, except from a few villages, and were able to provide aid and succour to those who required them. The governor inspected the flood-hit areas in September.

While the district was reeling under the effect of the floods, I earned the displeasure of MLA Hari Singh Nalwa in a curious case of alleged embezzlement. Generally, MLAs are sympathetic towards sarpanches and plead for them, but Nalwa felt the opposite towards a young sarpanch of a village called Oonjha in his constituency.

The sarpanch told me that he had been suspended a couple of years ago; the BDO had enquired into the charges and had sent a report, exonerating him of the allegations, had been received in my office. I perused the file: there were several charges of defalcation against him. The BDO had analysed each charge and the evidence related to it carefully and found no substance in any of them and had recommended the reinstatement of the sarpanch. The district development officer had endorsed the BDO's report. I saw no reason to differ and ordered his reinstatement.

Immediately, Nalwa came to meet me. Fuming, he said that I had committed a grave error by reinstating a scoundrel. I told him that all the charges of defalcation had been found baseless, no dishonesty had been proved and the young sarpanch appeared to be a good worker. Nalwa alleged that the man had bribed the BDO; I shrugged my shoulders.

The chief minister landed at Karnal airport after a few days: He wanted to make an aerial survey of the flood-affected areas and took me along with him. After the survey, we landed at the Safdarjung airport. I accompanied the CM to Haryana Bhawan. When we entered the CM's suite, Hari Singh Nalwa was already sitting there. While sipping tea, Nalwa broached the topic of the young sarpanch whom I had reinstated. I explained the whole matter to the CM.

Nalwa then took out a sheaf of papers from his pocket and told me that they contained new allegations against the sarpanch. I took the papers from him and said that I would have them enquired. Nalwa retorted angrily, 'Enquiry can be done later; first you have to suspend him immediately!'

No one had ever spoken to me in that dictatorial manner and I felt insulted. Turning to the CM, I handed the papers to him and said, 'Sir, please find a new DC for this job.' I rose and left the room, got into my car and returned to Karnal.

Two months later in January 1981, I was transferred to Chandigarh as State Transport Commissioner.

There were over 2,000 buses in the Haryana Roadways fleet when I became State Transport Commissioner, and it was considered to be an efficient public enterprise. It carried about 7 lakh passengers in a day and there were 10 depots in the state, administered by Haryana Civil Service (HCS) officers. The depots ran buses on common routes at different timings and there was a healthy rivalry among them.

The main problem was cheating by bus conductors in issuing tickets, causing loss of revenue. Random checking was done by mobile inspectors and the bus conductors found guilty were placed under suspension by GMs. The suspended employees used to submit mercy petitions to the CM, taking a few of his supporters along with them and in many cases a 'directive' was issued from the CM's office to reinstate them. These directives had piled up on my desk.

One day, I was summoned by the CM. I asked his PS what the occasion was. He told me that it was about the directives sent to me for reinstating the bus conductors, so I carried the bundle with me. The CM complained that I was not carrying out his orders, I showed him the bundle and explained that it wasn't possible to do so. He was himself greatly surprised to see the huge pile. He carefully examined them, selected three and gave them to me and said, 'You reinstate these.' The directives were few and far between after that.

I was actually wearing two hats at that time. Apart from being the operator of the state transport, I was also the regulator of motor transport in the state, controlling goods transport by trucks. There were four Regional Transport Authorities (RTA) which registered all new vehicles and issued temporary permits to private trucks for operating outside the state. They also collected tax from incoming trucks at state barriers. They were hotbeds of corruption.

In a bid to streamline goods transport in the country, the Union Ministry of Transport devised a scheme of National Permits which were to be issued to such trucks as had obtained the highest number of temporary permits. The sign 'N/P' was to be painted boldly on such trucks and they were to be allowed unhindered passage throughout the country. Four hundred national permits were given to Haryana.

I asked the RTAs to prepare a list of trucks which had obtained temporary interstate permits in the last two years and sent the staff officer, Jagga, to check these lists and prepare a combined seniority list. In the meanwhile, the chief minister gave me a long list of trucks. He told me they had to be issued national permits. I argued that only those which had been carrying goods outside the state and had obtained the highest number of temporary permits were eligible. But my argument did not cut much ice with him. I explained to him that it was a judicial order and if ineligible trucks were issued national permits, the high court would reverse it. 'So what?' he said, '*Apni tau baat rah jayegi.*' 'No, Sir,' I replied, 'my own reputation is at stake. But I will try to accommodate where there is a minor difference.'

While the process of selection was going on, the CM went to the US for a fortnight for eye treatment. I issued the permits according to the composite seniority list, while accommodating about 30 most deserving names from the CM's list.

Bhajan Lal was furious when he returned. Within a couple of days, I was transferred and appointed Officer on Special Duty (OSD), Land Use Board.

◆

The chief minister was also the chairman of the Land Use Board; the OSD functioned as its secretary. Several ministers and secretaries of important departments were its members.

Land use was undergoing constant change in Haryana; new urban centres and industrial complexes were coming up, highways were being broadened and new roads being laid. The Board's office received information from all departments about these developments and maintained updated statistics. Once a year, the Board held a meeting where the secretary made a presentation, underpinning the changes which had taken place during the year. His office was located in a sprawling private building in Sector 17.

The Board's office was, more appropriately, a 'cell': I discovered that it consisted of a superintendent and two assistants. It was a part of the office of the Joint Secretary of Rural Development, Sharad Maheshwari, who was junior to me by a few years.

At that time, I was living in a government house which was allotted to me a few years ago, close to the periphery of the Rose Garden in Sector 16. On a sunny September morning, I took the meandering footpath through the rosebeds and reached Sharad Maheshwari's office and told him that I had come to relieve him of the heavy burden of the Land Use Board. He laughed heartily and called for coffee. His assistant brought my joining report and the superintendent came and introduced himself.

Maheshwari offered to set up a nice room for me, adjacent to his own. 'That would be a waste,' I replied. 'I don't intend to sit here all day, twiddling my thumbs. I'll come in the morning, have a cup of coffee with you, see if there were any letters for me and be off, if that's not very inconvenient for you.' Maheshwari chuckled in amusement.

While returning, I watched a charming dance performance by a monkey couple in the plaza. Savitri was surprised by my early return. I read the newspapers, had an early lunch with her and went up to the bedroom for a siesta. The girls returned from school in the afternoon. I woke up hearing their merry chatter and came down. They were surprised to see me and squealed with delight. In the evening we all went for a stroll in the Rose Garden.

My dormant creative faculties were aroused by this new leisure. I began writing 'middles' for *The Tribune.* Its editor Prem Bhatia liked my flippant pieces and I began churning them out regularly. I sent some to my old friend, B.G. Verghese, who published them in *The Indian Express*.

The biggest advantage of this new routine was a daily stroll in the Rose Garden in the company of my children, in the evening. We would bend down and fill our lungs with the fragrance of the roses, discuss their comparative merits and then select the three best varieties among the ones inspected by us that day. This exercise required smelling the roses over and over again. What bliss!

•◆

One evening, some time in June 1982, while we were having tea with our neighbour, Chief Judicial Magistrate Sadhu Ram Bansal, he advised me to request the chief minister for a good post. I smiled and said, 'I have never had such a good post and I am thoroughly enjoying it. It's like a dream—no work and full pay! What can be better than this?'

'Don't be funny; this is no post for your calibre.'

'There is nothing either good or bad; only thinking makes it so, as Shakespeare said,' I responded.

'You are kidding, Varma Sahib. All officers go to the chief minister and request him for a good post. In fact, Mr Ojha (Principal Secretary to CM) has asked me to speak to you.'

'That's very kind of him, but you know that I've never asked anyone for a post. I am not boasting, but it's true that God has given me so much, far more than I deserve, without me asking Him for anything. You ask Savitri, I never do any *puja-paath. Ooper wale ke aage haath nahin failate, toh bandon ke aage kya haath failana?*'[131]

Savitri frowned at me and changed the topic.

•◆

[131]When you don't beg even from God, why beg from mere men?

A few months later, Bhajan Lal added some new ministers to his cabinet, including Bansi Lal's dashing son Surendra Singh. At the swearing-in ceremony, Surendra Singh told me that his father had asked Bhajan Lal to give me a decent job. I smiled and replied that he had already given me a very good job. Surendra Singh had a hearty laugh.

Within a couple of days, in September 1982 I was appointed MD of the Haryana Warehousing Corporation (HWC). Having been Director of Agriculture, I was fairly conversant with the activities of HWC.

Before the start of the next procurement season, after the harvesting of the Ravi crop, the chief minister convened a meeting and observed that there was, invariably, a glut in the mandis[132] due to the arrival of large quantities of wheat and stressed the need for expediting the procurement process. I pointed out that HWC had warehouses in all major mandis but our staff was not involved in the procurement process. I suggested that like the Agro Industries Corporation, HWC should also be involved in procurement to expedite it. The CM agreed and allotted 10 per cent of the total procurement to HWC. Consequently, our balancesheet recorded significantly higher profits that year.

◆

One of the perks of my job was an expense account for entertainment of guests of the Corporation. On a Saturday evening, I asked my staff to send printed dinner invitations to my wife and children by name. The girls were thrilled; they had never received such an honour before. They thought it would be a big party and wondered who else was invited. I quipped, 'Let's see.'

Only five of us turned up, but the party was a roaring success.

[132]Wholesale markets

At the end, I raised a toast to the chief minister, saying, '*Bhala ho Bhai Bhajan Lal ka!*' (God bless Bhai Bhajan Lal!)

The younger guests responded, 'Hooray!'

•◆

I availed another Leave Travel Concession for a journey to the Andaman and Nicobar Islands in November 1983. We travelled by train to Madras, where my batchmate Selveraj was Chairman of the Madras Port Trust. We stayed at the seaside Port Trust guest house for a few days and explored the city, discovering South Indian cuisine, soaking in the culture and romping on Marina Beach and enjoying the sea breeze. From Chennai, we boarded a ship named Nancowri, and sailed for the Andaman and Nicobar Islands.

It was our first sea voyage. We stood on the deck as the ship left the dock, watching hundreds of people wave goodbye from the shore. We watched the shore gradually receding into the horizon, before disappearing altogether.

Eventually, the blue canopy of the sky and sea stretched around us in all directions; it seemed like we were in the dead centre of the universe. The motion of a train becomes evident from the trees rushing past and that of a plane is indicated by the clouds and the earth gliding past, but there is nothing to register the ship's advance till it nears land. No matter how fast the ship moved, it appeared stationary. It was a strange phenomenon.

Towards the evening of the second day of our voyage, we neared the Nicobar Islands. Some people alighted, others boarded. The next morning we docked at Port Blair, where we visited the Cellular Jail; the seven wings of this three-storeyed British-era prison intersect at a central watchtower. We were reminded of the sacrifices of the many freedom fighters who had been sentenced to solitary confinement here.

On our journey back to the mainland, my daughters befriended the cabin crew and told them that they were visiting from Chandigarh.

24

PROMOTION AND ADMONITION

In 1984, our entire batch, barring me, was promoted to the super timescale of the IAS. I received a 'love letter' from Chief Secretary P.P. Caprihan, saying that while the overall assessment of my work in the previous year was 'Good,' my integrity was considered 'Doubtful' according to the last confidential report.

I made a representation refuting the allegation and asked that any specific act of dishonesty be pointed out, so that I may rebut it effectively. After a delay of a few months, my representation was accepted and on 13 June 1984, I was transferred from HWC and appointed Commissioner and Special Secretary of Administrative Reforms in the super timescale of the IAS, and I was reimbursed the arrears of my salary.

Six years back, in June 1978, Devi Lal had posted me OSD Administrative Reforms. This was just a 'cell' in the Chief Secretary's office. Now Bhajan Lal appointed me its Special Secretary deeming it to be a full-fledged department.

In October 1984, Prime Minister Indira Gandhi was assassinated by her Sikh bodyguards and her son Rajiv Gandhi succeeded her. He spearheaded a programme of reforms in the government, aimed to eradicate corruption.

The former Union Home Secretary in the central government,

S.M.H. Burney, had been appointed the governor of Haryana, and in August 1985, he delivered an address to the ministers and secretaries, stressing on the importance of rooting out corruption. As special secretary of administrative reforms, I drafted the minutes, and after approval from the chief secretary, circulated them for necessary action to all secretaries to the government, making sure that they were marked 'secret and confidential'.

The next morning, *The Statesman* carried a lead story on its front page about the governor's address, quoting the minutes verbatim. The report gave a slant that the governor was pointing an accusing finger at the Bhajan Lal government. Its correspondent, Prem Kumar, was my friend, and lived in a government house opposite mine. He had a penchant for scoops of this sort.

Bhajan Lal was livid; he suspected that I had intentionally leaked it. He asked the chief secretary to enquire. Caprihan called me and I told him that I was as clueless as anyone else. I added that the minutes had been delivered personally to the secretaries, maintaining secrecy.

Caprihan called Prem Kumar, but he refused to divulge his source. A few months later, Prem Kumar told me that his source had been M.G. Devasahayam, a former Army officer who had been assigned to the 1964 batch of the IAS and had eventually become a secretary.

A few days after this incident, I was appointed Secretary of the Housing, and Printing and Stationary Departments.

At this time, Prime Minister Rajiv Gandhi had announced a 20-Point Programme, emphasizing on socio-economic issues like poverty eradication, employment generation, housing, health and drinking water. I was appointed the commissioner of this programme implementation; I had to collect monthly data about the progress achieved by concerned departments and transmit it to the Union government.

In December 1985, I again availed of a Leave Travel Concession to visit Lakshadweep[133] Islands on the western coast of the Indian peninsula.

We visited Cochin, now Kochi, for a couple of days before taking a ship to Kavaratti Island, headquarters of the Lakshadweep Union Territory. We stayed with Omesh Saigal, an old batchmate who was the Administrator at that time.

As Administrator, Omesh was the Chief Secretary, Chief Minister and Lt Governor rolled into one. He used to attend the chief ministers' as well as governors' conferences in Delhi. Once, in a chief ministers' conference, Chief Minister Bhajan Lal had taken umbrage at Omesh's lengthy speech, who had then proceeded to point out that the territorial extent of Lakshadweep was far greater than that of Haryana. By inference, he had indicated to Bhajan Lal that he was entitled to longer speaking duration.

Omesh used to fly the tricolour on his sleek official car when going in the morning from his house to his office about 2 kilometres away on the other side of Kavaratti island, meandering through the palm trees, and returned for lunch in style. Mrs Saigal was a cheerful lady who enjoyed her stay in Lakshadweep, unmindful of her seclusion. She was also a great hostess and offered us delicious Punjabi food during our stay.

The Saigal children were of the same age as ours. We spent a fun-filled week with them, swimming, sailing and coral-watching in glass-bottomed boats.

•◆

The post of Managing Director of the Central Warehousing Corporation (CWC) in the government of India was vacant at that time. Although I had not applied for the job, I was called

[133]Sanskrit: Laksha Dweep—one hundred thousand islands.

for an interview by the Public Enterprises Selection Board and was selected for the job.

This new appointment appeared like divine intervention; finally, I escaped the stultifying atmosphere of the Haryana government. I drove to Delhi posthaste and took over my new assignment on 13 May 1986, the very day I was relieved by the Haryana government. The post had been vacant for the last six months and I got into action like a hungry tiger.

Alas, it proved to be a 20-day wonder!

•◆

Meanwhile, the political cauldron had again started boiling in Haryana.

In an attempt to undo some of the damage done to Sikhs in the aftermath of the assassination of Prime Minister Indira Gandhi, Rajiv Gandhi reviewed the award that Indira Gandhi had given in January 1970, on the division of Punjab and Haryana.

He signed the Rajiv-Longowal Accord with Sant Harcharan Singh Longowal, President of Akali Dal. Indira Gandhi's Award had stipulated that Chandigarh would go to Punjab after a new capital city for Haryana was built within five years with the Centre's financial support, and the Hindi-speaking areas of Fazilka and Abohar would be transferred to Haryana in lieu of Chandigarh by creating a six-kilometre-long strip for geographical contiguity. The new accord watered down several clauses of the Indira Award which favoured Haryana.

In his anxiety to please Punjab, Rajiv Gandhi caused widespread resentment in Haryana. Devi Lal seized the opportunity and began holding political rallies which attracted mammoth crowds. Haryana Assembly elections were due in less than a year and Rajiv Gandhi realized that Devi Lal would sweep these elections. To forestall Devi Lal's resurgence, and to counter Bhajan Lal's growing unpopularity, he sent Bansi Lal to Chandigarh.

Bansi Lal was the Union Transport Minister at that time, controlling the Railways, Road Transport and Shipping. On 4 June 1986, he rang me up and asked me if I would like to come back to Haryana as his Principal Secretary. He knew about my transfer to Delhi, as I had called on him after joining my new post. Although I had a great job in Delhi, I was tempted by his offer. I requested him for some time to think about it.

I discussed the offer with Savitri. She had grown up in Chandigarh and her parents lived there. She had been dreading the prospect of moving to Delhi. Her choice was very clear.

I was unsure of being relieved from my post, especially since the office had been vacant for the last six months, and I expressed my misgivings to Bansi Lal. When he assured me that he would arrange everything if I accepted the offer, I realized how greatly he prized my work. I accepted his offer without hesitation.

By the end of that day, I was relieved of my charge, and I drove to Chandigarh in Bansi Lal's convoy.

◆

Bhajan Lal's sudden ouster and Bansi Lal's return as chief minister caused an unprecedented turmoil in Haryana's politics. An equal amount of turmoil was caused in the bureaucratic circles by my return from the government of India within less than three weeks, that too in the avatar of the CM's principal secretary.

Last month, Chief Secretary Caprihan had been preparing to chargesheet me for misconduct, at Chief Minister Bhajan Lal's behest. However, after receiving the letter of my appointment from the government of India, he immediately shelved the chargesheet and promptly relieved me as good riddance.

Caprihan must have known about Bansi Lal's return to state politics, but my return as his principal secretary was a shock.

After Bansi Lal's gala swearing-in ceremony, he turned to me and reluctantly extended his hand, mumbling congratulations. I could discern a faint, forced smile softening his stern countenance.

◆

Bansi Lal concentrated on the completion of the Sutlej-Yamuna Link (SYL) Canal, which was to bring Haryana's due share of water from the Anandpur hydel channel in Punjab. Indira Gandhi had laid SYL's foundation in April 1982 in Punjab and considerable progress had been achieved in its 91-kilometre stretch in Haryana.

Bansi Lal started construction in double shifts, in the hope of completing the canal in Haryana before elections. However, a larger section of 121 kilometres lay in Punjab and work on that stretch had come to a standstill after terrorists had shot dead the chief engineer.

◆

By virtue of being the CM's principal Secretary, my predecessor B.S. Ojha had also been the President of the Haryana Olympic Association. Deputy Commissioners are presidents of District Olympic Associations and they elect the state president, and I was eventually elected in Ojha's place. This was an unexpected perk for a man like me, who had merely played gillidanda in his school days and had no time or inclination for other games or sports during his academic career.

The next Olympic Games were to be held in Seoul in South Korea. I led the Haryana team, along with M.S. Malik, DIG CID, who was the general secretary of the association. We travelled business class in a Thai Airlines flight to Bangkok. It was my first international flight, and after a couple of days in Bangkok, we went to Seoul.

The huge Indian contingent was led by former Union Minister

V.C. Shukla, President of the Indian Olympic Association. Our team put up an impressive show at the inaugural march past, but was pitifully ineffective in performance—not even a bronze medal! In comparison, the hosts, despite being a tiny country, put up a spirited performance.

•◆

Soon, the Haryana Assembly elections came around. Although Bansi Lal had earned the reputation of being the 'vikas purush' of Haryana, he proved ineffectual in the political arena and couldn't even retain his own seat. All his ministers were trounced, only Tayyab Hussain won in Taoru. It was Devi Lal all the way, and his Lok Dal-BJP alliance won a record four-fifth of the seats in the Assembly. 'A political hurricane has lashed Haryana!' *Hindustan Times* commented.

Change in the political complexion of the government invariably results in the overhaul of the administrative machinery: officers manning important positions are relegated to the sidelines. This change is not very marked in the central government, where it remains confined to the PMO and the secretaries attached to the ministers, but it is particularly noticeable in the states, where there are wholesale transfers of officers in almost all major departments.

•◆

Having been Bansi Lal's principal secretary, I was the most likely target of Devi Lal's wrath. However, now in his second ascendance to power, he appointed me the Chairman of Haryana Electricity Board—the most challenging job in government at that time. My appointment surprised all my colleagues; it surprised me most of all. Indeed, I had never suspected the old man of harbouring such admiration for my capabilities! When I called on him, he told me: '*Kaam tau Misra aur tum karte the, aur naam Bansi Lal ka hota tha.'* (The real work was done by you and Misra, and the credit went to Bansi Lal).

Electricity boards have since been 'reformed' and independent corporate entities for production, transmission and distribution have been created. In those days, the Board was a gargantuan conglomerate and Devi Lal gave me a free hand to run it.

We were not able to meet even half of our power demand at that time, from our own generation and our shares in NTPC and hydel power projects. The rural feeders, therefore, remained cut off from morning till evening. Devi Lal told me to stop this injustice to rural areas immediately, but our engineers were not prepared. The charge per unit from the industrial sector was ₹3, against a mere 30 paise from the rural sector. The Board's financial condition was already critical; opening the rural sector during the day would be disastrous. The Board would sink, the senior engineers who were Board members warned. However, simultaneous power supply to rural areas was the main agenda of Chief Minister Devi Lal and he had asked me to accomplish it at once. We went ahead and did it within a week.

I called on the chairman of the Central Electricity Board, who hailed from Haryana, to bear with us and allow excess withdrawals from the grid.

I informed Devi Lal that the discrimination against the rural sector had been removed. He didn't quite believe it. While going on a tour, he would ask his driver to go into a random village and stop at the chaupal. On seeing the chief minister's cavalcade the village folk would assemble at the chaupal in no time. The CM would ask in his booming voice, *'Kyon? Bijli aati hai?'* (Do you get electricity?) A man would stand up and press the switch, switching on the bulb, and say, *'Dekh le, tau, chass ri sai.'* (Look here, Uncle, it's on.) The CM would rise to go then, saying, '*Mauj karo*!'(Enjoy your self!) and the crowd shouted, 'Tau Devi Lal Zindabad!'

One evening when I returned from office, he gave me a call inviting me to his house. He was sitting on the terrace near a heap of watermelons. 'I have brought these for you from your state Rajasthan. I know you love them.' He asked his attendent to slice one melon. He took the slice from him and tasted it. 'No,' he told him, 'cut that one,' pointing out another melon. He tasted the slice but wasn't quite satisfied. 'No, cut that one.' He tasted the slice and said, '*Yeh khilao Sahib ko.*' (Serve this to Sahib). For about half an hour he feted me in this manner with watermelons as a reward for the improvement in power supply to the villages. As I took his leave, he asked the attendant to fill up my car's boot with melons.

Our field officers used their clout to get postings in the industrial and urban centres; no one wanted to serve in rural areas. I streamlined that, transferring staff who had been sitting in urban areas for three years or more to rural areas, and vice versa.

The Board was short of staff and needed 200 electrical engineers. We invited applications from fresh graduates from the best institutions in the country, made a merit list and recruited the top 200 candidates, forgoing the formality of holding an interview. It saved about 3 months, the time required to call and interview the thousands of applicants, and prevented the bias that came into play during interviews.

Work on constructing a new 210 MW machine had started a few years back; it was expedited and the machine was commissioned within two years. The Board was functioning from hired offices; the construction of Shakti Bhawan in Panchkula had started some years ago, but the project was mired in numerous problems. I got our own civil engineering unit to complete the job and Shakti Bhawan was inaugurated by the chief minister within five months of my appointment. The Board began functioning under one roof, benefitting from the synergy of greater cohesion among its administrative units. In the two and a half years that I was there, the Board's operations showed marked improvements.

◆

My tenure at the Electricity Board afforded several opportunities of foreign travel. The first of these was a conference in Brighton. I stayed in a hotel near Hyde Park and used to take a train in the morning for Brighton.

One Sunday morning, I decided to jog round the entire Hyde Park. It was very enjoyable, but the Park seemed to be never-ending. I gave up when I came to the pretty blue lake called the Serpentine: I had never seen anything more beautiful.

After the conference was over, I visited an innovative hydroelectric power station in Wales. During the day when there was high demand for power in the grid, it generated hydel power from a reservoir at a higher level and stored the used water in a reservoir at a lower level. After midnight when power demand in the grid was minimal, the water from the lower reservoir was pumped up to the upper reservoir to complete the cycle.

I also visited a dairy farm beside the hotel where I had stayed the night. The owner of the farm had about 200 cows and they roamed free in the farm. When the owner rang a bell at milking time, they lined up under a shower and proceeded to the milking area in rows of four. The owner attached the milking apparatus to their udders; he milked them in this manner, thrice a day. After the operation was over, he offered me a glass of fresh milk to drink. Many years ago, I had tasted fresh milk at the Aarey Milk Colony in Mumbai. This milk from the Wales farm was out of this world! Shamelessly, I drank three glasses.

From Wales, I went to North Yorkshire to visit the Drax coal-fired power station on River Ouse. Drax had six machines of 600 MW each. The control room was a circular hall; a lone young man sat at the switchboard, looking at images on the wall. He was controlling all the six machines. In response to my query, he told me that all the six machines were functioning at 100 Plant Load Factor (PLF). I gaped! I just couldn't believe it; it was too good to be true!

At my Panipat coal-fired station, the control room of a 110 MW machine was manned by about 10 senior/junior engineers. With their combined expertise, the machine never exceeded 50 PLF, and they were mighty pleased about it.

I went to the director and asked him to show me the coal they were using. He gifted me a packet of smooth coal brickets supplied by British Coal, which gave an even flame. The 'coal' we received from Coal India was full of ash and stones. A man would precariously perch on the conveyor belt and pick up these stones and throw them into a mountain of stones that had formed under the conveyor belt. Despite his vigil, many stones escaped, the mill was damaged and the operations stopped for weeks.

On my return, Union Power Minister Vasant Sathe called me because we had defaulted in our payments to Coal India. Coal India's chairman Narayanan was also there. I told Sathe about the quality (or rather lack of it) of the coal we received from Coal India, with its liberal mix of huge stone boulders and ash, and offered to show Mr Narayanan the mountain of stones at Panipat, which was a two-hour drive. Then, I presented the minister the packet of coal brickets that British Coal supplied to Drax. Sathe examined the brickets, showed them to Narayanan and giving me a wink, said: 'Bright cookie!'

Another memorable trip was to the Seagre Conference in Paris. On this trip, I took my daughter Vandana along. We attended an inaugural gala dinner at the Trocadero Palace near the Eiffel Tower. On another evening, we were taken on a cruise called 'Bateau Mouche', on the River Seine; dinner was served on deck as we passed the beautifully lit-up famous monuments of Paris. The concluding dinner was organized in an enormous steel structure that had been constructed during an international industrial exhibition. We enjoyed a five-course dinner to the accompaniment of strains of music.

Vandana and I explored the unending galleries of the Louvre and saw its most prized possession, the Mona Lisa. We also went to see the Musée d'Orsay, which has a rich collection of the Impressionists, and later discovered the Picasso Museum, which houses rare paintings of the great Spanish genius.

25

CHANGING PORTFOLIOS IN THE STATE SECRETARIAT

Having accomplished his dream of becoming Haryana's chief minister, Devi Lal's focus shifted to the Centre. During the Parliamentary elections of November 1989, he contested from Rohtak in Haryana, as well as Sikar in Rajasthan. He won from both places and gave up the Sikar seat.

Rajiv Gandhi's reputation as Mr Clean had been tarnished by his former defence minister V.P. Singh's disclosure that middlemen like Quattrochi, who were close to Sonia Gandhi, had received hefty kickbacks in the Bofors deal. The Congress party under Rajiv Gandhi's leadership failed to get a majority in Parliament; it only won 177 seats. The National Front formed by Devi Lal, V.P. Singh and Chandra Shekhar won 146 seats, BJP got 86 seats and the Communists 52.

The Opposition parties formed the government on 1 December 1989, with V.P. Singh as Prime Minister, Devi Lal as Deputy Prime Minister and Atal Bihari Vajpayee as Foreign Minister; the Communists provided support from the outside.

In Haryana, Devi Lal bequeathed his rule to his eldest son, Om Prakash Chautala, who was sworn in as Chief Minister on 2 December 1989. After a few days, he transferred me from my hectic job in the Electricity Board and appointed me Secretary of the Public Health Department. I was happy to return to the relaxed environs of the Secretariat on 23 December 1989.

Chautala was not a member of the Haryana Assembly and had to get elected to it within six months. He decided to contest from the Meham assembly seat which had been vacated by his father. It was a part of the Rohtak parliamentary constituency and was considered the safest option.

Devi Lal was an acknowledged leader of the Jats and Rohtak was their garh. However, he was a Bagri Jat from the Sirsa region; the Jats of Rohtak had welcomed him to contest for Parliament but they resented Chautala's intrusion. A local Jat leader, Anand Singh Dangi, challenged Chautala.

Elections were held in February 1990; staring at defeat, Chautala resorted to booth capture. As he was Chief Minister, the police looked the other way, but television had reached Indian homes by then. It captured scenes of a young man being mercilessly beaten to death by Chautala's goons. It was daylight mayhem in Meham. The Election Commission cancelled the election.

The elections were rescheduled for 20 May 1990. However, in the early hours of the morning of election day, the police found the dead body of Amir Singh, Chautala's 'covering candidate', lying by the wayside in adjacent Bhiwani district. In view of a candidate's demise, the election had to be countermanded.

The finger of suspicion pointed towards Chautala, as Amir Singh had been closeted with one of Chautala's sons till 11 p.m. the previous night, in the Meham PWD rest house. The national press cried foul against Chautala, who had resorted to such horrible tactics to avoid defeat. The Janata Dal public affairs committee asked Chautala to resign from chief ministership and B.D. Gupta was sworn in as chief minister on 23 May 1990, proving the adage *'Billi ke bhagya se chhinka toota'*[134]. Gupta had emerged from

[134]The milk pot hanging from the ceiling fell because of the cat's good luck.

the wilderness to join Devi Lal during his agitation against the Rajiv-Longowal Accord, and the latter had made him deputy chief minister when he became chief minister.

Chautala realized that he had to abandon the Meham route if he wanted to win. He asked one of his party MLAs, Vidya Beniwal from Dariba Kalan, to resign from her seat. When the by-election to fill the vacancy took place, Chautala won.

A few months later, Gupta transferred K.S. Tomar, SP Bhiwani. Amir Singh's dead body had been found in Tomar's jurisdiction and Gupta had suspected his involvement in the dark deed. However, Gupta's action drew the ire of Devi Lal.

He summoned Gupta to Delhi and asked him to resign and Gupta meekly did so on 12 July 1990, when Chautala again became Chief Minister. This time, Bommai, the party president, took umbrage and Chautala had to quit within five days. Another interim candidate, Hukam Singh from Charkhi Dadri, was then made Chief Minister.

Just a few days later, on 31 July 1990, V.P. Singh dismissed Devi Lal from deputy prime ministership. A week later, on 7 August, Singh implemented the Mandal Commission Report, giving 27 per cent reservation in government jobs to the backward classes. Till that time, only the Scheduled Castes and Scheduled Tribes had received the benefit of positive affirmation.

REFRESHER COURSE AT HARVARD UNIVERSITY

A month before these upheavals in Haryana and the country, the government of India had selected me for a six-week summer course at Harvard University, in June 1990. It was meant for officers heading important public utilities and corporations. Ironically, I had been transferred from the Electricity Board, by then.

There were about two dozen participants from Asian and African countries, and we stayed at Rockefeller Hall, where we were served breakfast before the lectures. We had to fend for ourselves for all other meals, and I resorted to eating microwaved meals which I bought from a nearby supermarket. On the first day of our stay, the thick smoke from the kitchen activated the fire alarm and the fire brigade arrived, honking furiously. Three Malaysian delegates were cooking a chicken dish. The caretaker gave a piece of his mind to the culprits.

The delegates from Pakistan stayed in hotels, not at Rockefeller Hall, as they had come with their wives. They were a friendly lot and joined us at breakfast before the lectures. One day, a delegate from Nigeria came to me, 'Mr Varma, I always see you sitting with these Pakistanis, cracking jokes with them, while I believe your countries are not very friendly towards each other. I've never seen you sitting with your fellow Indians.' He pointed towards three Indian delegates sitting at another table. I laughed and pointing towards the Pakistanis, told him that they spoke my language and I felt drawn towards them. 'But those Indians over there are from South India and I don't understand a word of their language. I can converse with them only in English!'

•◆

Early in the morning, I used to walk to Harvard Square, go to River Charles and jog along it for a while. On holidays, we used to take the Underground at Harvard Square and go to Boston, saunter in the main street for a while and then enter one of the malls to pick up something from the last counter offering the biggest discount.

The main thrust of the course was on privatization of public utilities. Prof. Mellons asked me to speak on India's giant-sized public corporation. I presented a paper on the FCI and maintained that it was performing a gargantuan task of procuring surplus foodgrains from various states of India and making it available to far-flung areas at affordable prices. I concluded that the FCI was indispensible and cannot be privatized.

One day, John Kenneth Galbraith was invited to deliver a lecture. I had imagined that a junior professor like Prajapati Trivedi would chauffeur the world-renowned economist and former ambassador to India, in his car. However, the tall and lanky Galbraith, who was in his eighties, ambled in quietly and sat near Professor Mellons. He made no sho-sha[135] about being a VIP guest speaker. He spoke, about the Great Depression of the 1930s and John Maynard Keynes advocating state intervention, and received a standing ovation at the end. I was happy that his talk corroborated my argument that state intervention was crucial at the present juncture in India.

On 4 July 1990, Independence Day in the USA, we joined a crowd of spectators at Boston to watch the spectacular fireworks on the bank of River Charles.

•◆

The mild-mannered Hukam Singh from Charkhi Dadri, who was imprisoned during Emergency when I was Deputy Commissioner, had become Chief Minister. Bhagi Ram was the minister of the Public Health Department. When I called on him after returning from Harvard University, he told me that his Ellenabad constituency was still deprived of adequate water supply facilities. Haryana was a pioneer in the country in rural electrification, road construction and in the supply of potable drinking water to far-flung hamlets in the state. I knew Ellenabad from my brief tenure there as SDM Sirsa. It is at the extremities of Haryana on the Rajasthan border. I

[135]Pomp and show

asked Engineer-in-Chief Chawla to go to Ellenabad and prepare a special project for strengthening the system. He got it prepared and discussed it with the minister. I got it approved in the Supplimentary Estimates and the implementation started.

However, I fell out with Bhagi Ram regarding a matter of promotion of a Superintending Engineer Sardana. Unlike all his other colleagues who had started their career at Class II level as Sub-Divisional Officers (SDO), Sardana was directly appointed at Class I level as XEN through Haryana Public Service Commission. He was later promoted as Superintending Engineer (SE) superseding the existing XEN's in the department.

Not being content with his accelerated promotion as SE, he said in a representation that he should be deemed senior to all exiting SEs, Chief Engineers and even the Engineer-in-Chief. His representation was rejected by the government. He filed a writ petition in the high court against the decision. The high court dimissed the petition and he filed an appeal in the Supreme Court, where the matter now rested.

After Bhagi Ram became Public Health Minister, he made a fresh representation for reconsideration of his case. The file was put up by the joint secretary to me giving the back history of the case. I sent it to the minister stating that his plea had already been rejected by the high court and the matter was sub-judice in the Supreme Court and as such his representation deserved to be rejected.

Bhagi Ram differed with me and returned the file saying that his orders should be complied with. Under the Rules of Business issued by the Chief Secretary in a case of difference of opinion between a minister and secretary, the latter may refer the matter for decision to the chief minister. Under this provision, I sent the file to the chief minister through the minister. Hukam Singh called the meeting in his room where Bhagi Ram, Chief Secretary

Kulwant Singh and Advocate General Mohunta were present. When I entered the room, Hukam Singh stood up and accepted my greetings with a warm handshake. I explained the case briefly and said that the officer whom the minister wanted to appoint as engineer-in chief was 13th in the seniority list of the department. The CM then looked at Bhagi Ram, who said that the government had the right to correct the seniority list. He looked at Advocate General Mohunta, who opined that the seniority matter could be re-examined in depth. CM looked at me and I said that the officer could move the Supreme Court for an early hearing and get the matter decided in his favour. CM looked at Mohunta again. To my surprise, Mohunta said that there was no problem and he would get the Supreme Court judgement with a month. I exclaimed that I would have no problem in complying with the Supreme Court's order.

The meeting ended and I got up to leave along with the rest. CM gestured me to stay back when everyone else had left the room. He told me with a smile that Bhagi Ram had banished his '*diwala*' (poverty) by taking a hefty sum from the officer. '*Usne Mohunta ko bhi pata liya tha. Aapne achchha thikane lagaya in badmashon ko*' (He had aligned Mohunta also to his side. You have nicely set these rogues right).

Hukam Singh continued for about eight months, till the dust settled on Om Prakash Chautala's misdeeds. At a hint from Chautala, he resigned on 22 March 1991, and the party MLAs unanimously elected Chautala as their leader. He was sworn in as Chief Minister for the third time by Governor Dhanik Lal Mandal.

A few days later, Chautala recommended the dissolution of the Assembly, hoping to remain caretaker chief minister till fresh elections were held. Unluckily, three of his MLAs deserted him in the meanwhile. The governor asked him to prove his majority in the House but he declined and, as a result, President's Rule was imposed in Haryana on 5 April 1991.

Chautala was a non-starter three times, but his clout in government remained undiminished. The government of India had appointed a judicial commission under Justice D.P. Madon to probe Amir Singh's death. Despite Justice Madon's repeated requests, the Haryana government did not provide him any staff or an office, forcing him to remain non-functional. He resigned in utter frustration, saying, 'I have wasted over four months of my life in breaking my head against ministerial indifference and bureaucratic ignorance.'

◆

General Elections were held in 1991, while Haryana was under President's Rule. The Congress secured a clear majority with 51 seats. As a fallout of Chautala's misrule, Devi Lal's Samajwadi Janata Party (SJP)'s tally was reduced to 16. Bansi Lal's newly floated Haryana Vikas Party (HVP) got 12 seats and BJP two. Bhajan Lal bounced back as Chief Minister. He transferred me from Public Health Department and appointed me Secretary of Animal Husbandry and Fisheries departments.

At the national scene, Rajiv Gandhi had died a tragic death at Sriperumbudur while holding a public meeting and Narasimha Rao had become Prime Minister, presiding over a minority government. Rao's government was tottering because of a no-confidence motion, but Bhajan Lal saved it from collapse by his proverbial resourcefulness.

Telltale photographs of Bhajan Lal entering Jharkhand Mukti Morcha chief Shibu Soren's house, carrying a swanky briefcase, had appeared in the national newspapers. His political stature was at its peak.

◆

Animal husbandry was a major department, in comparison to the fisheries department; Haryana being home to famous breeds of cows. Fisheries was minor one. However, my insignificant assignment as Secretary of the fisheries department brought an unexpected dividend by way of a foreign tour. A team of fisheries experts from Israel had visited Haryana and suggested that we adopt an advanced fish-production technology developed by Israel.

At that time, Shakrulla Khan was the Fisheries Minister. He had already gone on the Haj and been to Mecca and Medina. He now wanted to visit the Al-Aqsa Mosque in Jerusalem, which is regarded as the third holiest site of Islam. The king of Jordan had built a beautiful mosque with a gold-plated dome on the spot where Prophet Muhammad was believed to have ascended to heaven.

Shakrulla Khan got a tour sanctioned by the Chief Minister, ostensibly to see Israel's fisheries development programme. He was to be accompanied by the secretary and director of the department.

There was just one weekly flight to Tel Aviv in those days, operated by an Israeli airline, which meant that one had to stay for a week in the country. The Indian mission booked us a hotel in Tel Aviv and on a Sunday evening, we landed there.

We visited their innovative fisheries production sites at different places. They had large production centres of a few hundred hectares or so, which were almost fully mechanized.

Basically, while we just introduced fingerlings in our natural ponds and harvested at maturity, in Israel, they had constructed a series of large cemented tanks in a 100-hectare site. They introduced millions of fingerlings in one pond and provided nutrient-rich feed and transferred them to an adjacent tank having a larger area through an interconnected duct. As the fish grew in size, they went on transferring them, as they needed still larger living space, till the fish attained the marketing size.

They had laid out heavy duty nets at the bottom of the marketing tanks. The fish were lifted by mechanical winches and poured into aerated tankers for export.

No manual labour was required in any operation at any stage of growth. All operations with regard to hatching, breeding, rearing and production were digitally controlled, leaving no scope for human error.

They claimed that they produced about 40 tonnes of fish from a one-hectare block and their monthly output was thousands of tonnes, most of which was exported. What a contrast from our primitive method of rearing fish in village ponds resulting in measly production!

In the meanwhile, we visited Jerusalem. Shakrulla Khan went to the Al-Aqsa mosque while I went to the Wailing Wall, the sole remnant of the great temple where Jesus used to pray. Afterwards, like a faithful Christian, I walked through the narrow Via Dolorosa, the Path of Sorrows, which Jesus had taken, carrying the heavy cross, to go up to the hill of Calvary where he was crucified. The Church of the Holy Sepulchre stands at the spot of crucifixion; the rock on which the cross was fixed has been covered by a huge sheet of glass.

I am not a religious person, but I knelt and touched the rock instinctively and a shiver ran down my spine. Next, I saw the open grave from which Jesus is believed to have exited, but it did not inspire me.

I went to Bethlehem after that, the birthplace of Jesus, and entered the magnificent Church of Nativity which stands over the cowshed where Joseph and Mary had taken shelter for the night. No service was taking place at that time but I sat in a pew for a while and felt happy.

The next day, our guide showed me the spot in River Jordan where John the Baptist had baptized Jesus, after which we proceeded to the small town of Nazareth where Joseph and Mary lived, and saw the Sea of Galilee where Christ had performed the miracle of 'fish and loaves'. The so-called 'Sea of Galilee' is actually a huge lake, formed by the River Jordan. Interestingly, it lies 200 metres *below* sea level!

I went beyond to see the Dead Sea, which is a large lake at the dead end of River Jordan. There is no outflow from the Dead Sea and the entire inflow evaporates very easily. Its salinity is nine times that of an ocean, which allows humans to float in it without any effort. Tourists were reading novels while floating in water. It occurred to me that the possibility of floating effortlessly in the Dead Sea probably gave the idea of Christ performing the miracle of walking on the Sea of Galilee to the composers of the New Testament.

We visited all the fisheries sites and did some sight-seeing and still had three whole days left. Shakrulla Khan suggested a trip to Egypt to see the pyramids. Cairo was just a short flight away from Tel Aviv. I sent a fax message from the embassy to K.K. Sharma, Special Representative of the Haryana government in Delhi, to allow us to visit Cairo to see the fisheries in the Nile delta. Within a few hours, we had the government approval, which we conveyed to the embassies in Israel and Egypt.

We flew to Cairo in the evening: it happened to be Ramzan time and the last three days of fasting were left.

The next morning, when we went to see the Great Pyramid of Giza on the outskirts of Cairo, it seemed that the entire populace of Cairo had congregated on the vast sandy expanse. The conical peak of the pyramid was piercing the blue sky. This is Egypt's biggest pyramid, built by King Khufu, who reigned in the twenty-sixth century BCE, 2,000 years before the Buddha! Shakrulla Khan and Director Chowdhary mounted the gaudily dressed 'ships of the desert' for joyrides. I was drawn by the alluring symmetry of the pyramid and went closer to admire the huge chiselled blocks of stone which were placed in layers to give a perfect conical form to the pyramid. It seemed a super-human creation!

I joined a group to see the tombs of King Khufu and his queen inside the pyramid. We walked in single file in the dark and narrow passage inside the pyramid and reached the chamber of the Queen's Tomb revealed by the guide's torch. Getting back, we ascended higher and reached the Kings' Tomb at the top. It was larger then the Queen's Tomb. There was a little hole at the zenith which allowed a streak of light to peep in.

As we retraced our steps, on a sudden impulse I sat down on the stone floor in a yogic posture, took a deep breath and began chanting 'O-O-M!' My voice echoed in the darkness. The group sat down around me in silence. I chanted for a minute or two and then we came out of the pyramid, following the guide. Neither had I chanted in my life before that day, nor have I ever chanted afterwards. I don't know what came over me in the brooding darkness of the pyramid. When we came out, the group surrounded me and exclaimed that it was wonderful.

The Sphinx was not very far from the Great Pyramid. The Sphinx and a small pyramid beside it were built by Khufu's son Khafre. The guide said that the Sphinx's face was modelled after King Khafre, but it had suffered erosion and looked like a woman's face to me.

In the evening, I visited the Cairo museum and saw the solid gold artefacts recovered from King Tutankhamun's grave: his gold face mask, the gold-plated beds with heads of bulls and lions and his golden throne. The hall dazzled in a golden glow.

The next day, we drove along the Nile to Alexandria, the city founded by Alexander the Great on the Mediterranean Sea. We saw the impressive Fort Quetbey, which has been built on the site of the great lighthouse of Alexandria, it was one of the Seven Wonders of the Ancient World and was eventually destroyed by tidal waves.

We then saw Pompey's Pillar, standing forlorn amidst the ruins of a fort. I wanted to visit the palace of Cleopatra but the guide said that it had all been submerged. We finally came to the charming waterfront along the Corniche, the city's most fashionable street, and had lunch in a restaurant.

Of all my foreign visits, I prize my Egyptian safari the most!

26

PINNACLE OF MY CAREER

The next General Elections were held in May 1996. The Congress party, under Bhajan Lal's leadership, suffered a crushing defeat. Bhajan Lal too was defeated; only nine MLAs survived. Bansi Lal's Haryana Vikas Party and BJP had formed an alliance to fight the elections. HVP won 33 seats and the BJP secured 11. Bansi Lal formed the government in coalition with the BJP and the support of a few independent MLAs. He appointed me his Principal Secretary.

•◆

Bansi Lal had fought the election on the promise of introducing prohibition. Just after being sworn in, he announced that from 1 August 1996 (after 2 months), total prohibition would be enforced in the state, outlawing the manufacture, transportation, sale, possession or consumption of alchoholic beverages of any kind. During this tenure, he was almost entirely engrossed in matters related to prohibition, every day making detailed enquiries from field officers on how many persons had been caught, the progress of cases in the courts, convictions, etc. and paid scant attention to other matters of import which I discussed with him. He seemed to have left it all to my judgement.

Problems in enforcing prohibition were mounting: Haryana is a small state with a porous border, surrounded by Punjab, Himachal

Pradesh, UP, Delhi and Rajasthan, and easily accessible from all sides at innumerable points. Bootleggers, both inside and outside the state, had a field day. New liquor shops cropped up some distance away from the Haryana border, and people from Haryana began flocking to them. In the first year, over 40,000 people were rounded up and about 35,000 cases registered. There was hardly any space left to store case property or lodge offenders. Rural women, who had enthusiastically voted for Bansi Lal because of his promise to stop drinking, found their men decamping to neighbouring states for their tipple. The remedy seemed to be worse than the disease. Rumours were rife that liquor smuggling was being patronized by the sons of ministers.

•◆

When Bansi Lal took over in May 1996, M.C. Gupta was Chief Secretary. He was three years senior to me and was due to retire at the end of July after attaining the age of 58, which was the age of retirement at that time. There was a move in the government of India to raise the ceiling of retirement by two years. Gupta requested Bansi Lal to let him continue for a couple of months beyond July; it was expected that the announcement for raising the age of retirement would be made by that time. However, no decision was made till September, so Bansi Lal extended Gupta's tenure till January 1997, which was the maximum he could allow.

When M.C. Gupta retired at the end of January 1997, I was promoted to Chief Secretary and L.M. Jain was appointed Principal Secretary to CM. I had finally reached the pinnacle!

There was a certain thrill in occupying the chair in that room. I remembered the first time I had entered that room 28 years ago in January 1969, to call on Chief Secretary Sarup Krishen after my appointment as Director PR. How time flies!

I had been almost at the bottom of our batch when I had

first entered the Secretariat in May 1965 as a probationer. It was unthinkable that I would end up as Chief Secretary!

A member of the Haryana Public Service Commission (HPSC) was to retire towards the end of 1997 and Bansi Lal asked me if I would like to take his place. I politely declined the offer; after being chief secretary, I had no interest in any other job. Bansi Lal was surprised by my refusal and told me that it was a constitutional post with a five-year tenure and I would become Chairman, HPSC after a year or so. But I had seen HPSC chairmen cringing before chief ministers; they cannot but feel beholden to their benefactor and do his bidding. Besides, I had my own ideas about what I wanted to do after retirement.

In May 1998, three months before my retirement, the government of India finally decided to raise the age of retirement by two years. I was reminded of a popular adage which my mother used to quote, '*Bin mange moti milen; mange mile no bheekh.*'[136]

When Parliamentary elections were held in February 1998, Bansi Lal's Vikas Party and BJP got only one seat each out of 10 in Haryana, indicating a steep fall in the government's popularity. Atal Bihari Vajpayee became Prime Minister, but his government lasted only 13 months and the Lok Sabha was dissolved in April 1999. However, Vajpayee remained as caretaker Prime Minister.

For the upcoming Parliamentary elections of September-October 1999, the BJP decided to align with O.P. Chautala's Indian National Lok Dal (INLD) and began distancing itself from Bansi Lal. Bansi Lal had scrapped prohibiton at the end of March 1999

[136]You get pearls without asking, but not even alms by begging.

and was upset by this development.

After securing an electoral alliance with the BJP, Chautala could count on the 11 BJP MLAs who had been supporting Bansi Lal. He now needed another 13 MLAs to topple Bansi Lal, and started poaching on his camp.

In July 1999, as many as 17 members of Bansi Lal's fold deserted him and Chautala became Chief Minister. The untimely collapse of the Bansi Lal government was caused by the BJP severing its uncomfortable alliance. Indeed, it was an uncomfortable alliance. Bansi Lal had been a trenchant critic of the BJP throughout his political career and Atal Bihari Vajpayee felt more comfortable in the company of Devi Lal, who had been incarcerated during Emergency like him.

I called on Chautala and told him that he could give me a sinecure and appoint whoever he liked as chief secretary. Although not highly educated, Chautala spoke in a flowery, sugar-coated Hindi. He praised my erudition and administrative acumen and assured me that he couldn't even entertain the notion of replacing me.

However, a few days later, M.S. Gill, who was the Chief Election Commissioner at that time, told me that Chautala was seeking his permission to transfer me. Gill had told Chautala that the model code of conduct was in place because of the impending Parliamentary elections, and the chief secretary could not be transferred.

In the 1999 Lok Sabha elections, the BJP and INLD combine won all 10 seats in Haryana. This emboldened Chautala and he recommended dissolution of the Haryana assembly. Fresh elections were held in February 2000 and his party secured an absolute majority. He did not need the BJP's support any more.

Chautala could have replaced me after the Lok Sabha elections, but his father probably told him not to disturb me. Whatever the reason, even though he used to tease me and crack jokes with me during cabinet meetings, he always showed due respect towards me. I retired on 31 August 2000.

Just a week later, on 7 September 2000, a week after my retirement, we moved to our flat in the Haryana Officers' Co-op Housing Society, which had been completed a few months before. In 1995, when I had been Secretary of Animal Husbandry, I was elected President of the Society by its 200 members. The Haryana Urban Development Authority (HUDA) had allotted a five-acre plot to the Society in Panchkula and the flats had been allotted to the members in April 2000.

When I look back, I am filled with amazement at the witchery of happenstance in my life. In the first few years after my allotment to the Haryana cadre in 1966, I came in contact with and enjoyed the confidence of main dramatis personae who were to shape the destiny of the new state of Haryana.

Rao Birendra Singh, Chaudhary Devi Lal, Bansi Lal and Bhajan Lal were the principal actors on the Haryana stage in the three decades that spanned my career. Of them, only Devi Lal harboured some animosity towards me but, despite that, he too seemed to have a secret admiration for me. Although I worked zealously in all my assignments, I consider my work as Chairman of the Haryana Electricity Board as the crowning achievement of my career in the IAS.

27

FAMILY

God gave us only daughters, no son. My wife Savitri held a grudge against God on that score. In her family too there were only daughters, no son; she was the eldest of five sisters. She hungered for a son. I had no such complex; we were two brothers and a sister.

Indeed, one of my greatest pleasures in life has been rearing our little daughters. Actually, Savitri reared them; I only derived the pleasure.

Our first child, Vandana, was born on Sharad Poornima in Rewari when I was SDM. Our second child, Jyotsana, came within a year of Vandana's arrival, when we had moved to Chandigarh. Savitri conceived again and we had our third daughter. She suffered from spastic paralysis and did not survive beyond six months. Savitri conceived once again and delivered a robust baby girl. We named her Upasana.

Barring a brief interlude in Bhiwani, our daughters studied at the Sacred Heart School in Chandigarh. All three of them excelled in their studies; they were toppers in their class and were head girls of the school, in their final year.

When they were in kindergarten, Vandana and Jyotsana introduced me to the wonder world of nursery rhymes. They babbled snippets of rhymes they had learnt in school, but being innocent of them, I couldn't make out what they were singing, although I had done my master's in English Literature. I realized that they were singing garbled rhymes, but having never learnt nursery rhymes, I was at a loss to understand. Eventually, I bought records of nursery rhymes and a record player from Delhi, and we began playing them at home. Singing the rhymes with them was sheer bliss!

I also bought a standard book of rhymes which added to our stock. Once, we had gone on a vacation to Shimla, where in the rest house I held a competition of singing nursery rhymes between the two of them and promised to give a toffee for every rhyme they sang. The contest was close; I think I had to give about 60 toffees to each of them!

◆

When Vandana finished high school in 1982, terrorism was at its height in Punjab. For her 'Plus 2', we got her admitted to the special residential school on the national highway at Rai which was started by S.K. Misra during Bansi Lal's time. There too she excelled. She was appointed Head Girl and topped in academics. As at Sacred Heart, I was a VIP in Rai School too because of her. Thereafter she joined the Chandigarh College of Architecture for B.Arch. She was an outstanding student and stood second in the order of merit of the University.

We celebrated her marriage with Navneet Sehgal after she finished college. Navneet was in the UP cadre of the IAS and was posted as SDM, Etah at that time. Later when he was transfered to Dehradun, Vandana enrolled herself at Roorkee University for M.Arch. She would commute to the University by bus every day and returned home late in the night. She was rewarded for her painstaking endeavour; she topped the University in M.Arch two years later. She joined the Government College of Architecture, Lucknow, as a lecturer after some time. Years later, she took a four-year sabbatical to do her PhD from the School of Planning and Architecture, Delhi. Today,

Dr Vandana Sehgal is the Principal and Dean of the Faculty of Architecture and Planning, APJ Abdul Kalam Technical University, UP. She has started post-graduate classes in her college and also guides students for PhD in Architecture.

Vandana's husband, Dr Navneet Sehgal, had worked as District Magistrate in Jaunpur, Gonda, Faizabad and Lucknow. Later, he was Secretary to Mayawati, when she was the chief minister. Subsequently, during the tenure of Chief Minister Akhilesh Yadav, he was posted as the CEO, Uttar Pradesh Expressway Industrial Development Authority. He completed and commissioned the 302-km, six-lane Expressway from Lucknow to Agra, with a landing facility for fighter planes, in a record time of 22 months. Currently, Navneet is the Additional Chief Secretary in-charge of the Department of Micro, Small and Medium Enterprises (MSME) and the Department of Publicity and Information in Yogi Adityanath's government.

She and Navneet are blessed with two sons, Shiv and Dhruv. Shiv did his graduation in Law and Politics from Cardiff University, UK, and came back to India to launch a start-up called 'Polstrat'. Dhruv graduated from the University of Warwick, UK, and is currently working for PricewaterhouseCoopers (PwC) in Gurgaon.

•◆

Jyotsana studied at the Govt College for Girls (GCG), Chandigarh after high school. She graduated in 1989 with Honours in Economics, French Literature and Sanskrit. Earlier in 1988, she was also awarded the Diplôme Supérieur in French Language by Alliance Française de Paris which she attended in evening. She enrolled in Punjab University in 1991 to do her master's in Economics. While still in the final year of her M.A., she appeared in the IAS examination, choosing Economics and French Literature for her higher papers. She cracked the IAS and joined the Academy in 1992, when my batchmate Naresh Saxena was its Director.

She was allocated the Bihar cadre and was SDM of Patna for two years. After that, she went to Nalanda on promotion as ADC. When the new state of Jharkhand was carved out of Bihar, she was allocated the Jharkhand cadre.

Jyotsana served as District Magistrate of Lohardaga for a couple of years, at a time when it was facing internal unrest. Later, she became Director of Welfare at the state headquarters in Ranchi. After a year, she came to Delhi as a Deputy Secretary in the Ministry of Economic Affairs.

In 2009, she joined the Asian Development Bank (ADB) in Manila. Currently, she is posted in Dhaka as second-in-command of the ADB mission.

Jyotsana's first marriage was a fiasco and ended in divorce after a few years. She later married Anupam Ray of the Indian Foreign Service and they had a child whom they named Trishala, and whom we called Gungun. Some years later, when Jyotsana discovered that Anupam was cohabiting with a Jewish woman in New York, they separated. She took custody of her daughter and sent her to University College, London for higher studies.

◆

Like Jyotsana, Upasana too joined GCG Chandigarh in 1989, after topping the merit list of her school. For her BA, she chose Economics, Sociology and French Literature and passed her final examination in 1994 with flying colours.

She joined Punjab University for a master's in Economics, like Jyotsana. There too she excelled and topped the University merit list in 1996, setting an all-time record by scoring the highest marks in all four subjects and winning all four gold medals!

When the Punjab University convocation was held, Upasana had already left to study at the London School of Economics (LSE). Proud as a peacock, I walked up to the podium and received the medals on her behalf from the Chancellor!

At LSE, Upasana studied for a post-graduate diploma in Econometrics in 1997, and M.Sc. in Development Studies in 1998.

On her return she worked at the World Bank office in Delhi. In 2003, she married her old university friend Rajiv Madhok and went to live with him in Singapore, where Rajiv was in-charge of Airtel. Taking a huge loan, she enrolled for MBA in Singapore with INSEAD and studied at their Singapore, campus for six months. For the next six months she went to study at their Fontainbleau campus. After a while, Upasana joined BNP Paribas in Singapore. They were blessed with a daughter, whom they named Zara. A Filipino maid they had employed took good care of the new-born baby. I too stayed for a couple years with them in Singapore in those days. Holding little Zara's hand, I would walk her to the mall in front of our condominium and we'd play the game of going up and down the automatic stairs in the mall and loiter in the showrooms.

Rajiv had completed his MBA with specialization in international business in 1998. He took up his first job, before marriage, in West Africa where he was mainly responsible for procurement and export of commodities. He came back to India in 2000 and joined the Bharti Group at Singapore (Airtel). He was responsible for multiple product launches including the very popular ring-back tones. His next stint was with Onmobile based out of Singapore where he was responsible for international business development from Brazil to South East Asia.

He came back to India in 2008, to start his company Oorja as well as head the business at One97 (Paytm) where he was also on the board directors. Post 2012, he ran Oorja, successfully creating path-breaking platforms for telecom operators. The company pivoted to creating a marketing automation software which was sold in 2018.

As a serial entrepreneur, Rajiv is now on to his next venture

Poshtik, making multigrain flour, promoting health and nutrition in the country. After some time, Upasana too got an offer from the International Finance Corporation (IFC) of the World Bank in Delhi. She resigned from her BNP Paribas job and joined the World Bank Group and relocated to Delhi to be with Rajiv. Later, they were blessed with a baby boy, whom they named Roshan.

Recently, Zara became the Head Girl of the junior section in the Sanskriti School where she and Roshan study. I had a feeling of *deja vu* when I attended her investiture ceremony in the company of her parents.

28

WANDERLUST: TREKKING EXPEDITIONS

The happenstance of joining the Punjab cadre
Brought me to Chandigarh, the City Beautiful,
Which became my brave new habitation.
It shaped my life in a new mould,
Opened new vistas and a new horizon.

On formation of the new state of Haryana,
I found myself among multi-tasking mandarins,
Working in tandem with grass-root visionary leaders,
And did my bit in shaping a new Haryana,
Found love, happiness and fulfillment.

But for my sojourn in the City Beautiful
I may never have ventured into
The Himalayan region and discovered
The joy of trekking, which developed
Into an enduring passion over the years.

Else I would have never known what's a babbling brook,
A thundering cataract or an awesome crevasse,
Never set foot on million-year-old glaciers,
Or seen snowy peaks blushing at dawn
At their reflections in blue dreaming lakes,
And marmots frolicking with their fawn.

CHOOR DHAR

There was a Civil Services Mountaineering and Trekking Association in the Haryana Secretariat. Under its aegis, we organized a trekking expedition for the families of officers during the school holidays of June 1990. An expedition was planned to the Choor Dhar peak in nearby Himachal Pradesh. The group included Ajit Sharan, Sanjay Kothari,[137] Ashok Lavasa[138] and S.K. Saxena among others, along with their wives and children. Balwan Singh from the Electricity Board also joined with his family. Savitri had scoffed at the idea, so I went by myself. I used to go for regular walks to the Sukhna Lake, but had never gone on a trek.

We went by bus to Nohra Dhar via Solan, stayed for the night at the rest house, and set off after breakfast the next morning.

It was hot and humid when we started climbing by a kuchha path. Suddenly, clouds gathered, bringing a whiff of cool air. In an hour or so, it began to rain and there was nowhere to take shelter. We were drenched and the path became slippery, but the perseverance of the group, especially the children, was astonishing, and we trudged on.

Soon, we understood why the peak was named Choor Dhar. The route circled around the mountain as we climbed, resembling bangles, or choori, that women wear.

We reached the top at about 4 p.m. and found a small temple and a little hut there. The ascetic who lived in the hut was happy to see us, and let us rest in his hut and made tea for us. He was suffering from consumption and Balwan Singh asked him to come to Chandigarh and promised to get him admitted to the hospital in Panchkula.

---

[137]He rose to be Secretary to the President of India.

[138]He was working as an Election Commissioner. Has now joined as Vice President in ADB at Manila.

We had actually planned to return to the rest house at Nohra Dhar in the evening, but that was impossible; we had to spend the night on the mountaintop. As evening fell, it became quite cold. We did not have sleeping bags, a must for trekkers. We huddled together on the floor of the hut through the night, enveloped in the warmth of fellow-feeling.

The next day, we trooped down to the rest house at Nohra Dhar, bathed and had lunch. We reached Chandigarh late at night. It gave us our first bittersweet taste of adventure.

The ascetic did come to Chandigarh, and after receiving treatment for a couple of months, he recovered and went back to his abode at Choor Dhar.

HAR KI DOON

In June 1991, we planned an enterprising trek to Har Ki Doon—'God's Valley'. It was almost the same team as the previous year, except that the Saxenas had dropped out. In a mini bus, we went on the Dehradun Road via Nahan and reached a road junction called Yamuna Bridge. From there, we went to Sankri, via Purola and Netwar.

We left our minibus at Sankri and walked 12 kilometres on a narrow hill track to reach a village called Taluka. After the previous day's journey by bus, this walk was welcome, and prepared us for the two days of trekking ahead of us.

Taluka is a sleepy hamlet, nestled beside a tranquil pool of water. From the rest house, we could see the River Supin sparkling in the distance and hear its roar. The next day, on the way to Osla we crossed this tumultuous river twice. Osla is the last inhabited village. We stayed in the rest house on the way. The village was, in fact, tucked on a steep ridge about a kilometre high. The inhabitants of the village traced their kinship to the combatants of the hoary Mahabharata war. They claimed to be descendents of the Kaurava princes, who were vanquished and slain in the Mahabharata war at Kurukshetra. Their ancestors, they believe, had escaped to this remote spot in the Himalayas. In their small old temple in the village they worship Duryodhan, the eldest Kaurava prince, as their principal deity.

The next day's trek lay through verdant, flowery meadows. River Supin flowed at a distance on our right and soon we saw its tributary, Rupin, merging with it. Incidentally, Rupin and Supin are the originators of the fabled River Saraswati! Snow-clad peaks glimmered in the distance. The bright sunshine and gradual ascent made the trek pleasurable. After about four hours, we came upon a majestic waterfall, thundering down from a cliff. There was a steep climb beyond it through a thick forest. Climbing higher, we passed through pretty Bhojpatra trees with their paper-thin bark, which was used in ancient times to prepare sacred scrolls. There were no trees beyond them.

In another half an hour, a glorious view of the Kala Naag, Swarga Rohini and Bunder Poonchh peaks and Kedar Dome loomed ahead of us. We could see the small forest rest house in the distance[139]; we had arrived!

Sunshine lingered on the peaks and then all of a sudden the sky was aflame, the peaks glimmered with a golden glow, the rippling stream caught the radiance. It was an ethereal moment. Wordsworth's poem came to mind:

> …when meadow, grove and stream,
> The earth, and every common sight
> To me did seem
> Apparell'd in celestial beauty.

[139]The regular tourist lodge was not there at that time, it was built much later.

Soon we began to feel the chill and took refuge in the rest house. The chowkidar had lit a fire in the fireplace which made it warm and cosy. There was hardly enough space to accommodate everyone, so Balwan Singh and I slept in the small enclosed verandah. Neither he nor I were adequately clad. I just had a sweater under my khaki jacket. I pulled my knees close to my chest and had a fitful sleep.

The next day's descent was child's play. I stopped at the great waterfall, stripped and stepped into the pool under the cascade. The shower was benumbing, and blissful!

OVER SAACH PASS AND INDRAHAR PASS

Three months later, in September 1991, we planned an ambitious trek from the Kullu valley to Chamba valley and eventually crossing into the Kangra valley by going over the mighty Dhauladhar range. We had to cross the Rohtang Pass, descend and go along River Chenab to Kilar, just a few miles short of the Kashmir border, and from there trek up to the 14,500-feet-high Saach Pass in the Pir Panjal range and cross into Chamba valley. From there, we wanted to go to Bharmour and, God willing, scale the Indrahar Pass in the Dhauladhar range to cross into the Kangra valley and reach Dharamshala and meet the Dalai Lama.

It was a small party: my colleague Raj Roop Fulia, a lean, devout bachelor with a soft smile, Balwan Singh from the Electricity Board, and Rakesh and Sukhija from the Secretariat service. Rakesh was a trained mountaineer and Sukhija an affable, ever-smiling companion.

While the road from Manali to Rohtang has a gradual climb and pretty waterfalls on the way, beyond the Pass the road has a sudden fall and is bare, less-travelled and poorly maintained. We hurtled down this road and had tea at the Khoksar rest house on

River Chenab. Crossing the river by an iron bridge, we came to its confluence with River Bhaga, which gave the Chenab its other name, Chandra-Bhaga. Our path lay along the Chenab, towards Kashmir.

By evening, we reached an old British-era rest house tucked under tall deodar trees on the outskirts of Killar. It was called Cherry Bungla and was pretty as a picture. A diminutive, quick-footed chowkidar gave us hot water to wash and served piping-hot tea. Later, he cooked a simple meal for us and in the morning gave us hot water to bathe in—he was an angel in a humble, humdrum garb!

I hired a porter in the morning to carry my rucksack, while Fulia, Balwan, Rakesh and Sukhija carried theirs. We had to cross the Chenab to go up to Bindra Bani. The road along the river had been washed away by rains and was under construction. It was an uphill climb through a rugged terrain and by evening we reached the snow point at about 10,000 feet. We found shelter in a cave at a place called Dunai and ate sandwiches sitting around a small fire that we made.

We set off again in the morning. Balwan, Rakesh and Sukhija walked ahead. Fulia, with a huge rucksack balanced on his shoulders, and my porter, a mere boy who climbed the hilly path like a mountain goat, gave me company. It was a clear sunny day and by noon we reached the top of Saach Pass. Hooray!

After a short rest and some tea in a tent, we soldiered on. The Chamba side of the Pir Panjal range was piled high with snow, but it was also greener. Suddenly, we were enveloped in dense fog (or was it a wayward cloud?) and couldn't see beyond a few yards. The boy walked close to me but I couldn't see where Fulia was and called out to him. My voice resounded in the fog. He called out in reply, and his voice seemed to be coming from far away: it was uncanny. We called out to each other for the fun of it, our voices echoing in the silence of the hills.

By noon, we reached a place called Satrundi. We had meals at a rest house there. Our minibus, which had left us at Cherry Bungla, had reached Satrundi by road. The bus took us to Bharmour for the night. Fulia and Sukhija decided to return from there; Balwan and Rakesh stayed behind.

Bharmour is a small town between the Pir Panjal and Dhauladhar ranges, and the valley of the Chenab and the Ravi. It is famous for a cluster of Chaurasi (84) Shaivite temples dating from the seventh to tenth centuries. The Mani Maheshwar Temple is the most impressive one and there are others dedicated to Bhadrakali, Ganesh, the Nandi Bull and lesser gods and goddesses.

The next day, we stayed in a small roadside 'lodge' on River Ravi. It was a wooden structure built on stilts. The turbulent river flowed about 20 metres below its wooden floor where we had spread our sleeping bags. The lodge was run by a gutsy Himachali lady who served us tea and cooked a homely dinner for us.

A rather elderly man with a short white beard offered to carry my baggage the next morning, on our way to village Kwarsi, about 20 kilometres away on a hilly road. I was doubtful about his ability but to my surprise he walked faster than me and we reached our destination at dusk. We spread our sleeping bags in the wooden balcony at the back of an old house. The balcony overlooked a common courtyard which had a small temple under a tree. As I was preparing to go to sleep, I saw an ensemble of about a dozen male and female dancers, dressed in colourful Himachali costumes, beginning to dance in the temple courtyard in bright moonlight. It was a slow charming dance and I wondered if I was dreaming!

I was even more amazed when, on closer inspection, I spied my old porter among the male dancers! He had transformed from a lowly porter into a graceful dancer. I hadn't seen him carrying the festive costume. He probably belonged to Kwarsi. What a sprightly and spirited old man he turned out to be!

Rakesh had requested an instructor of the Bharmour Mountaineering Institute, N.R. Thakur, to accompany us on our expedition to Dharamshala. Thakur and I started off after breakfast, Balwan and Rakesh were to join us a little later with our baggage and my sleeping bag. Unfortunately, they never caught up with us, although we waited for them at a few places on the way. It was quite a tough trek for me. I had eaten two boiled eggs for breakfast and was carrying four more, which I ate on the way.

Eventually, we reached the snow line and advanced slowly upwards. As we climbed the last snow-filled ascent to the summit, the sun dipped below the horizon. There was no question of returning now; we had to go over. I felt the thrill of accomplishing my mission of going over the majestic Dhauladhar range, which I had seen many times from the Ridge at Shimla.

We began to descend slowly as the light dimmed. Observing my unsteady gait on the steep descent, Thakur held my hand and supported me. Darkness was falling and I felt apprehensive. Thakur's little torch seemed too feeble. Then, suddenly, the full moon rose and it became as bright as day. My uneasiness vanished and I involuntarily thanked God. I am not a devout person but I felt He was taking care of us.

The path had stone steps but the descent was unending. We had been going downhill for about three hours and I was at the end of my tether. A little later after the steps ended, we came upon an unfinished shack. I had no strength left in me to go further and we decided to call it a day. What a long long day it had been!

However, I did not have a sleeping bag. Rakesh had to bring it with my bag. Thakur unzipped his and asked me to put my right leg inside it. Then he inserted his left leg and we became somewhat like Siamese twins, joined in the middle wrapped in one sleeping bag. We spread ourselves on a stone slab. I will never forget that night; nor will he, perhaps.

At daybreak, we began our descent, reaching Triund after an hour or two, which has a good rest house. We bathed in hot water and had double omelettes for breakfast.

There was lovely sunshine and we walked jocundly on the downhill path to the Mountaineering Institute at McLeodganj. The director gave me their best room, in which the Dalai Lama had lived for a few years, when he had sought refuge in India after fleeing Tibet in 1959, before he moved into his present abode. I wanted to meet the Dalai Lama, but he had gone abroad.

The next day, Balwan and Rakesh also arrived, and we celebrated our reunion. They had strayed from their path and had to return to Kwarsi.

GANGOTRI-GAUMUKH

In June 1992, we decided to go to Badrinath and, from there, trek to Gaumukh, the mouth of the Gangotri glacier. Starting early morning in a minibus, our team of about 20, including kids, reached Rishikesh in the evening. The next day, we had lunch at the lovely lake formed by the Tehri Dam, and reached Badrinath in the evening. We saw the morning aarti in the Badrinath temple and began the 20-kilometre trek to Gaumukh. It was a pleasant and enjoyable walk along River Bhagirathi, through fir, spruce and deodar trees. That night we stayed at the Garhwal Mandal rest house at Bhojbasa, 4 kilometres short of Gaumukh.

The next morning, after crossing long stretches of sandy riverbed and jumping over boulders, we came face to face with the awesome Gaumukh, where the Ganga gushes out of an enormous mountain of frozen snow. I stood watching in wonderment: rivers usually begin as mere trickles, but the Ganga emerges as a full-blooded, boisterous river from the glacier's womb.

To the right of Gaumukh stands a snow-clad mountain which looks like a towering pyramid and is called Shivling. A fellow traveller told me that one could go up the Gangotri glacier and look at Shivling from close quarters. To me, it looked like Ganesh in sitting posture, with a snowy cap on his head. He had two large elephant ears and his trunk came down over his large belly.

Yes, I told myself, I'll go up the glacier one day and have a close look at Mount Shivling and venture beyond. Nowhere in India or elsewhere had I seen such a soul-stirring sight.

SANGLA VALLEY

We went to Sangla valley in Kinnaur for the first time in September 1992, when my youngest daughter Upasana had joined us. She was in her third year at that time. Our large contingent consisted of fellow officers like Satish Chaudhary, Ashok Lavasa, Roshan Lal, Hardeep Kumar, their familes and a few others.

We reached Rampur Bushahr by a minibus in the evening and stayed in the Circuit House on the bank of the Sutlej. Rampur Bushahr used to be the capital of the former ruler of a state by the same name.

The morning after our arrival, we went up a hilly road to Sarahan to see a temple dedicated to Bhimakali, the presiding deity of Rampur Bushahr. When we reached the top of the hill, we were rewarded by an awesome view of the Himalayan Range.

In the afternoon, we left for Sangla. After crossing the Sutlej by a bridge, the road skirts over a steep mountain. For 10–15 km, the road has been cut into the rock face. For city folks like us, going through that narrow passage was quite an adventure. Sangla is a quiet village on River Baspa; we stayed there for the night.

The next morning, we went on a lovely trek in a lush green valley along a gurgling rivulet. After a while, we reached a pretty lake full of lotus blooms, which mirrored the snow-clad peaks. Finally, we reached Chitkul, the last inhabited village on the China-Tibet border.

We continued trekking and reached Nagasthi, where the Indo-Tibetan Border Police (ITBP) had constructed tin huts. They provided us shelter for the night. The next day, we trekked towards the border, up to a place called Ranikanda, and returned to Nagasthi for the night. The next morning, we thanked the station commander for his hospitality and trekked back to Sangla.

BASE CAMP-BANDARPOONCH

In May 1993, our experienced mountaineers from the Haryana Secretariat, Rajiv Midha, Rakesh Panwar, Ravinder and a few others, decided to scale the Bandarpoonch Peak (6,102 metres), which is also called the White Peak, under the aegis of the old Civil Services Association. They had set up their base camp at Kiar Kothi.

Novel Lavasa, Balwan Singh and I decided to see how they were faring. We went by bus to Sankri and trekked to Taluka. The next day we reached Osla, and on the third day, rather than taking the straight path to Har ki Doon, we crossed River Rupin, took the path to its right and, in a few hours, reached the picturesque Ruinsara Lake late in the afternoon. It's a like a large turquoise gem, set in a rugged ring of green hills.

We camped near the lake that night, and were lulled to sleep by the soft rippling sound of its waves in the silence of the hills. A hoopoe was calling his mate, 'Hoo pu-pu! Hoo pu-pu!' from a tree near us for a long time. I dozed off listening to his haunting call.

The next morning, we took a round of the lake and found a small spring. We bathed under it and resumed trekking. We crossed the snow line to reach the camp at Kiar Kothi camp by noon. Other groups had also gathered there: they were attempting different peaks, Swargarohini, Black Peak or Bandarpoonch.

Kiar Kothi is on a steep ridge, about 200 metres above the Bandarpoonch glacier. The glacier spreads out like a monkey's tail and provides access to the cluster of dazzling peaks.

Balwan stayed back and Novel Lavasa and I set off with a porter who had come there to take supplies to the base camp. We descended to the glacier and then walked on it for about two hours to reach the base camp of our team at about 18,000 feet above sea level. That was the highest point I had ever trekked to! Snow peaks glimmered all around us. It was an ethereal site. They made tea for us and erected a new tent for our stay.

Rajiv told us that they had already made an attempt to climb the peak but had to return when the weather turned inclement. We ate a simple dinner together. Then, they spread thick mattresses for us and provided extra blankets. I slept fitfully and when I woke up in the morning, I found to my amazement that I had sunk about 9 inches deeper in the snow! Novel's mattress had sunk similarly on the other side of the pole. It was like being in an ice grave.

It was a bright and sunny morning. After breakfast, we wished the team good luck and returned to Kiar Kothi. Balwan had already left. The next morning, we walked back to Osla and the day after we reached Sankri and returned to Chandigarh the next day.

DODITAL

Next year in June 1993, during the summer holidays, we headed to Dodital. Our group comprised Satish Chaudhary, Ashok Lavasa and his family, Roshan Lal, S.S. Dhillon, Balwan Singh and his wife, and our coordinator Rakesh and a few others.

From Uttarkashi, we continued on the Gangotri road till

Sangam Chatti, where we alighted from the bus and the trek began. We crossed a dry riverbed and tracked for a few miles. By evening, we reached a place called Agora. There used to be a forest rest house at this place, but unfortunately it had been destroyed in a severe earthquake in 1991. We pitched a tent on high ground.

The next day, we reached Dodital; it is a celestial blue-green lake, surrounded by a ring of snow-clad mountains. Tall green trees stood on its one-kilometre-long periphery which were reflected in its tranquil waters.

A mythical story is prevalent about this dreamy lake which explains how Lord Shiva's son Ganesh came to possess an elephant head. They say that one fine morning Parvati wanted to bathe in the lake. She called her son Ganesh, and told him to stand guard and not allow anyone to come near the lake till she had come out and dressed.

As it happened, Lord Shiva came there at that instant from his wanderings. Little Ganesh was standing at the mouth of the channel emanating from the lake; he barred his entry. Shiva was furious and immediately severed the child's head with his trishool; the head rolled down into the stream.

Parvati came out and, seeing her son's headless body, began to howl. Shiva was repentant and wanted to attach the child's head to the body, but couldn't find it. Then he saw a baby elephant trailing his mother. Shiva severed the baby's head and attached it to Ganesh's body and Ganesh was reborn with an elephant's head on his shoulders. Looking at the lake's loveliness, I felt it was indeed worthy of dalliance of celestial nymphs.

Satish and I strolled around the lake and met an old sadhu with a white jata, sitting at his dhooni (smouldering fire), smoking pot. He offered his chillum[140] to us; Satish took a puff.

---

[140]Clay pipe

The next morning after breakfast, as we sat at the edge of the enchanting lake, Ashok Lavasa asked me, 'Sir, when do we bathe in the lake?'

'That's a very good question!' I replied.

I was in my shorts. I stood up at once, removed my T-shirt and dived into the lake. It felt like a thousand scorpions had stung me. I came out immediately, vigorously rubbed myself and then dived again. My body had got over the shock and I could stand it better now. Meanwhile, Ashok had also dived into the lake, followed by his wife Novel, Balwan Singh and many others. Swimming for a few minutes in the ice-cold water was really invigorating.

The next morning, a few of us trekked up to Bakkar Top and went to the Yamunotri shrine from there. While returning we were picked up by our friends who came by bus.

REGISTRATION OF NATIONAL ADVENTURE CLUB (NAC)

We created a new forum for the promotion of adventure sports, the National Adventure Club (NAC), which was registered under the Societies Registration Act on 1 September 1993, under my presidentship. Its founding members were Ajit Sharan, Vivek Mehrotra, Ashok Lavasa, P.K. Gupta, Y.S. Malik, Rajan Gupta, Ram Niwas and Balwan Singh, among others. Its principal objective was to create a spirit of adventure in the country's youth and promote adventure sports through an annual national adventure festival in Chandigarh.

In February 1995, NAC organized the first adventure festival, in which about 400 college students from different states participated. They were initiated in skiing, rock climbing, rappling and river rafting for a week, in places like Manali, Narkanda and Khada Patthar. Since then, every year, NAC invited about 400 youth to this festival at Chandigarh. They were taken to different locations for a week's experience of adventure activities, courtesy NAC. After the formation of the NAC, all our adventure activities took place under its aegis.

The 25th Silver Jubilee festival was held in February 2019, in which a contingent from Bangladesh participated, giving the NAC an international status.

•◆

LEH-LADAKH

The world beyond River Chandra Bhaga, Leh-Ladakh, was a mystery to us. We set off to explore it from Manali one bright sunny morning in June 1994. By noon we were at Tandi, the confluence of Chandra and Bhaga, and began the uphill journey along River Bhaga and reached Keylong.

The dusty, narrow and crowded lanes of Keylong didn't impress us much. After eating some noodles, we took to the highway again. We were told to look for the face of the 'Lady of Keylong' etched in snow on a mountain peak ahead of us.

'What hogwash!' I said to myself.

Suddenly, Fulia exclaimed, 'Look there, sir! A woman's face!'

He was pointing towards a snow-covered peak. Indeed, one could discern a woman's face in the snow on the peak. As we neared the peak, the contours of the face became clearer.

The sighting was a good omen. We had been told that the 'Lady of Keylong' was elusive and mostly remained hidden behind clouds or mist; she revealed herself only to lucky travellers.

I had requested the commander of the Army units stationed on the highway to give us shelter. We stayed in their camp at Jispa for the night. The next morning, an Army jeep escorted our vehicle over Baralacha La[141] and beyond. The landscape was unearthly—dry, barren hills with patches of snow lingering on them! Wispy clouds drifted across a deep blue sky. The serpentine road had recently been cleared of snow. As we neared Baralacha, we passed through high walls of snow on both sides of the road. We saw the emerald green Surya Taal on our right, the source of River Bhaga. We stopped to pay homage at the tiny temple of Baralacha Pass, with its colourful prayer flags fluttering in the wind.

We stayed in an Army hut at Sarchu that night and set off early next morning. We reached Pang by midday, and reached Tanglang-La at 15,000 feet, the highest pass on the road. From there, it was an easy downhill journey. Crossing Upashi, we arrived at Leh in the evening.

We stayed with an Army unit in Leh for three days and explored the quaint town and market; the decrepit old royal palace on the hillock testified to its old lineage. We also visited the nearby Thiksey Monastery. Serenity pervades this monastery, perched on a hilltop. We paid homage to the huge golden statue of Maitreya Buddha. There were cute child lamas wrapped in red and yellow robes. Inside the hall, the lamas sat in rows, mumbling prayers as they rocked in unison. But I was intrigued to see a painting of a demon-like figure holding a woman in coitus posture.

While returning from Manali, we took the road to Naggar, which had been the old capital of the Raja of Kullu for over a thousand years. We wanted to visit the place where the great Russian painter and theosophist Nicholas Roerich had spent the last part of his momentous life, gazing at the Himalayas and painting its moods in vibrant colours.

After visiting Roerich's house, we went to see the five-centuries-old castle of the Raja of Kullu, constructed in stone and wood. This

---

[141]'La' means a high mountain pass

building had withstood the terrible earthquake of 1905, which had levelled thousands of buildings in the region and is now a heritage hotel managed by the Himachal Tourism Corporation.

BASE CAMP: KEDAR DOME

Our montaineering team made another high-atltitude attempt in June 1995, on Kedar Dome. Rajiv Midha, Rakesh Panwar, Ravinder and company had already gone and set up base camp beyond Tapovan at Khada Patthar, at 16,000 feet.

I had promised to visit the base camp. I requested for a week's leave to go to Kedhar Dome and to visit the team, but Chief Minister Bhajan Lal did not approve my leave. I called on him and made a personal request and he allowed me to go.

I also wanted to see Mount Shivling at close quarters. So, when I reached Gaumukh, Rakesh arrived to escort me to the base camp.

Going up the mountain of snow from which the Ganga was emerging was an ordeal. I was breathless after a few steps and had to stop. Besides, it was slippery. Rakesh held my hand and in about an hour, we were able to cross it. From there, there was another steep ascent to Tapovan, the base of Mount Shivling. The snow-covered Shivling was dazzling in bright sunlight. That took another half an hour. I sat on the rock, gazing at its Ganesh-like form, mesmerized by the view.

A saintly South Indian lady called Mataji lived in a small cave nearby. She did not go down to Harsil even in winter, when even the idols of the Badrinath temple moved there for a winter sojourn. Rakesh took me to Mataji's cave. She was very loving and affectionate, and made hot coffee for us on her stove.

After our short stop, we set off towards Mount Shivling and went beyond. The path beyond Mount Shivling was covered in snow.

After a slow walk with some stops, we reached the base camp late in the afternoon and were greeted by Rajiv Midha and company.

I spent the night in their tent, and returned the next day, after wishing them good luck.

◆

HINDUSTAN-TIBET ROAD

A large contingent of our National Adventure Club set off on an expedition later in 1995, aspiring to complete the entire circuit of the great Hindustan Tibet Road. We wanted to go along the Sutlej, all the way to Tabo Monastery and return via Kaza and Manali to Chandigarh.

We reached the circuit house at Rampur Bushahr on the first day. The next day, we passed through Kalpa and proceeded on a lonely road along the river. We passed Jeori and Tapri and reached Karchham in the evening, where we set up camp. Another day's drive brought us to Puh, a village tucked on a hillside. Here, we got the unfortunate news of a devastating landslide on the road ahead, that had taken a toll of hundreds of lives. There was a rest house at Puh where we stayed for the night before turning back.

◆

Bansi Lal became chief minister on 11 May 1996 and appointed me his Principal Secretary. My adventure trips came to an end. But NAC that we had founded flourished because of my increased clout. We were able to get more donations now. Every year in July when snowfall occurs, we held adventure festivals. I was appointed Chief Secretary on 31 January 1997 and although O.P. Chautala ousted Bansi Lal on 21 July 1999, I remained C.S. till my retirement on 31 August 2000.

◆

The first thing I did after my retirement was to go to Tapovan and sit gazing at Mount Shivling.

Rakesh accompanied me there in early September and I was happy to meet Mataji again. As I sat in my tent, looking at nature's wondrous creation, it dawned on me that there were not many in the world as blessed as I was.

THE DREAMLAND: BHUTAN

In May 2002, we went to Bhutan—a dreamland tucked high up in the Himalayas. We reached Jalpaigudi by train and hired a minibus to go to Thimphu. Entering Bhutan at Phuntsholing, we drove on the road to Thimphu through rugged, mountainous terrain. On the way, we passed the beautiful Paro valley and the driver pointed out the road going to the airport to the left. The road ascends through a hilly region and finally, we sighted Thimphu, far away in a valley.

We had made reservations in the government guest house of Thimphu, a palatial building offering royal hospitality, and stayed there for four days.

We spent a day exploring the town and saw young men engaged in archery practice; archery is the national game of Bhutan. Then, we went to see the impressive Taschichho Dzong, the seat of government administration, situated at a commanding height, overlooking a river.

The next day, we went to see a Buddhist monastery perched atop a hill. A congregation of male and female lamas sat in separate groups; they were a jovial lot, chatting and laughing among themselves. Monkhood sat lightly on their shoulders.

I believe that there is a dress code in the country which is strictly followed by everyone. We saw women wearing hand-woven long skirts, called kira, intricately embroidered with colourful patterns. However, there was a touch of modernity about the way young girls wrapped their kiras tightly: with their fair skin and features, they almost looked European.

Indeed, we glimpsed a subtle juxtaposition of ancient tradition and modernity. Serenity and peace pervaded everywhere and there was a marked exuberence about everyone, young and old. It was evident that the happiness quotient of the people was quite high.

DESERT SAFARI

During the Christmas holidays of December 2002, a large contingent went on a desert safari to Bikaner, Jodhpur and Jaisalmer. My daughter Upasana joined us on this trip.

The sandy landscape starts in Hisar district, which is at the edge of the Thar Desert. We stopped to see the 'rat shrine' of Karni Mata on the way to Bikaner. Hundreds of rats scampered around the temple compound, scrambling over the idol and nibbling at the offerings placed before the idol. The temple was built by the king of Bikaner and enshrines a mystic woman, Karni Devi, who was deemed to possess godly attributes.

We stopped at Bikaner and visited the Junagarh Fort, the old residence of the king. We also saw the new palace called Lalbagh, built by the great former ruler Ganga Singh, which has now been converted into a five-star hotel.

We proceeded to Jodhpur from there, visited the majestic Mehrangarh Fort Palace and the Umaid Bhawan Palace, which is also a famous hotel now. I met my old friends in the English Department of Jodhpur University, P.C. Joshi, M.C. Joshi, George John and his brother Abraham, and introduced Upasana to them. George was the Head of the Department and hosted a dinner for us.

Finally, we reached Jaisalmer, the ultimate destination to experience the beauty of sand dunes, and stayed in tents pitched on the sand. Dunes, shaped and carved by desert winds, stretched to the horizon. Many tourists were enjoying camel safaris; Upasana and I did the same. There were long lines of camels giving joy rides, as far as the eye could see.

A camel safari is both thrilling as well as a pain in the ribs. The awkward gait of the camel causes riders to be jerked up and down. However, if one gives the camel full rein, allowing it to run on its long legs, one understands why it is called the 'ship of the desert'.

The traditional singers of Jaisalmer, called 'manganiars', put up a delightful performance in the evening. Women in colourful long skirts and men in huge safas sang and danced around a bonfire in the enveloping silence of the desert: it was magical.

Early next morning, before sunrise, Upasana and I went up the dunes, barefeet. There was no one else, just the dunes and us. We climbed to the crest of a high dune, sprawled on the rim and rolled down. Again and again, we ascended the mound and rolled down till the sun came up. Then, we returned to the tent, covered in sand, but were filled with happiness such as we had never felt before. While returning, we visited the Maharaja's Palace in Jaisalmer.

◆

RAFTING ON THE INDUS

On one of our several trips to Leh, we went river-rafting on the Indus and finished at the confluence of the Indus with the Zanskar River. I noticed a striking contrast between the colours of the two rivers. The water of Zanskar is deeper blue. It reminded me of the Yamuna merging with the Ganga at Prayag; one can clearly make out the bluish stream of the former as it merges with the latter's whitish water.

While returning by our mini bus, we visited several Buddhist monasteries such as Alchi and Lamayuru, saw monks dressed in red robs, attending prayer meetings and gazed at intricate and mysterious statues and paintings.

NUBRA VALLEY

Another time, rather than going towards Leh from Tanglang-La, we turned to the left and went into the Nubra valley. After the zigzag way down from the high Pass, the road straightened out in the valley. To my surprise and great delight, there were lovely white sand dunes along the road, like in Jaisalmer, on a vast stretch of sandy ground. Tourists were having joy rides on the two-humped Bactrian camels. The Bactrians looked so cute. We could not resist the temptation and enjoyed the rides for an hour or so. They are much gentler than their Rajasthani brethren. Besides, one feels more secure sitting comfortably between the two humps. The Bactrian, to my mind, is an improved model of the camel.

SIACHEN GLACIER

On a later occasion, the great Satish Chaudhary, who became Chief Secretary later on, arranged our visit to the Siachen Glacier, courtsey General V.S. Tonk, former Deputy Chief of Army Staff. Siachen Glacier is approached from the Nubra Valley. We took a flight to Leh which was routed via Srinagar. From Leh, we drove to an Army guest house in Nubra valley. The next morning, an Army vehicle took us through slush and snow, to the snow-filled ground where the Siachen glacier starts.

It was a bright sunny day, though there was a nip in the air. We walked with slow steps through the snow and reached the glacier. The Army personnel gave an impressive demonstration before us. I was amazed at their dexterity and perfectly coordinated actions at the height of about 20,000 feet, where we found it hard even to breathe. After about half an hour, we came down from the glacier and were brought to the guest house.

The walk on the Siachen glacier was akin to a lunar walk for the likes of us!

NATHU-LA AND RAFTING ON THE TEESTA

We planned a trip to Gangtok, the capital of Sikkim. The governor of Sikkim at that time was Chaudhary Randhir Singh, who hailed from Haryana. I requested him for accommodation in the Raj Bhawan guest house for our party. My youngest daughter Upasana accompanied me, and we stayed in the Raj Bhawan for a few days.

One morning, we drove to Nathu-La, situated at a height of over 14,000 feet on the Chinese border. The pass had been closed after the Indo-Chinese War of 1962, and was reopened in 2006, when friendly relations were re-established between the two countries. It lies on the trade route with China and is important for the economy of Sikkim.

On our way back, we stopped to admire the picturesque Changu Lake, about 15 kilometres from the pass. It is held in reverence by the Sikkimese people and, like Nathu-La, it remains under a thick blanket of snow in winter.

The next day, we went rafting on the beautiful Teesta, and the day after, we drove to Kalimpong, where we stayed in the circuit house. We roamed in the beautiful town, visited a church and a monastery and then went to a lovely park on a hillock for a glimpse of the Kanchenjunga. We also visited a nursery of orchids and cacti and saw some huge, amazing specimen of cacti.

PANGONG TSO

In 2001, we headed for Leh-Ladakh again. The destination was Pangong Tso. Ram Niwas, Balwan Singh and Rakesh were part of our group, among others.

With the permission of and help from the local Army Commander, we reached the beautiful Pangong Tso. Situated at over 14,000 feet, this brackish water lake is more than a hundred kilometres long but only a few kilometres wide. We were told that two-thirds of it lies in China and one-third in India. Recently, there was a fracas with China over the Line of Control.

The impulsive Balwan was so charmed by the Pangong Lake that he jumped into a channel coming from the lake with his clothes on, not realizing that its water was freezing cold. Immediately, he began shivering, his teeth began chattering. An Army jawan, escorting us, jumped into the channel and pulled him out. His skin had become red; they removed his clothes and vigorously rubbed his body to revive him.

I wanted to visit the grave of Haryana's brave son Maj. Shaitan Singh, who had died in Chushul during the Indo-Chinese War and was awarded the Param Veer Chakra for exceptional bravery. Chushul is on the Line of Control between India and China. We stayed in an Army outpost at Chushul that night. We returned to Leh after paying homage to Maj. Shaitan Singh in the morning.

TSO MORIRI

Next year in 2002, we went to another lovely lake in the same area, called Tso Moriri. My colleague Virendra Nath, who had settled in Faridabad after his retirement, joined our expedition. Unlike Pangong Tso, this lake is entirely in India. The 20-kilometre-long lake is fed by springs which originate in the high, snow-clad mountains around it. 'Tso' means 'lake' and 'Moriri' means 'mountain'; the name is indeed apt!

We stayed in a rest house on the lake's bank and enjoyed boating on its tranquil and transparent waters. We roamed in the desolate environs, and in the evenings, had a drinking session.

◆

PINDARI GLACIER

In April 2003, we made an attempt to go to the Pindari Glacier in the Kumaon Himalayas. My daughter Jyotsana had gone on this trek in April 1993 with a group of IAS probationers. She had told me that the way passed through forests of stunning rhododendrons.

We boarded the Ranikhet Express from Chandigarh in mid-April and reached Kathgodam in the morning. A bus took us to Kausani that night, the village in which our great poet Sumitra Nandan Pant was born. Kausani is nestled in the lap of nature and commands a stunning view of the Himalayas. No wonder the beauty of nature has passed into Pant's poertry.

The next day, via Almora and Bageshwar, we reached a place called Loharkhet, which was the starting point of the trek. It was a tough trek over rivulets and through oak and rhododendron forests. The rhododendrons were in their full glory, laden with bright red flowers. Even in the forests of Himachal Pradesh there are plenty of rhododendrons, but we generally go there in September-October when the flowering season is coming to an end. Here we were in mid-April, at the peak of the flowering season. What a memorable feast for the eyes!

There is a gradual ascent of about 3,000 feet from Loharkhet to Dhakuri, where we stopped for lunch. From there, we descended by about 1,500 feet to reach Khati. The next day's trek took us to Dwali, 14 kilometres away, at a height of 8,600 feet, and took almost the whole day. The fourth day's trek to Phurkia was short, only 5 kilometres, but our progress was slow due to the high altitude and we took about three hours to reach the rest house.

Phurkia was our last stop. We had to go to the glacier in the morning without backpacks and return. There was bright sunshine in the morning and we set off for the glacier after breakfast. The path was covered with snow but we bravely marched on. Unfortunately, the weather changed suddenly; icy winds began blowing, mist descended and we made a hasty retreat. In fact, we were not properly equipped for a walk on the glacier; none of us had windcheaters or crampons.

The next day, we started the trek back and reached Dwali in the evening. After one more day of easy trekking to Loharkhet, we returned via Nainital to Kathgodam. Our mission remained unfulfilled, but we had an enjoyable trek and had feasted our eyes on a riot of rhododendron flowers.

CHAUKORI, KHALIA TOP AND PATAAL BHUVANESHWAR

In April 2004, we took the night train to Kathgodam once again on a tour suggested by Ram Niwas. This time we went to Chaukori, one of the loveliest places I have been to. It offers a ringside view, as it were, of the majestic Himalayas, particularly the Panch Chuli peaks.

We stayed at Chaukori for a couple of days and journeyed to Munsyari by bus. The next morning, we trekked to Khalia Top by a steep stone-paved path through a sparse forest, the path being in a state of disrepair. Ours was a large group of about 20 persons—men, women and kids. I particularly remember a huffing and puffing Sanjeev Kaushal urging his daughters to climb. I think we did it in half a day and pitched two tents at the top. We stayed in those idyllic surroundings for two days, enjoying the magnificent views of the Panch Chuli peaks and lighting a campfire every evening for long sessions of singing and revelry.

Trekking back to Munsyari was easy. From there, we went to see a strange and mysterious place called Pataal Bhuvaneshwar. After a long journey on a winding hill road, we stayed in a lodge for the night.In the morning, we entered the incredible cave of Pataal Bhuvaneshwar, 90 feet below the surface of the earth! We went down an iron ladder, one by one, holding a chain, and landed near a monstrous seven- or nine-hooded stone-carved serpent! The hood was about 10 feet wide in my recollection, a foot or two higher than my height. Water was dripping over it from the overhanging rocks. The mighty serpent's curvaceous, undulating body stretched into a narrow fissure, washed by a tiny stream running alongside. We walked over it in the dripping cave for about 50 feet. The serpent's body appeared to be chiselled by human hands. The cave widened where a little pond of water had been formed. Water dripped from the curious-looking rock features that hung from the ceiling. The cave had been discovered a few centuries back. I surmised that a local king had got the enormous form of the Shesh Naag chiselled by craftsmen, but the local people believed it to be a natural creation.

In Chitrakoot, I have seen a large cavern in a hill with water running at the base and large statues of Lord Rama chiselled near the ceiling.

SANGLA VALLEY AGAIN

So charmed were we by Sangla valley that we went there again in 2006 and 2007. This time we trekked up a steep hill through fragrant woods and stayed at Reckong Peo, perched high on a hilltop, the headquarters of the Kinnaur district. The view of the

Kinner Kailash peaks is even more stunning from there.

While returning from these treks, we travelled via Narkanda and stayed in the beautiful Circuit House there. We enjoyed its commanding views of the Himalayas from our bedrooms. We made short daily treks to the Hatu peak in its vicinity.

THE ELUSIVE TABO MONASTERY

We decided to visit the Tabo Monastery, which had eluded us so far. Virender Sibal, my senior in the Punjab cadre, who had retired after a distinguished career in Delhi and had settled in Chandigarh, heard about our trip and desired to go with us. He had been the SDM of Kaza in the beginning of his career, under M.S. Gill, the former chief election commissioner and Union minister, who was deputy commissioner of Keylong district at that time. Sibal wanted to revisit his old haunt. Sibal reminisced that he had often trekked all the way from Rohtang Pass to Kaza!

The number of participants swelled, as there was no trekking involved. Satish Chaudhary, Ashok Lavasa and his wife, Hardeep Kumar, S.S. Prasad, Kamal Sehgal and of course Virender Sibal, were part of the large group.

In July, we drove to Rohtang Pass and set off for Khoksar, but some of our companions, unaccustomed to the hilly drive, became unwell while crossing the Rohtang Pass. After spending the night at Khoksar, we took the snow-ravaged road upstream River Chandra the next day. We stopped at Chhota Darra that night. On the third day, we started for Kunjam Pass, which is situated at over 15,000 feet and remains under snow from October to June. Like Tanglang-La, it is among the highest motorable passes in India and its numerous hairpin bends test the driving skill of motorists.

After crossing Kunjam-La, the road was winding but in good

condition. When we crossed a milestone indicating the arrival of Kaza, I noticed that we were approaching a lovely township with sloping roofs painted in bright colours: red, green and yellow.

I was sitting beside Sibal, and I exclaimed, 'Here is your Kaza!' He couldn't believe it; his Kaza had just 13 modest houses, while this appeared to be a prosperous, sprawling township of multi-storey houses.

Kaza looks like a neat modern town, with a lovely avenue of tall trees, cafes and shops. We went to the rest house and our ailing companions were taken to hospital. Sibal went in search of the one-room 'house' he had lived in. He couldn't find it; he got lost in the jumble of new houses that had cropped up there. He did not know who to ask, as he didn't remember the owner's name. Luckily, he met an IAS officer from the Assam cadre who belonged to Kaza and was constructing a new house. He helped Sibal locate the house that had replaced the one he had lived in. He was happy and came to the rest house and told me about it

I accompanied Sibal to his old house and met the IAS officer, a pleasant gentleman who had come on a month's holiday to build a new house. He invited us to dinner. Their drawing-room covered with ornate wall-hangings, looked like the hall of a monastery; we ate dinner there, the four of us sitting in a row along the wall.

We were told that the road to the Tabo Monastery was damaged, so we decided to return. Our ailing companions had bounced back to health and we returned the next morning after breakfast.

From Kunjam-La, we decided to leave the bus and trek to Chandra Tal. It was a most enjoyable trek, we were jumping and skipping all the way downhill in the glorious sunshine. The blue and emeralad lake was nestled in the lap of snow-covered cliffs.

We had told the bus driver to reach Chandra Taal and pitch a tent near the lake. We ate sandwiches sitting on the silvery sands on its shores. Suddenly, Ashok Lavasa asked the same old question he had asked me at Dodital, 'Sir, when do we bathe in the lake?' My response was the same. I changed into my swimming trunks and dived into the blue waters. Ashok and his wife Novel did the same and many others followed suit. We had a blissful and memorable swim.

THE VALLEY OF FLOWERS

In August 2007, we embarked on our most adventurous trip to the Valley of Flowers. It had been so named by a team of British mountaineers who had lost their way back from an expedition to Mount Kamet and had chanced upon these meadows full of exotic blooms.

It had seemed to be an easy trek of about 15 kilometres from Gobind Ghat to Ghangharia, which was just a few of kilometres from the Valley of Flowers. Even the Choor Dhar trek, at the beginning of our trekking career, had required a much longer climb. Compared to that, this trek seemed like cakewalk to us. Little did we know that the trek to the Valley of Flowers would test our capabilities and stamina to the utmost and become our swansong.

Our contingent consisted of Satish Chaudhary, Ram Niwas and Dhanpat Singh from the IAS, Devender Singh, Commissioner Central Excise, Lucknow, Sarvesh Saini, a solicitor from the UK, V.P. Gupta, a Sessions Judge from Haryana, Ashok Sharma, an advocate from Delhi, Kamal Sehgal, an advocate from Punjab and Haryana High Court, Dr Satbir Singh CMO, Chandigarh, Prof. Ashok Khanna and Rakesh Pawar, an ace trekker and our organizer.

We stayed at the Garhwal Mandal rest house at Kodyala on the first day. The next day, we camped at Joshimath, which was a

Jyotirmath[142] established by Shankaracharya twelve centuries ago. On the the third day, we reached Gobind Ghat before noon. Leaving our mini bus, we crossed the suspension bridge over River Alaknanda and began the trek to Ghangharia.

It was a tough uphill climb in scorching heat, but we pushed ahead valiantly. All of a sudden, clouds appeared and it began to pour. We were surprised by this dramatic change in weather, because we had heard that August and September were the best months for trekking to the Valley. In those days, there were no smart phones that could have forewarned us about the impending rain.

None of us had a raincoat or an umbrella. The rain pelted down mercilessly and we were drenched to the bone. Trekking in this inclement weather took much longer than expected. However, all of us reached Ghangharia safely before nightfall. Our clothes were all soaked, even the ones in our bags! We got them dried at a dhabawalla's oven: he made more money by drying our clothes that day than by selling food!

After spending the night at the Garhwal Mandal rest house in Ghangharia, we trekked about 5 kilometres to reach the Valley of Flowers the next day. Shrubs of wild strawberries and creepers of tiny roses welcomed us on the way and led us into a vast dreamland of flowers.

The Valley extended for about 10 kilometres and was a natural nursery of Alpine flowers—orchids, poppies, marigolds, violets and primroses. This flowery abundance reached up to the top of the hillsides on both sides of a gurgling stream. The overall impression was that of an exuberant riot of colours. White, pink, red, yellow, mauve and purple flowers were fluttering in the breeze with gay abandon.

We leisurely strolled admiring them and reached a spot where

---

[142]Abode of light

the stream had formed a little lake. While returning, we dilly-dallied in the lanes, discovering flowers of myriad colours, shapes and sizes. There were even multi-tier flowering plants, displaying several rings of pretty flowers on the long central stock. The Valley afforded us an experience of a lifetime.

The next day, we descended to Gobind Ghat and wanted to go up to Badrinath by our minibus, but were told that the road ahead had been damaged by heavy rain. So, we went to the Auli ski resort, instead. Since there was no snow at that time, the resort wore a deserted look, but it's a picuresque spot surrounded by snow-capped mountains and we had an ample stock of the elixir from Scotland and some accomplished songsters among us, and had a memorable evening.

Real adventure awaited us on our way back the next day. At a place called Garud Ganga, our bus came to a sudden halt; the road ahead had disappeared in a massive landslide. We found ourselves on the brink of a flooded ravine in pouring rain. Dusk had fallen by then and we took shelter in a tiny roadside tea stall under a tin shed.

What saved us was a crate of Chivas Regal Devender Singh had brought with him. We had already consumed a few bottles but half of the stock was still intact. There was a strange thrill in sipping the elixir, sitting on rough-hewn benches under a shed without walls as the unrelenting rain provided music by drumming on the tin roof.

It took a lot of time cooking our simple meal. But we had all the time in the world, sipping the drink, chatting and listening to Dhanpat Singh's wisecracks who is a storehouse of jokes. Satish Chaudhary took out his mouth organ and the tune of the popular song *'Hai apna dil tau aawara, na jane kispe aayega'* rang out in the solitude of the hills. He then recited gazals of Ghalib and Bahadur Shah Zafar. Ram Niwas had brought his harmonium with him.

A regular mehfil environment was created when he took it out and began singing Haryanavi raginis and then sang Mehdi Hasan's *'Ranjish hi sahi, tu dil ko dukhane ke liye aa, aa phirse mujhe chhod kar jaane ke liye aa.'*

The rain had subsided and one of our friends left the shed to empty his bladder, standing on the edge of the road. That very instant a huge boulder came hurtling down the hill just about 10 yards from him. God is guarding us, I said to myself.

It was nearing midnight when we ate our simple dinner of daal-chapattis. We slept hunched up on bus seats or in the shed by joining the benches.

There was no prospect of taking the bus any further. Leaving the bus, we left in the morning and walked through slush for about half a mile to get to the road. We heaved a sigh of relief when we got there. But soon we met another landslide and had to go through slush again. We encountered four landslides in the 10 kilometres to reach Rudra Prayag. We got taxis there and reached Kodyala, our old haunt for river rafting. The next day our cars reached Kodyala from Chandigarh.

The Valley of Flowers would count as our most memorable as well as arduous trek; sadly, it was also our last.

RAFTING IN THE GANGA

We had started rafting in the Ganga before we began our trekking expeditions. In April 1990, we went for our first rafting expedition on the Ganga. We went to Rishikesh and from there to Kodyala, which is the starting point for rafting expeditions, and stayed in the cottages of the Garhwal Mandal on the bank of the river.

The rafting company provided us the rafting gear—a helmet, a swimming jacket and a paddle. We took a plunge in the ice-cold

Ganga to acclimatize, before getting on the raft. It is controlled by the guide sitting at the back of the raft with a master paddle in his hands, but the rest assist in moving the raft by plying their paddles, sitting on both sides of the raft to balance it.

Rafting is smooth sailing but for the rapids, which create turbulence in the river, turning the water foamy and milky. That is why it is called 'white-water rafting'. There are many rapids in the Ganga between Kodyala and Rishikesh. Except for one rapid near the sheer cliff called The Wall, there is no chance of the rafts capsizing. In between two rapids, when the river is calm, one can jump into the river and swim alongside the raft.

I like to swim and be in the lap of Ganga as much as I can. It affords an ineffable pleasure, especially when one swims on one's back, looking at the blue sky.

A few days before going on one of our expeditions, all my teeth had been extracted as they were severely affected and I had got dentures fixed. When I dived from the raft into the river my mouth was open and my upper denture flew out. 'O my God,' I thought, 'I'm done for!' Luckily, I saw the denture floating in the river and in a split second, in a reflex action, my right hand reached under it and caught it before it could sink to the river bed. I heaved a huge sigh of relief. I would have gone hungry but for the alacrity of my hand.

Rafting has been our favourite sport and we have rafted in the Ganga many times in later years. On a few occasions, my daughter Vandana's sons, Shiv and Dhruv, had also joined us. We used to have a log fire in front of the cottages at Kodyala. Satish Chaudhary would take care of all arrangements. He was also our masterchef and spent a lot of time in the kitchen, cooking chicken in a large kadahi (pot). Besides, he is a soulful singer and would regale us with songs of Hemant Kumar as we sipped the elixir and savoured the chicken sitting around live fire. His sonorous voice would resound in the stillness of the star-studded night.

Tum pukar lo, tumhara intezaar hai!
Khwab chun rahi hai raat, beqarar hai,
Tumhara intezaar hai, pukar lo!

The last time we rafted on the Ganga was in April 2015. Before approaching The Wall, the guide asked us to disembark and walk on the shore as the chances of the raft capsizing in it were high. All other rafts in our group were disembarked. However, we thought we were experienced rafters and continued sitting in the raft. The raft capsized and we were thrown overboard. It was my first such experience. I bobbed up and began to swim towards the shore. There were a few ladies, too. The guide reached out to them first and helped everyone later. The Wall has a circular flow of water like a whirlpool near the cliff which sucks a person in if he/she falls into its vortex, but our raft had cleared the suction zone before capsizing.

It dawned on me then that unless you fall into a rapid, you never experience the real thrill of rafting.

BUS JOURNEY TO NEPAL

Unlike our visit to Bhutan, where a large part of our journey was done by rail, we went the whole way to Nepal in a bus, right from Chandigarh. Undoubtedly, there was a touch of madness about us.

It was a large group of about 25 people—men, women and kids—rollicking and rambunctious, lively, noisy and fun-loving. We stayed in Haryana Bhawan, Delhi on the first day. The next day, we went to Agra and were in time to have a glimpse of the Taj Mahal when its dome was lightly kissed by the golden rays of the setting sun. On the third day, we halted at Sitapur and the next day entered Nepal at Nepalgunj.

We stopped in the Nepalgunj market for tea and cold drinks. To our amazement, we found that alongside Coca Cola bottles, the shopkeeper had beer bottles in the fridge! In India, you could buy beer only from a theka.[143] We rejoiced and sipped beer while the ladies and kids had Coke.

Driving on the straight, broad road from Nepalgunj to Kathmandu passing through a forest of tall trees, was a pleasure. There was hardly any traffic. The ladies started singing film songs and everyone joined in. We drove non-stop for 4-5 hours and reached a place called Butwal late in the evening and stayed there that night. The road turned northward from there and by the next evening, we were in good old Kathmandu. Eureka! We had arrived!

We checked into a hotel and went to a restaurant for dinner. I was particularly pleased to see that the Indian rupee was much prized in Nepal. We did not have to get our money changed into Nepalese currency; it was gladly accepted at a premium.

The next morning, we went to Durbar Square, where the Royal Palace is situated. It was like stepping into a different world. There was an old world charm about the place. We visited the Kumari Temple, where a little girl, eight or nine years old, is enshrined as a goddess. She appears in a window at an appointed hour to give darshan to her devotees in the square. A new goddess is installed before the present Kumari attains puberty. What a shock it must be to her when from a goddess she is reduced to a mere girl, I thought. The poor girl must be cursing her coming-of-age.

Next, we joined an unending stream of worshippers at the Pashupati Nath Temple, the most revered abode of Lord Shiva, on the bank of River Bagmati. Later, we went to Patan Bhaktapur,

---

[143]Authorized vendor for liquour

which used to be the seat of an earlier dynasty. There is a sky-high five-tiered pagoda-style temple here, which can be reached by wide marble steps.

Another colossal structure is the Buddhist stupa of Swayambhunath on a hillock. It is the most popular tourist site in Kathmandu and serves as a symbol of religious harmony. The large eyes painted on the high tower of the stupa gaze at you from a distance and seem to possess a magnetic power.

After staying in Kathmandu for two days, we moved to Pokhra, where there is a lovely, boundless lake, stretching to the snow mountains. We pitched our tents by its side. The blue-green lake mirrors the Annapurna and Dhaulagiri ranges. The view is captivating. The most prominent peak reflected in its waters is called Matsyapuchhe (Fish Tail).

We sat in a circle on the grassy banks and invited the kids to present an item each—song, dance or a skit, whatever. Talent was overflowing, girls surpassing the boys. Then Ram Niwas's four-year-old son Aksh stood up and began singing a popular film song, swaying his legs and hands. He got the loudest applause! All of a sudden, clouds descended and it started raining; our tents were blown away by the wind. We had to take shelter in a hotel.

Next morning the retreat began. There is a straight road from Pokhra to Butwal. We reached there in the evening, but rather than staying at that nondescript place, we drove to nearby Lumbini, the birthplace of Gautam Buddha. I believe a beautiful garden has, since, been created and a few monasteries have sprung up, but at that time, the place was almost in its pristine state, with just a small pond near an old banyan tree and a place to stay for pilgrims. Across the road, there was a row of makeshift shops, catering to the pilgrims.

Lumbini was a bonus for us; it was not a part of our itinerary. I rejoiced being there, seeing the pond in which Queen Mayadevi had bathed and the place where she had delivered her baby. There was no place to stay there; some of us slept in the bus, some on the roof and some spread themselves on the ground.

We returned the way we had gone, via Nepalgunj, Sitapur, Agra and Delhi and Chandigarh. It was the crowning adventure safari of my life.

29

THE BIRTH OF AN AUTHOR

I had a lot of free time after my retirement, and it increased when my better half Savitri left for her heavenly abode in 2004. I had bought the whole set of the Rig Veda in four parts with Hindi translation from Jaipur after retirement. I opened the first part and began reading it.

The hymns of the Rig Veda were composed by rishis dwelling in their idyllic ashrams on the bank of the Saraswati. They were memorized by the descendants or disciples of the composers and were passed on from one generation to the next, orally. They were written down and compiled around the Buddha's time. It's a wonder how they had preserved their original, uncorrupted form.

The Rig Veda is a collection of 1028 hymns, composed by hundreds of rishis. It is arranged in ten sections called 'mandalas'. The hymns are addressed to Vedic-age gods like Agni, Indra, Varun, the Maruts, Rudra, Soma, etc. and were meant to be recited at ritual sacrifices. Each hymn is a complete poem by itself. They preserve 'the timeless world of myth and ritual', to borrow a phrase from Wendy Doniger[144].

I must admit that I do not know Sanskrit, let alone Vedic Sanskrit which abounds in archaic idioms and phrases. I have gleaned the meaning hidden in these ancient, esoteric poems partly through Hindi translations (which generally give a warped

[144]Wendy Doniger, *The Rig Veda*, Penguin Books, London, 1981, p. 16 (Intro.).

meaning), but mainly from Wendy Doniger's English translation of 108 selected hymns.

The Rig Vedic deities are luminous celestial entities, mostly formless. Only Indra and Vishnu have anthropomorphic attributes. Indra is the most important deity in the Rig Veda; there are about 250 hymns dedicated to him while just three hymns invoke Vishnu. The Rigvedic rishis vied with each other in singing Indra's praise, celebrating his victory over the serpent Vrtra and other demonic lords like Vala, ensconced in high impregnable forts. Indra killed them and released the waters and the cows from their captivity.

The Rig Veda had been closely guarded by our pundits. Only during British rule, when the East India Company appointed Max Mueller to translate the Vedas into English, did they come into the public domain. Mueller had links with the Brahmo Samaj and wished to usher in a reformation of Hindu society like its promoter Ram Mohan Roy.

The common belief prevalent among Hindus about the Rig Veda is that it is full of holy prayers and sacred sermons. In common terminology, 'Vedavakya'[145] is regarded as divine and sacrosanct. The reality, however, is far different. The Rig Veda is an astonishing amalgam of the sacred and profane, of the 'other worldly' and 'worldly'.

'Almost every hymn in the Rig Veda,' observes Wendy Doniger, 'expresses at some point a wish for the good things in life… The Rig Veda is a sacred book, but it is a very worldly sacred book.[146] The rishis don't seek to renounce the world. The gods are invoked to give the worshipper health, wealth, power and sons! Indeed, the Vedic invocations are 'joyous celebration of human existence'.

Reading the Rig Veda was a revelation to me. I found the hymns

---

[145]Words of the Vedas

[146]Wendy Doniger O'Flaherty, *The Rig Veda*, Penguin Books, London, 1981 Page 229.

to be wonderfully refreshing, like a breath of cool air from distant Himalayan realms. There are hymns that embody an inspired vision and arise from soulful contemplation. There are also hymns that puzzle and surprise and trouble the mind, and there are profane hymns without any inhibitions.

The rishis even laughed at themselves. There is an ingenious hymn dedicated to frogs, which mocks the Vedic priests who chanted the hymns like the chorus of frogs during the rains.[147]

Imagine my surprise when by reading the Rig Veda I came to know that the Vedic rishis not only offered the Soma juice to the gods but also regarded Soma as a god and were its devotees. There are as many hymns in the Rig Veda in praise of Soma as there are in praise of Indra, their supreme god. They carefully cooked a young bull's tender flesh, offered the choicest portions in yajna to Agni and, through him, to the other gods, besides satiating them with Soma. Thereafter, they gladly savoured and supped the remains themselves and imbibed the draught of Soma. After reading the hymns of Rig Veda, my guilt complex about being a tippler and a non-vegetarian vanished completely.

I also read the Valmiki Ramayana in its English translation. I was told that the Valmiki Ramayana was a more authentic source of the story of Lord Rama; the poet Valmiki is thought to be a contemporary of Rama and portrays him realistically, like a human being.

However, I found the Bala Kand of Valmiki Ramayana filled with fanciful tales from the Puranas. After reading it, I realized that unlike the Rig Veda, the Valmiki Ramayana had been bowlderised by the pundits and miraculous episodes had been woven into this *'itihas*

[147]Rig Veda: 7.103

kavya'[148] which transformed Rama from a prehistorical prince into a mythical avatar. I decided to erase the gaudy, fanciful embellishments in my rendering, revealing the simple beauty of this timeless tale and restoring its pristine glory.

In fact, I got the idea of rewriting the Ramayana story after reading John Brockington's *Righteous Rama: The Evolution of an Epic.* He is an eminent Sanskritist, and his book is based on his doctoral thesis at the University of Oxford. Brockington detected the spurious verses embedded in Valmiki's epic by determining their age, by examining sentence construction and syntax, and classifying them whether they were pre- or post-Panini.

I was encouraged in my endeavour by Prof. Brockington and his erudite spouse Mary Brockington, who is an eminent Indologist in her own right. Not only did they provide valuable guidance, during its writing, they obliged me by writing the Foreword of my book, *Before He was God: RAMAYANA Reconsidered Recreated.*

My daughter Vandana, who is a professor of architecture and a reputed painter, created the illustrations for my book, which enhanced its beauty and appeal exponentially. The book came out in 2010. Its Hindi version, *Ishwaratva se Poorv: RAMAYANA*, was published in 2014.

After that, I worked on my next book, *Life in the IAS: My Encounters with the Three Lals of Haryana*, which was published in 2017. Since then, I have been working on my memoir.

•◆

A week after Upasana and Rajiv's wedding on 31 October 2003, Savitri told me that she had been experiencing some pain in her stomach for some time. I took her to Dr Chawla, head of the hepatology department at PGI, Chandigarh. He got her ultrasound

[148]Historical poem

test done and saw, to his horror, that her liver was riddled with spots. He was tongue-tied.

Savitri asked him, 'Is it cancer, Doctor Sahib?'

The good doctor was amazed by her query and put a counterquestion, 'You knew it, madam? Why didn't you come earlier?'

'I knew it, Doctor Sahib, but I didn't want to *open my chapter* before my daughter Upasana's marriage. Her marriage was solemnized last week; it doesn't matter in the least now.'

'But we could have done something if it had been detected early, madam.'

'That is alright, Doctor Sahib.'

Upasana and Rajiv had been engaged about five months ago and we wanted an early marriage. But the pundits said that according to the shastras (religious scriptures) the marriage season was over. *Tara doob gaya* (the star has gone down), that's what they had said. The earliest date for their marriage accordingly was fixed on 31 October, when they were married.

Dr Chawla tried to find the source of infection but could not detect it. I told him that I could take her to the US for treatment. He replied that it would be of no avail; they would say the same thing.

She left for her heavenly abode on 2 February 2004. Her fast friend Santosh Bansal told me that she had confided in her about acute pain in her abdomen and she suspected cancer. 'Why don't you tell Varma Sahib about it?' Santosh had asked her. She gave her the same answer, 'I don't want to open my chapter before Upasana's marriage.'

What a self-sacrificing person Savitri was!

•◆

During my childhood, our leisure time was spent in playing games like chhupam chhupai[149], kabaddi and gillidanda. Later, I used to play tennis on the hard courts at Sukhna Lake when I lived in Chandigarh. In the last 10 years before my retirement, my physical activity was limited to a walk along the lake.

During his tenure as Home Secretary, Chandigarh, U.T., Rupinder Singh Mann created the first golf course in Chandigarh near the Sukhna Lake, He used to ask me to come and try out the sport, reassuring me that I would love it. I scoffed at the idea, saying that it was a game for elites like him, not for a commoner like me.

However, during Bansi Lal's last tenure, an ambitious project to create an excellent sports complex in Panchkula was formulated. Unauthorized stone crushers were operating on both sides of the River Ghaggar, fouling the atmosphere of the new township of Panchkula. Bansi Lal ordered the removal and relocation of the stone crushers. A grand sports stadium on the eastern bank and a world-class golf course on the western bank of the river were created. The golf course was executed by Bhaskar Chatterjee, Principal Secretary of Town and Country Planning Department, who was a keen golfer as well. Before the stadium and the golf course were completed, Bansi Lal was ousted by O.P. Chautala. The stadium was named Tau Devi Lal Stadium and a towering statue of Devi Lal was installed at its entrance.

I was Chief Secretary when this project was initited. When the golf course became functional in 2003, I became a member, bought a golf set, took some coaching and began playing the game. To my utter surprise, I found that golf was a much simpler game than my childhood game of gillidanda. In gillidanda, the player, had to strike the gilli with the danda to make it airborne and hit it in a split second, while in golf, the ball rests on the tee or on

[149]Somewhat akin to Blind Man's Bluff

green grass in fairways and one can play it unhurriedly with any of the eleven clubs designed to send the ball at varying distances. The game was about a proper swing of the clubs and cool concentration.

My son-in-law Navneet Sehgal brought a state-of-the-art putter for me from New York and my other son-in-law Rajiv Madhok got me a top-quality 5-wood club from Singapore which improved my putting and long drive immensely. In about two years I became sufficiently adept in the game and was part of the foursome that had qualified to play a tournament in Dubai. I had graduated from my childhood game of gillidanda to golf!

I have called my memoir *From Gillidanda to Golf* because it sums up my progression and my transformation in life. On most days, as the sun's golden orb peeps out from behind the Shivalik Hills, I tee off on the golf course on the bank of the good old Ghaggar, which is the sole remnant of the 'Ambitame, Naditame, Devitame' Saraswati, on whose banks the Vedas were composed.

It is controversial whether the authors of the Rig Veda came to India from across the Himalayas or were original inhabitants, but it has been established beyond doubt that they lived on the banks of the Saraswati *before* it disappeared around 1900 BCE. They composed the Vedas there, performing yajna and chanting the verses, and reached the shores of the Ganga after the Saraswati's disappearance.

I feel a whiff of the Vedic age as I tee off at the Panchkula golf course on the Ghaggar.

INDEX